The Digital Archives Handbook

The Digital Archives Handbook

A Guide to Creation, Management, and Preservation

Edited by Aaron D. Purcell

ROWMAN & LITTLEFIELD
Lanham • Boulder • New York • London

Published by Rowman & Littlefield
An imprint of The Rowman & Littlefield Publishing Group, Inc.
4501 Forbes Boulevard, Suite 200, Lanham, Maryland 20706
www.rowman.com

Unit A, Whitacre Mews, 26-34 Stannary Street, London SE11 4AB

British Library Cataloguing in Publication Information Available

Library of Congress Cataloging-in-Publication Data

Names: Purcell, Aaron D., 1972– editor.
Title: The digital archives handbook : a guide to creation, management, and preservation / Aaron D. Purcell [editor].
Description: Lanham, Maryland : Rowman & Littlefield, [2019] | Includes bibliographical references and index.
Identifiers: LCCN 2018041539 (print) | LCCN 2018047935 (ebook) | ISBN 9781538122396 (Electronic) | ISBN 9781538122372 (cloth : alk. paper) | ISBN 9781538122389 (pbk. : alk. paper)
Subjects: LCSH: Electronic records—Management—Handbooks, manuals, etc. | Digital preservation—Handbooks, manuals, etc. | Archives—Collection management—Handbooks, manuals, etc. | Archives—Access control—Handbooks, manuals, etc.
Classification: LCC CD974.4 (ebook) | LCC CD974.4 .D538 2019 (print) | DDC 070.5/797—dc23
LC record available at https://lccn.loc.gov/2018041539

Printed in the United States of America

For Clio

Contents

List of Figures and Tables

Preface

An email from a records officer about a transfer of electronic files, a hard drive from a prize-winning journalist, or a mystery box of floppy disks found in a backlog collection is an everyday challenge for today's archivists. Professional archivists in a variety of archives programs face daily challenges related to digital materials maintained by their programs or destined to be part of their digital collections. The reality of managing digital archives is not a new concept for archivists, but the deluge of electronic information and rapid changes in technology have intensified challenges that previous generations of archivists did not face.

But where can archivists look for advice on managing digital archives? Many sources on managing digital materials focus on electronic records that denote government or official archival materials. This rigid term ignores a wide variety of digital material being created by other types of donors far outside of official records schedules, public laws, and institutional legal requirements. Sources on the challenges of legacy media and digital curation are either far too technical or consist of overly specific case studies.

As a remedy to this literature gap, *The Digital Archives Handbook: A Guide to Creation, Management, and Preservation* explores the challenges of managing digital archives. This handbook is written by archivists who have developed methods to provide access to a diverse range of digital materials found in government, private, and academic archives. The chapters discuss the core components of digital archives:

- the technological infrastructure that provides storage, access, and long-term preservation
- the people or organizations that create or donate digital material to archives programs and the researchers who use the collections
- the digital collections themselves, full of significant research content in a variety of formats representing a range of genres with a multitude of research purposes

A common theme throughout the book is that the people and the collections that make up digital archives are just as important as the technology. Further, this book emphasizes the importance of donors and creators of digital archives. Building digital archives parallels the cycle of donor work—planning, cultivation, and stewardship. During each stage, archivists work with donors to ensure that the digital collections will be arranged, described, preserved, and made accessible for years to come.

The chapters provide both general and format-specific advice for archivists. Following a brief introduction, the first section reviews processes and practices. In includes chapters on acquisitions, appraisal, arrangement, description, delivery, preservation, forensics, curation, and intellectual property. The second section is focused on digital collections and specific environments in which archivists are managing digital archives. These chapters review digital collections in categories including performing arts, oral history, architectural and design records, congressional collections, and email.

Archivists must take proactive and informed actions to build valuable digital collections. Knowing where digital materials come from, how those materials were created, what materials are important, what formats or topical areas are included, and how to serve those collections to researchers in the long term is central to archival work. *The Digital Archives Handbook: A Guide to Creation, Management, and Preservation* is designed to generate new discussions about how archival leaders of the twenty-first century can overcome current challenges and chart paths that anticipate, rather than merely react to, future donations of digital archives.

Acknowledgments

All writing projects represent a journey. An idea sparked at a conference or during the early morning commute may take a dozen years before the words hit the page. During the journey there are intermittent periods of waiting, long hours searching for the right words, a variety of supporters cheering from the sidelines, and an array of unexpected challenges. For edited books, there are other twists and turns. The purpose of an edited volume is to bring a group of strong voices to shared pages in some sort of coherent and consistent way. Each contributor brings his or her own style, strengths, and schedules to such a project. That variety strengthens the finished product even if the voices are not always in stereo or the voices take a long time to say what they need to say.

The origins of this book began in 2015. It took another full year before the contents, purpose, and contributors took shape. Then it took another two years of drafts and editing to bring the completed chapters to the end of the journey. The ten authors who followed me were patient, gracious, and willing to let me edit their work. My goal was to enhance their words, when I could, and to shape each puzzle piece to create a larger picture. I thank them for letting me lead this journey and for articulating so well the challenges and approaches to digital archives.

Many thanks go to Charles Harmon at Rowman & Littlefield. He supported this project from the very beginning and gave me the time I needed to complete the work. I must also thank colleagues for listening to my thoughts on donors over the past few years and for their willingness to read outlines and drafts of this manuscript. Steve Tatum once again did a fantastic job with the cover image. I deeply appreciate the enthusiasm of the eight students in my archives class who shared their hands with the world. Those students include: Liz, L.T., Marlee, Drew, Emily, Kathryn, Jeff, and Kelly. My fellow archivists at Virginia Tech also deserve acknowledgment for their support and for not questioning the many blocks of editing time on my calendar. Finally, my family deserves praise for pushing me to be professionally alive. I dedicate this book to Clio, our family's muse who brought light to all our days.

Introduction

Aaron D. Purcell

Digital collections are everywhere. Each day we leave behind our digital footprints when we send an email, upload and share photos through social media, read an online article, purchase airline tickets, or check the balance of our banking account. In our professional lives, the digital footprint is larger and more complex. Organizations (whether private, government, public, academic, nonprofit, for-profit, or a family business) create a massive amount of digital material. The use of cloud-based storage systems rather than in-house servers has accelerated the trend for employees, business owners, and institutions to have a "keep everything" policy. The sheer volume of digital materials is frightening. It is too common and too easy to keep thousands of emails in an inbox believing that "someday I will sort through them all." That day is always tomorrow.

Of course, the bulk of digital content created by individuals or organizations has limited long-term value. A paid invoice from ten years ago, a personal email about picking up groceries after work, or a preliminary draft of a quarterly report does not age well. For a moment, these digital materials are important, but quickly the information loses its value. Rather than send these digital files to the "recycle bin" as a regular practice, we move on to creating new digital files to meet the next round of personal and professional demands. In fact, Amazon.com, Google.com, and other large companies encourage this behavior so they can mine our undeleted content. We are great at creating digital content but lousy at managing it.

Our digital footprints also contain a small portion of files that age well. These materials are what make up digital archives. Annual reports, email correspondence during or about a significant historical event, final structural plans for a building, high-quality recordings of theatrical performances, data sets, and social media reactions to important cultural events are some of the types of digital collections with potentially long-term value for researchers and others. Identifying the important files out of the hundreds if not thousands of unimportant ones is challenging. Often these materials have unintelligible file names that only make sense to the person who created them. An awareness of the important and unimportant, especially when we depend on institutional or individual memory for answers. Further, rapid technological change and software obsolescence result in the inability to access older files without significant intervention and technical expertise.

Each day the digital footprints of individuals and organizations grow larger and larger with no end in sight. Very few individuals and organizations place value on organizing, selecting, deleting, and thinking long term about their digital files. Even the IT experts who upgrade systems and build secure technical infrastructure have little interest in considering existing content and how today's digital files will be used in another six months. Somehow people, including many archivists, are more concerned about a room full of filing cabinets stuffed with paper files than multiple terabytes of data on hard drives, servers, or in cloud storage. The unseen nature of digital material makes it easier to ignore the long-term technical challenges that await us.

Archivists are one of the few professional groups dedicated to collecting, selecting, managing, preserving, and providing long-term access to digital archives. Approaches to building digital archives are still quite new. The digital environment is tremendously different from a paper-based world, and adapting analog practices for digital material is not often possible or advisable. Despite the challenges, archivists build digital archives from a variety of sources. As part of that process, archivists educate the creators of digital materials on the importance of long-term access. Closer work with donors and a proactive approach to collecting digital material results in collections that have significant research value and often supplement existing analog collections in archives programs.

Archivists recognized the challenges of digital archives several generations ago. The late 1970s and early 1980s were an important period for archival theory and practice. In a post-American-bicentennial glow, archivists established new archival programs, offered different types of training, and embraced the idea of active documentation strategies for multiple layers of the nation's history. The archival literature of this time was extraordinarily rich. It was during this period that Gerald Ham introduced the concept of a postcustodial era for archivists and pushed the profession to document a more diverse patchwork of American society.[1] Archival educators and practitioners, including Trudy Huskamp Peterson, Frank Burke, and Frank Boles, wrote and presented on new trends, practices, and theories in archives. Their articles and books continue as required readings for any aspiring or seasoned archivist. Collectively, these scholars recognized a changing role of archivists in society, which would be shaped by technology and an abundance of information.[2]

One of the best snapshots of this pivotal period came from Edward Weldon. His presidential address at the 1982 Society of American Archivists meeting, published the following year in the *American Archivist* as "Archives and the Challenges of Change," focused on three observations that are still prevalent in the work of today's archivists. First, Weldon discussed the significance of the baby boomer generation in reshaping American society and approaches to documenting those cultural shifts. Today, the baby boomers retain influence over all walks of American life and have key leadership positions in the archival community. Second, he pointed to a proliferation of new organizations and government agencies that were producing records at an alarming pace. To tame the records monster, he suggested a broader and more grassroots approach to archival work and an abandonment of practices that overdocument the highest levels of society. Weldon's third and most significant observation was that the postindustrial information revolution would change society and the archival profession in untold ways. As the instrument of change, the computer would alter how information is created, stored, and shared. Weldon made the wise choice not to predict exactly how affordable digital technology would cause gray hair and sleep loss for archivists. He did, however, suggest that to overcome challenges in the information era, archivists must partner with librarians, records managers, and technical experts rather than charting a separate set of solutions.[3]

Weldon's observations from over thirty-five years ago serve as an excellent reminder that several generations of archivists have faced the deluge of electronic information and new technology. Perhaps the biggest obstacle, which Weldon discussed at length, was individual and institutional resistance to change. As technological change marches forward at its own rapid pace, archivists and especially their institutions are slow to adapt. As a corollary effect, the volume of the fire hose of digital information increases daily. Government officials, scholars, students, leaders of organizations, bloggers, community activists, and basically anyone with a cell phone or access to an internet connection creates more digital files each year than he or she did the year before. Identifying who and what is important has become even more muddled than when Weldon and his generation of archivists stared into the archival black box at the beginning of the electronic age. Just as important and complicated is how archivists collect, preserve, and provide access to digital materials.

In the years and decades that followed Weldon's heyday, archivists encountered a range of digital challenges. At the same time, the volume of analog materials also increased at an unprecedented rate. More simply, the paperless society of the new century that many dreamed of did not occur when the clock struck midnight on December 31, 2000. Instead, many of today's archivists are still overwhelmed by paper-based collections and wade into electronic records issues only when faced by a crisis. As further evidence of this reality, the most significant and still highly debated archival theory and practice of recent times is minimal processing of large paper-based collections.[4] There have been many successes with electronic records projects, technical training, shared standards, and digital access tools that archivists should be proud of. But after nearly two decades into the new century, the profession is still struggling to keep up with technology, to work with records creators, and to consider how, if at all, paper-based archival theories work in a digital environment. It is also clear that archivists have not built enough bridges to the related fields of libraries, records management, and information technology, as Weldon suggested.

The good news is that whether archival materials are in analog or digital format, archivists ask three simple questions. First, who is donating the material? Second, what material is being donated or transferred? Finally, how has and how should the material be managed and preserved? In other words, who is the donor, what kind of "stuff" do they have, and how will archivists deal with the material in the long term? The "who, what, and how" questions encompass the full range of archival work and the answers simplify many of the challenges of creating, managing, and preserving digital archives.

I found the simple "who, what, and how" questions helpful for organizing *Donors and Archives: A Guidebook for Successful Programs* (2015).[5] The book contains some discussion of digital donations, but the focus is on donor relations and building a strong donor program. Just after the book was published, I took the stage as a panelist at a Midwest Archives Conference meeting to talk about the challenges of working with one of my donor communities that are creating large amounts of digital content. My co-presenters discussed their issues with electronic records creators, how to best store and curate the digital files, and approaches to recovering lost data from obsolete media. Clearly, there was much more to say on donations of digital content, but I knew that multiple voices needed to tell that important story.

After the conference, I organized a group of archival practitioners and experts to write a handbook on digital archives. They represented different types of archival programs but shared many of the same digital challenges. I asked them to write about their experiences with digital materials, the practices they follow, what resources they use, where their collections come from, how researchers use their collections, and finally, what they think about the near future of their area of expertise. As I worked with each of them in the following months, the core components of digital archives became clear—the technological infrastructure that provides storage, access, and long-term preservation; the people or organizations that create or donate digital material to archives programs and the researchers who use the collections; and the digital collections themselves, full of significant research content in a variety of formats representing a range of genres with a multitude of research possibilities. As the chapters took shape, the book emphasized that the people and the collections that make up digital archives are just as important as the technology. The result is a detailed practical guide to digital archives that fills in a significant gap in the professional literature.

The archival literature on managing digital materials is uneven. Overview archival sources provide a laundry list of options for managing electronic materials in archives with a strong focus on the technological needs. These sources, however, provide little information about implementation and maintenance. At the other end of the spectrum, there are case studies and books on archival trends that describe how archives programs within a very specific context overcame their digital challenges and which choices were made. The "we done good" or "lessons learned" sources have merit, but such contributions are so specific to an organizational context that they cannot be duplicated with success elsewhere.[6] Other sources provide advice about managing personal or individual collections of digital content. These sources focus on a particular type of creator, format, or technology, which limits the extent of their reach.[7]

A major shortcoming of the archival literature on digital materials is the emphasis on official electronic records only. Archivists working in a variety of settings must manage official materials as mandated by law, retention schedules, or organizational policies; however, there is a much wider range of important digital materials that are not the traditional official records. Each day, archivists in government, higher education, and private archives programs work with digital materials that are "official" and "unofficial" records of documentary evidence. No longer can archivists compartmentalize their digital efforts to one type of record, format, or institution. A more holistic approach to building and managing digital archives is required.

Approaches to building digital archives are still quite new. It is only in the past two decades that archivists have developed replicable practices for managing digital archives. The digital environment is tremendously different from the paper-based world. Archivists created standards and developed best practices for paper records, but to simply adapt those approaches in the digital realm is often not possible. As a related challenge, the differences in archives programs (e.g., purposes, funding, staffing, resources) make it difficult to create a one-size-fits-all approach for managing digital material. The purpose of this book is to introduce readers to current approaches to building digital archives, review common technical challenges for all archives programs, and highlight the most frequent types of digital collections and where they come from.

The Digital Archives Handbook: A Guide to Creation, Management, and Preservation is focused on the "who, what, and how" of digital archives. The chapters review the processes and practices of building digital collections while also providing insights into how archivists and archives programs work with specific types of digital materials. Chapters are written by archivists who are experts in their field and have direct experience with acquiring, managing, and providing access to digital archives.

The first section of the book targets general processes and practices. Lisa Calahan begins the journey with an exploration of the acquisition and appraisal of incoming digital collections. She describes experiences with the receipt and ingest of digital content at the University of Minnesota Libraries and how those processes are replicable for other archives programs. The second chapter, by Dorothy Waugh, focuses on the complexities of describing and delivering digital content for researchers. She uses examples from the Rose Library at Emory University, which boasts a digital archives unit and significant digital collections. In the following chapter on preservation of data, Bertram Lyons, who works for AVPreserve, describes the basics of the digital environment and how to begin a digital preservation program. Like other authors, he emphasizes the importance of preservation planning with donors before content is even created. Martin Gengenbach, an archivist at the Gates Archive, follows this discussion with more long-term strategies for the recovery and curation of digital content. His chapter reviews emerging digital forensics practices and the role that archivists must play in creating information systems that have a long-term component. The section concludes with an in-depth discussion of ownership, contracts, rights, and privacy concerns when providing access to digital archives. Heather Briston, university archivist at UCLA, reviews best practices and shares experiences of balancing access and privacy with digital materials.

The second section of the book targets specific types of digital collections and how archives programs manage these electronic materials. The first chapter in this section reviews performing arts collections. Vin Novara uses examples from the Smith Performing Arts Library at the University of Maryland to review the complexity of digital content created by artists and performers. The next chapter comes from Doug Boyd, who manages the Nunn Center for Oral History at the University of Kentucky. He not only describes the challenges of creating and curating oral history collections but also points to innovative tools and resources to help manage oral history initiatives. In the next chapter, Aliza Leventhal, an archivist for Sasaki Associates, explains how architects and designers have been using complex software for decades. She describes the numerous challenges of recovering and providing access to architectural and design records in the long term. Many archives programs collect political collections, which are often voluminous and carry special conditions of use. Danielle Emerling reviews common strategies for working with digital content from congressional collections, with examples from the University of West Virginia. Finally, Matthew Farrell from Duke University reviews one of the most ubiquitous digital formats of our daily lives—email. He includes different approaches to collecting email and how to provide access to researchers.

These ten chapters offer practical advice for managing digital archives. They carry similar themes that apply to all archives programs and include a few ponderings about the near future. First, the authors place great importance on the donor or creator of the material. Archivists must work with their donors early and often, planning for the acquisition of digital content even before that material has been created. Discussions with donors must be transparent. Archivists should inform donors what is possible or not possible, even if that information affects the terms and outcome of the donation. Donors serve as an important link in the chain of custody for digital archives.

The donors and creators continue as partners long after their digital material is available; archivists would do well to rely on them as long-term partners and collaborators.

Second, not all challenges of digital archives are technical or have a technical solution. The authors are at different points in their careers and play unique roles for their institutions. No matter where they are located on an organizational chart, the authors represent leaders for their archives programs and the profession. Further, the authors are well-trained archivists with specialized content knowledge. They know more than just how to build digital systems and arrange and describe a collection; they also know a great deal about the content itself. A solid understanding of the research value of incoming digital content and knowledge of the context in which that material was created (e.g., the details behind the creation of a special university task force on diversity adds contextual information to the final PDF report in the collection) are invaluable skills during all phases of managing digital archives. Sharing this knowledge with others in the program and the profession is crucial for overcoming the many challenges of maintaining digital archives. Building a team of archivists with content knowledge is just as important as having a group with strong technological skills. Such teams often start on short-term projects, with the expectation to make those positions and their associated skills become a central and programmatic part of the archives program.

Third, it is important for archivists to be current on technology and to be part of conversations with IT professionals in their institutions. Archivists do not need to be leading their organizations' IT programs, but they should at least be part of the discussions when larger decisions are being made. Archivists must not let the technology dictate what is possible for building digital archives. Too often, the limits of software or the IT budget confines the ability of archivists to be effective managers of their digital collections. It is true that resources must be allocated for software, hardware, server space, and technological development, but those choices must not limit which collections can be acquired or the how content can be accessed. Archivists are developing a variety of free open-source tools and software, which in the coming years will create new options and opportunities.

Next, the amount of incoming digital content will only increase as new technologies emerge. Individuals and organizations will produce more complex digital content in new formats at a much faster pace. A culture of "big data," and relying on data for decision making, such as solutions to global problems, will also mean that preservation, curation, and forensic recovery services will become more mainstream. Archivists and librarians have an important opportunity to play a significant role in developing those digital services and bringing digital education to a much larger audience. Technology will always be changing. Archivists must be current on these changes but not so fixated on bleeding-edge directions that they lose sight of the challenges of digital archives already under their care.

Another theme of this book revolves around the importance of use and the researcher. The use of digital archives by researchers is the main reason why archivists create, manage, and preserve digital archives. Just like analog collections, digital materials are intended to be used and not simply stored away for safekeeping. If collections are inaccessible, they serve little purpose and often become a burden on archives programs. Similarly, available digital archives are only useful if researchers are actually using them or have the correct tools to access them. Research using archival material is still at its core a tedious process, so technology does not necessarily make research easy, but it does make research possible for many digital collections. The needs of the researcher are central to the entire process of acquiring, managing, and providing access to digital archives. Often archivists are so consumed with designing the perfect system to access or store digital archives that they create systems and build content that only archivists would understand. Archivists must think like researchers if they want their digital collections to be used by researchers.

Finally, and in Weldon's footsteps, archivists must capitalize on developments in other fields and partner with experts from other professions. Archivists are not well equipped to change public perceptions about digital preservation unless they work in tandem with other professional groups, speaking the same language and the same message. Such partnerships will allow archivists to focus on more specific challenges, such as the changing nature of rights, creating better digital appraisal practices, developing more effective discovery tools, and promoting sustainable open formats for digital preservation. Through archival and nonarchival networks, archivists must share their approaches to these specific challenges. These and other areas offer the next generation of archivists the ability to further define the field of digital archives.

The success of today's archives programs is measured not by linear feet or terabytes of files but by how digital archives are acquired, accessed, and preserved. The chapters in this book provide readers with both theoretical and practical approaches to creating and caring for digital archives. They place emphasis on working with donors early and often. Building digital archives parallels the cycle of donor work—planning, cultivation, and stewardship. During each stage, archivists work with donors to ensure that the digital collections will be arranged, described, preserved, and made accessible for years to come.

Indeed, digital collections are everywhere. Archivists must take proactive and informed actions to keep valuable digital collections from becoming lost in the digital deluge. Knowing where digital materials come from, how those materials were created, what materials are important, what formats or topical areas are included, and how to serve those collections to researchers in the long term is central to archival work. This handbook is intended to generate new discussions about how archival leaders of the twenty-first century can overcome current challenges and chart paths that anticipate, rather than merely react to, future donations of digital archives.

NOTES

1. F. Gerald Ham, "Archival Strategies for the Post-Custodial Era," *American Archivist* 44 (Summer 1981): 207–16; F. Gerald Ham, "The Archival Edge," *American Archivist* 38 (January 1975): 5–13.

2. Trudy Huskamp Peterson, "Counting and Accounting: A Speculation on Change in Recordkeeping Practices," *American Archivist* 45 (Spring 1982): 131–34; Frank G. Burke, "The Future Course of Archival Theory in the United States," *American Archivist* 44 (Winter 1981): 40–46; Frank Boles, "Disrespecting Original Order," *American Archivist* 45 (Winter 1982): 26–32; Edward Weldon, "Archives and the Challenges of Change," *American Archivist* 46 (Spring 1983): 133.

3. Weldon, "Archives and the Challenges of Change," 125–26, 130–32.

4. Mark Greene and Dennis Meissner, "More Product, Less Process: Revamping Traditional Archival Processing," *American Archivist* 68 (2005): 208–63.

5. Aaron D. Purcell, *Donors and Archives: A Guidebook for Successful Programs* (Lanham, MD: Rowman & Littlefield, 2015).

6. The most recent and similar sources on management of digital archives include the Society of American Archivist's Trends in Archives series. The modules are intended to be brief treatments with eventual updates as new practices emerge. These sources provide prescriptive advice and are loosely connected by themes. Some of these modules examine components of managing and preserving donated digital content. Michael J. Shallcross and Christopher J. Prom, eds., *Appraisal and Acquisition Strategies* (Chicago: Society of American Archivists, 2016); Christopher J. Prom, ed., *Digital Preservation Essentials* (Chicago: Society of American Archivists, 2016).

7. Sources that focus on managing and organizing personal collections of digital content include Gabriela Redwine, Megan Barnard, Kate Donovan, Erika Farr, Michael Forstrom, Will Hansen, Jeremy Leighton John, Nancy Kuhl, Seth Shaw, and Susan Thomas, *Born Digital: Guidance for Donors, Dealers, and Archival Repositories* (Washington, DC: Council on Li-

brary and Information Resources, 2013), https://www.clir.org/wp-content/uploads/sites/9/pub159.pdf; Christopher A. Lee, *I, Digital: Personal Collections in the Digital Era* (Chicago: Society of American Archivists, 2011); Ofer Bergman and Steve Whittaker, *The Science of Managing Our Digital Stuff* (Cambridge, MA: MIT Press, 2017).

I

Processes and Practices

Chapter One

Acquisitions, Appraisal, and Arrangement

Lisa Calahan

Receiving digital archives is not an unusual challenge for archivists. In fact, digital materials are quickly becoming the most common type of donation to archival repositories. Yet standards and best practices for managing these donations are still in their infancy. Unfortunately, the easiest decision to make about incoming digital materials is to not make any decision at all. But, expecting the next generation of archivists to manage digital donations of the past is no longer a legitimate strategy. A more proactive approach to acquire, appraise, and arrange incoming digital materials minimizes later challenges and results in quicker access to electronic research materials.

As with all archival donations, the acquisition of digital material may be unexpected or anticipated. Archivists have traditionally used paper-based strategies for acquiring, appraising, and arranging digital materials. As a result, when digital materials are one component of an analog collection, it is common for archivists to focus first on paper records. At some point in the future, however, archivists must return to the challenges of the electronic files or media. Many times, digital materials, especially those contained on hard drives or disks, are separated from analog materials and become part of series related to electronic media (usually one of the last series listed in the collection's finding aid). Alternatively, digital files are stored on a server awaiting the careful review of an archivist.

Professional literature in the last twenty years suggested high-level best practices, stressed the time sensitivity of digital records, and encouraged archivists to act quickly. The message was not lost on archivists. The dooms-day literature warned archivists of the dangers of inaction or moving ahead haphazardly. However, the hard-line approach often has the opposite effect, and archivists may not act at all out of fear or lack of resources. Based on the guidelines supported by the literature, archivists follow a general set of protocols to successfully manage digital archives including the following:

1. Have policies and strategies approved by stakeholders
2. Have workflows and processes in place for management
3. Act quickly; time is of the essence
4. Have standardized processing activities and metadata creation policies
5. Bit-level capture or disk imaging is the professional standard
6. Provide a digital repository for management
7. Prove the authenticity and maintain the integrity of material
8. Leverage expertise in the larger local and professional communities
9. Create and maintain clearly defined submission information packages (SIPs), archival information packages (AIPs), and dissemination information packages (DIPs)
10. Provide resources and maintain a designated "clean" workstation
11. Check all accessions for viruses
12. Photograph all media
13. Regularly backup SIPs, AIPs, and DIPs
14. Create inventories for individual media[1]

Following this list of procedures and policies before the acquisition of digital archives is necessary but often not an option for many repositories. Archives programs without resources to foster a sense of digital awareness and prepar-edness create an environment in which their archivists become frightened by the prospect of acquiring and managing electronic records. This common scenario leads to the very inaction cautioned by well-meaning authors. The most important takeaway is that doing *something* is better than doing *nothing*.

Working with digital donations often requires a unique process, which is sometimes drastically different from accessioning and processing analog ma-terial. However, acquisition and appraisal best practices and ongoing ethical obligations for analog material should be followed for digital content. Devel-oping new practices and internal methods to manage digital records repre-sents an important moment to consider the realities of appraisal. Collecting decisions are based on an individual archivist's lived experience, and in the words of Verne Harris, "Every act is implicated in acts of constructing, representing, accessing, and disseminating what is held in custody. Every act of custodianship assumes an exercise of power."[2] The archivist's role in deciding what is kept as part of the historical record for society is more crucial with the accrual of digital records, and it is important to be aware of the implication of making acquisition and appraisal decisions in a profession that is predominately white, in which decision makers are in positions of political, social, and economic power.[3] As Mario Ramirez succinctly states, "*Being* an archivist does not somehow absolve them of also being a product of society and therefore subject to its prejudices and assumptions."[4]

With that in mind, archival strategies for receiving, appraising, and organizing digital materials will vary by institution, but there are some common steps for archivists to take and plenty of pitfalls to avoid. This chapter focuses on some of the common challenges of acquiring, appraising, and arranging digital donations. It discusses common approaches to these challenges and how one institution adapted those best practices to fit its needs and available resources.

BACKGROUND AND CONTEXT

Like most repositories, the Archives and Special Collections (ASC) at the University of Minnesota (UMN) Libraries has acquired digital files since the time when there were disks to put in boxes. The disks stayed dutifully in their folders and boxes, where they continue to reside until funding makes it possible to manage the legacy material. The same active ignorance cannot be prescribed with digital records today. Although ASC still receives the disks in a box, the department is much more proactive in addressing new digital acquisitions. Archivists must accept and plan to preserve history that is not created analogously—our world is a digital one.

For ASC, appraising, accessioning, and arranging digital donations required a team effort and consensus. The initiative began as a larger effort within the University of Minnesota Libraries of which ASC is a department . ASC is an academic archives program consisting of fifteen individual collecting units, each focusing on material from diverse communities. The units collect and preserve a wide range of materials to support interdisciplinary research for the university and surrounding communities. The department has approximately twenty-four full-time positions in addition to project staff, students, volunteers, and interns, who are integral to the work conducted by the department.[5]

Like many archives programs, the collecting units have a history of working independently with their own staff and unique collection development policies and internal standards for appraisal, acquisition, and processing. In fact, it was not until 2000 that the archival units were combined into one department and not until 2018 that all collecting units were housed in the same building. To better streamline and standardize internal processes, in 2007, UMN leaders created a central processing unit to help oversee the work of acquisitions and processing for the various collecting units. The decision to centrally manage acquisitions had several advantages for analog collections, but at that time, there were no guidelines in place for born-digital collections. The department still needed guidance to streamline and integrate digital collections into a uniform plan that would mirror department protocol for the central management of all acquisitions. Further, department leadership wanted to ensure that collecting units could focus on procuring digital donations, rather than creating their own internal procedures for managing them that did not match internal best practices or stewardship requirements.

In 2014, the libraries approved the creation of an Electronic Records Task Force (ERTF) to make institutional decisions about electronic acquisitions and management. The ERTF represented a centralized approach to manage the challenges of digital donations. The libraries charged the ERTF to review professional best practices, create and bolster university protocol and best practices, and create guidelines for preserving, ingesting, processing, and providing access to electronic records. Started in March 2014 and extended the following year, the ERTF included different stakeholders in managing digital content. The group included staff from several library departments responsible for the creation, storage, preservation, and access to digital material. After recognition by the University of Minnesota's University Council, the ERTF first worked on the creation and implementation of methods for acquiring, ingesting, and processing digital donations. Although originally chartered as a task force to represent all of the libraries' digital assets, it quickly became clear that the focus of the task force was better suited to address archival material.

The work of the ERTF began with conversations and meetings with archival staff and curators. The group determined that staff through the units of the UMN needed significant training on best practices for digital acquisitions and how to work more closely with donors of digital content. Through shareable documents, the ERTF promoted open conversations about the nature of electronic records and shared reasonable expectations of managing and preserving digital records. The group created staff guidelines in an easily digestible format to review the expectations of donors and the reality of what could be provided.

The ERTF mediates the various steps in a digital donation. With input from ASC staff and many UMN departments, the task force created documentation to help guide unit staff through conversations with donors about potential acquisitions, donation and acquisition strategies, preferred and preservation formats, and other considerations. ERTF members work with unit staff to better understand the source of the acquisition and what the priorities for the collection are. Once the ASC receives an acquisition, ASC staff adds the information to an electronic records accession log and the ERTF takes over. ERTF members are solely responsible for transferring the digital donation from the original or transitional media and performing ingest and accession procedures.

The experiences of managing born-digital records will be unique at every repository, but the task force model at the University of Minnesota Libraries offers a scalable approach for other institutions. By pooling available resources and bringing stakeholders together to make decisions, staff were able to create strategies for stewardship that met available staff and financial resources. Drafting best practices based on trial and error during the appraisal, acquisition, and arrangement processes allowed the task force to fully grasp the context of managing digital donations in a real environment.[6]

APPRAISAL AND ACQUISITION

The professional literature on appraisal and acquisition is often a separate discussion, but it is increasingly difficult in the twenty-first century to keep the conversation compartmentalized. Professional standards increasingly recognize and respect the ongoing role and influences of creators in addition to stronger documentation practices for archivists making acquisition and appraisal decisions. While the literature discusses the merits and shortcomings of archival appraisal, it is important to reiterate the insight of authors who challenge the status quo. Especially when managing digital donations, archivists must be aware that decision-making practices include inherent biases, particularly when it comes to appraisal strategies for preserving the histories of marginalized communities—who are often times doubly marginalized because of unequal and limited access to digital technology and content.[7] This is a key consideration when examining the appraisal and acquisition of records of marginalized communities and understanding the importance of recognizing erasure or the whitewashing of digital records.

When considering the influence of archivists on the preservation of cultural heritage, Kit Hughes argues that archivists must understand that their role in the creation process of records is more critical than fully realized. Hughes explains that archivists who are responsible for records management functions influence what records are created and kept, and Hughes believes archival appraisal serves as a key cultural function. She also states that "as contemporary recordkeeping moves further into digital realms and it becomes apparent that early intervention in the records-creation process is imperative if archives want to save any records whatsoever, the question of archivist involvement in the creation of the documentary record resolves itself—it is unavoidable."[8]

It is the urgency for intervention and action to preserve digital records that can be overwhelming. Unlike analog records, we know that bits can easily slip through our hands like grains of sand—preserving context and authenticity is not easily accomplished. Often, the urgency with which archivists must acquire and preserve digital records is not met with the additional resources to address digital records with realistic ambition. Likewise, Angelika Menne-Haritz explains that beyond the many questions regarding appraisal strategies, "the underlying premises of all of them is that archives aim at shaping as true as possible an image of society. But the raw material that we must work with does not conform to those ambitions."[9]

Because of the dichotomy between the ambition of best practices and reality, the application of theoretical archival appraisal standards for digital donations nosedives when practitioners attempt to match best practices to practical available resources. The massive quantities of digital material produced by creators are often too overwhelming for archives programs to manage, which makes it difficult for archivists to devote the bit-by-bit attention that professional standards outline. As Richard Brown and Daniel Caron explain in their 2013 article in the *American Archivist*, only a small fraction of the enormous quantity of digital content has historical or intellectual value, and they point to macro-appraisal as a potential adoption method for digital appraisal. Separating the chaff from the wheat is impossible given the vast amount of content. Their article stresses that appraisal should move toward the preservation of context of the record creator rather than the content of the records. They also emphasize the unsustainability of the practitioner's "blind faith" by relying on technological recall and the hope that the strengths of information technology will render appraisal unnecessary.[10] Further, Brown and Caron explain:

> Of the various elements contributing to the information management crisis, surely one of the most significant has been the "blind faith" . . . in the capacity of information technology to both handle the volumetrics of current information production and support the "precision of recall" necessary for effective public administration on a continuing basis. The operational manifestation of this information technology mythology—and it is truly mythology—is that it is unnecessary to consider the value of information resources from any lens or frame of perspectives . . . since the [practitioner] . . . has the storage capacity to keep everything and the computing power to render the "everything" instantly and precisely accessible through software search tools and applications.[11]

Inversely, the seminal writings of Ricky Erway for OCLC indicate that best practices should focus on item-level management of digital material. Erway's work concentrates on the creation of disk imaging to preserve at the bit level as well as photographing and inventorying individual digital media.[12] Likewise, the AIMS Project outlines workflows and processes and is caveated as a "framework," with the understanding that following the model is not an attainable venture.[13] In their 2011 essay on the case study of the Salman Rushdie digital archive, Laura Carroll, Erika Farr, Peter Hornsby, and Ben Ranker focus on the intense amount of attention that the collection required. As one of the first case studies on working with hybrid collections, archivists have held this as a gold-standard example (as they should). Yet, many archivists work in archives programs that are unable to devote significant resources to this level of digital archives management.[14]

Authors, including Brown and Caron, have emphasized the differences between what is realistically possible with available resources and professional best practices and what are the expectations. This disconnect feeds inaction and archival paralysis when making appraisal and acquisition decisions. Robert Sink argues that the archival profession does not benefit from "a single appraisal theory to guide archivists in making acquisition and disposition decisions."[15] Because of overly detailed best practices, urging archivists to preserve every bit, and overarching and overly broad appraisal theory, archivists are left with little guidance on appraisal practices for digital records.

The prescription that only bit preservation and retention of inaccessible proprietary and obsolete formats should be preserved continues to be a major stumbling block for many repositories interested in preserving and providing access to digital records. The preservation and management of digital records is much more intensive than their analog counterparts, but the mandate that all digital files should be managed and preserved equally represents an early misunderstanding by archivists of how donors create and manage digital records. More recent publications and conversations regarding the appraisal of digital records to fit the repositories' capabilities and internal strategies is a more realistic and iterative approach. [16]

Having a firm grasp of the professional literature on appraisal of digital records is an important and ongoing first step to implementing individual best practices and practical workflows. It is arguable, however, that it is more important to understand that appraisal literature will not reflect the reader's real-world management of digital collections. The bigger challenge is that available resources (i.e., staffing and technological infrastructure) at each institution often make professional recommendations unrealistic if not impossible. By following recommended best practices without the necessary support in place, archives programs become poor stewards of digital collections.

As the UMN experience demonstrates, sometimes being good stewards is more important than following professional standards. The importance of being a steward is often defined by the available resources the archives program has access to and the ability to say "no" when stewardship cannot meet a collection's preservation or management needs. This practical approach conflicts with the advice from the authors of *Born Digital: Guidance for Donors, Dealers, and Archival Repositories*, who argue that making appraisal decisions based on real resources, or working with donors to manipulate and organize files, is negligence. This important source suggests that all digital content be preserved in the short term for analysis in the long term. They recommend that archives programs preserve, bit by bit, every inaccessible file that may or may not have historic value. [17] For UMN, investment of scarce resources into an uncertain future is not a sustainable approach for accepting digital donations. Instead, all incoming donations receive some level of appraisal, and those decisions are well documented.

At UMN, appraisal is tied to acquisition and ingestion of content. Working with donors before the material arrives is crucial. Those conversations affect the level of appraisal necessary once the donation is complete. Building a close relationship with donors allows for candid conversations about the program's capacity and what types of materials are wanted and can be supported. Appraising the files before they arrive provides archivists with a better understanding of what type of intervention the collection will require. Having clear guidelines of the types of formats that are acceptable and supported makes appraisal decisions easier.

One of the pitfalls of actively collecting digital files and appraising post-donation is underestimating the quantity of digital materials that are created, duplicated, and shared. Brown and Caron question the archival value of the bulk of digital content being created. The authors also describe the logistical challenges of digital appraisal, especially the endless variety of programmatic and proprietary software needed to use, view, and manipulate records.[18] At UMN, archivists minimize these challenges by early engagement with donors when possible. These conversations promote a better understanding of types of material and records that have historical and archival value. Archivists must emphasize to donors which types of file formats the archives programs can realistically support. It is unwise for archivists to promise or allude to a promise of keeping certain file types and formats in the hopes of future technological developments that might make the content accessible.

Even with structured and intensive appraisal practices that include active donor participation before acquisition, it can be difficult to assess the complexities of the collection until after acquisition. The actual review of digital material and discussions with donors occur in many settings, including at the donor's home, at the repository, or virtually through file-sharing software. But, it is not until the ingest process that staff are able to obtain a deeper understanding of the complexities of digital collections. At UMN, collection review is built in as part of the ingest process. Archivists review file formats, check for duplicative material, and screen for personally identifiable information (PII). This process helps assess the condition and uniqueness of the files, and internal appraisal decisions are based on a series of questions and considerations. Archivists consider the ability to preserve and provide access to files, the volume of the donation, the relationship between digital and paper materials within a hybrid collection, the available information about the context and content, the ability to realistically transfer the files, and an understanding of potential preservation challenges. This review identifies files that were created by and stored within proprietary software, the level of organization, and any type of image identifier.

As an example of digital appraisal at UMN, archivists worked with a professional photographer to acquire a large collection of digital photographs. Typical for digital photograph collections, none of the files were organized, and the file names were the image identifiers assigned by the digital camera (i.e., dmg0001). Members of the ERTF used documented workflows and best practices to make definitive appraisal decisions. During the examination, even though conversations with the donor about file formats had already occurred, archivists discovered that all image files were kept in a proprietary editing database that could not be supported. That reality meant that archivists needed to work closely with the donor to convert the image files to TIFF files before the donation. Fortunately, the donor was amenable to spending countless hours of personal time to export the files out of the proprietary software and save them as TIFFs. The donor exported over 18,000 files (approximately 473 GB), organized the files, and saved them to a hard drive. Archivists still faced the challenge of naming and organizing the material, but the quality of the content justified the appraisal decision.

As a second example of appraisal, a nonlocal film production company wanted to donate a collection of digital audio and visual material. Archivists shared technical requirements with the company and requested more information on the size and file types of the potential donation. From the first conversations, archivists explained to the donors that staff would not be able to preserve any files that required proprietary software. Further, archivists recommended that the company convert the in-house production and proprietary files to MP4 so that staff could be confident that they could support and preserve the files. Even though this request slowed the donation by about nine months, the files arrived as a usable and accessible research collection. The cost benefit and immediate value to researchers was immeasurable.

These examples support Robert Sink's argument that "appraisal is not a single action to be applied to a group of records at a single point of time. The appraisal process is progressive. It takes place throughout our custody of records, and we ask different questions at different times in the process."[19] This is especially true as archivists making appraisal decisions based on the cultural heritage value, stewardship considerations, access points, and available resources.

Just as the range of collecting scope varies for each archives program, the types of digital records acquired are also vastly different. Each new accession brings its own issues and challenges, which means that best practices need to be flexible to suit the constant fluctuation of collection demands. The University of Minnesota Libraries developed its standards through a centralized committee (ERTF), which had input from multiple departments and from staff with different roles in the process. This collaborative approach is scalable for all types and sizes of archives programs.

The ERTF outlined issues to be aware of, from appraising material for content to limits on the ability to preserve and/or view all file types. The group also created a similar guide for staff to share with donors as a starting point for a conversation on what a digital donation might include, types of formats that could be accepted, and access expectations. In addition, the ERTF produced a brief survey for staff to share with donors to gain more information about their potential donation. Donors were asked to estimate the potential donation size, list types of formats, identify proprietary software, describe types of material found in the records, address any type of personal information, and list any requested restrictions on the material.

To supplement the work of the ERTF, leaders of ASC reinstituted an acquisition committee. The committee, which included staff with broad responsibilities for collection development, reviewed potential, large digital donations in keeping with ASC policies. In collaboration with the head of archival processing, the acquisition committee drafted a centralized accessioning protocol. This protocol required that all accessions—analog, born-digital, and hybrid—be reported on a centralized accession log, on which the collection could be tracked.

Once an accession log for the donation is completed, the collection is added to an ingest queue to be accessioned by either specific archival or unit staff or a member of the ERTF; the person assigned to ingest the collection often depends on available staff resources and the immediacy of the collection needs. As part of the ingest process, staff remove the files from original hardware devices. They load the files onto a "clean" hard drive, where they can be examined according to internal protocols. Preservation of digital content begins at this early stage. Archivists complete checksum reports on the files and conduct a series of reports to check for personal or private information, potential duplication, content not originally identified as topically relevant, and other common issues. Many times, archivists identify errors and issues that need to be discussed with the donor before further action can be taken. The ERTF shares this information with the unit responsible for the donation. It is then up to the unit to provide the resources to make processing decisions based on the recommendations of the ERTF.

ARRANGEMENT

The arrangement of digital collections represents the practical application of archival theory. At the same time, arrangement is the most nebulous and intangible process in managing digital records. Existing literature on processing digital records has focused primarily on preservation and access to content while largely ignoring the challenges of arranging digital files. Unlike analog material, digital files cannot be holistically reviewed. The principle of "original order," used for arranging paper records, does not fit well with the structure of digital files. Further, many digital collections have nested file structures, which make it difficult if not impossible to identify clear arrangement paths.

The question of arrangement and integration of minimal processing techniques with digital records is an ongoing professional conversation. The minimal approach to processing has become a common method for archives programs to quickly arrange large analog collections. Similar to the disconnect between high-level appraisal best practices for digital records, the application of minimal processing at first response seems to clash with item-level/bit-level management of digital records. In a 2010 article, Mark Greene states that professional literature on electronic records focuses so heavily "on theory and definition rather than on method and practice" that there is considerable confusion on what are acceptable practices for arrangement. Greene argues that, just as with analog records, minimally processing material and providing collection-level description is better than inaction, which, in principle, is the same argument made for minimally processing digital records. [20] In an article from 2014, Cyndi Shein provides a case study of successful use of minimal processing on the Getty Research Institute's digital records. She astutely points out that DAS workshops and electronic-records-specific education are "still fundamentally built upon existing workflows for physical archives." [21] Shein argues that "accepting 'minimal processing' and/or 'accessioning as processing' as viable options in the handling of born-digital materials meets a documented need for flexible and scalable workflows" that are based in a foundation of archival best practices and accepted principles. [22]

Initially, ASC archivists attempted to process all new acquisitions at the item level, believing that by doing so we were following recommended best practices. However, it did not take long for staff to realize that doing so was completely unsustainable and not the best use of staff resources. Instead, the ERTF recommended a tiered approach to processing digital material based on three levels to account for the different tasks and requirements for processing digital records. This tiered processing approach created levels of priority and arrangement recommendations for each collection. Arrangement decisions were based on the complexity of the records, the identified original order, the perceived research value, and available financial and staff resources.

At ASC, the tiered approach for processing analog and digital collections includes three levels. The first level is "minimal." A minimally processed digital collection receives a collection-level finding aid with minimal preservation steps taken—at most, the collection SIP is created, and no action is taken on removing duplicates or PII identified during ingest. No arrangement is recommended for collections at this level, unless the donor supplied an inventory, or it was created by an archivist at the time of accessioning.

The second level is "intermediate." These collections may have top-level folder arrangement and renaming conducted as needed, and duplicates are weeded and PII redacted where necessary. It is expected that the description will meet DACS requirements for a multilevel description with high research value series denoted with scope and content notes.

The third level is "full." These collections will have top-level folders arranged and renamed as needed, and subsequent folders or files may be arranged or renamed to aid access with all duplicates removed and all PII redacted. Each of these levels include room for interpretation, flexibility, and modularity depending on the collection and its contents.

At ASC, this tiered approach to arrangement has worked well for digital donations. Although preservation has different meanings and implications for analog and digital materials, some of the more routine preservation steps are built into the ingesting/accessioning process. In addition, having clear guidelines on what are acceptable *minimal* practices relieves the processing archivist of the burden of doing more than his or her internal resources can realistically support.

Since recommended best practices do not meet the realities of most archival programs, having clear processing levels helps remove internal roadblocks and reframes the focus of processing on accessibility and stewardship. The preservation needs of digital collections must be assessed early in the process of a donation and those needs are an ongoing commitment of resources, technology, and access tools. Archivists must understand that these high-level decisions affect the tasks of arranging and processing a digital collection.

At ASC, the arrangement function for digital donations is focused on ingest and making sure the files are preservation ready. The ERTF completes this preliminary work and leaves further processing up to the individual unit responsible for managing the collection. In most cases, ASC archivists do not complete further arrangement because the collections are enormous, the files are deeply nested, and resources are limited. In addition, internal data on researchers accessing digital collections does not support the need for further arrangement of the material.

Another perspective on applying analog arrangement patterns to digital collections is that the virtual retrieval of these files is far different from physically pulling folders of analog materials. When a researcher requests use of a portion of a large collection (e.g., five boxes from a five-hundred-box collection), archivists retrieve the specific boxes rather than the entirety of the collection. When a researcher wants to access a large digital collection (e.g., five individual files from five hundred nested folders), however, there is no reason for archivists to pull out the specific files. Rather, the archivists would provide researchers access to the entire digital collection to promote discovery of content by the researcher, an underlying principle of MPLP. This shift in thinking about access and retrieval decreases access barriers for researches and allows archivists to focus on other challenges of digital archives.

The experiences at UMN demonstrate that the arrangement of digital collections represents a process that is not so different from principles of minimal arrangement of analog materials. Most often, if arrangement occurs, it happens earlier in the donation process. The ERTF either identifies or completes a number of simple arrangement tasks that could be completed—identifying and removing duplicates when easy disposition decisions are clear, identifying and possibly removing personal and private information, simplifying overly nested folders, shortening folder titles, re-titling files and folders with special characters, and grouping arbitrarily named image files—during the accessioning process.

NEXT STEPS

The development of processes to manage incoming digital donations is still emerging across the profession. At the University of Minnesota Libraries, archivists took a centralized and committee-based approach to the many challenges of acquisition, appraisal, and arrangement. The Electronic Record

Task Force coordinated the crucial responsibilities involved in receiving and preparing digital collections for the multiple archival units and the creation of internal best practices based on realistic resources. These experiences demonstrate that working with donors early in the process resulted in faster and better access for researchers. That early involvement also included discussions about long-term preservation of data.

The variety of archives programs mirrors the uniqueness of each collection that they hold. Despite the wide range of institutional and technological environments, archivists are forging new standards for the work of digital donations. In just two years, the ERTF at the University of Minnesota registered significant progress in documenting workflows and best practices. These standards are applicable to other archives programs facing similar digital challenges with the understanding that use of these practices will depend on available resources and the level of institutional support.

In the coming decade, archivists must be better prepared for receiving more digital than analog content. This means that archivists must play a leading role in making institutional decisions about information architecture, educating records creators about archives, disseminating the lessons of their successes and failures to other archivists, and challenging appraisal and acquisition decisions based on white privilege. These types of activities empower other archivists to develop their own solutions to the multiple challenges of acquiring, appraising, and arranging digital donations. Responses to those challenges are important for the description stage, which is covered in the next chapter.

NOTES

1. These points are common themes in literature on the management of digital archives. AIMS Work Group *AIMS Born-Digital Collections: An Inter-institutional Model for Stewardship* (University of Virginia Libraries, January 2012): 85, https://dcs.library.virginia.edu/files/2013/02/AIMS_final_text.pdf; Lorraine L. Richards, "Teaching Data Creators How to Develop an OAIS-Compliant Digital Curation System: Colearning and Breakdowns in Support of Requirements Analysis," *American Archivist* 79 (Fall/Winter 2016): 371–91; Ricky Erway, *You've Got to Walk before You Can Run: First Steps for Managing Born-Digital Content Received on Physical Media* (Dublin, OH: OCLC Research, 2012), https://www.oclc.org/content/dam/research/publications/library/2012/2012-06.pdf; Ricky Erway, *Walk This Way: Detailed Steps for Transferring Born-Digital Content from Media You Can Read In-House* (Dublin, OH: OCLC Research, 2013), https://www.oclc.org/content/dam/research/publications/library/2013/2013-02.pdf.

2. Verne Harris, "Jacque Derrida Meets Nelson Mandela: Archival Ethics at the Endgame," *Archival Science* 1, nos. 1–2 (2011): 9.

3. Mario H. Ramirez, "Being Assumed Not to Be: A Critique of Whiteness as an Archival Imperative," *American Archivist* 78 (Fall/Winter 2015): 348. Updated SAA membership statistics are also available through *The 2017 WArS/SAA Salary Survey*, available at: https://www2.archivists.org/sites/all/files/WArS-SAA-Salary-Survey-Report.pdf.

4. Ramirez, "Being Assumed Not to Be," 351.

5. "Archives and Special Collections," University of Minnesota, https://www.lib.umn.edu/special.

6. The Electronic Records Task Force phase 1 and 2 resulted in the publication of two final reports that include more detailed information about the task force and outcomes. Carol Kussmann and R. Arvid Nelsen, *Electronic Records Task Force Final Report* (University of Minnesota, September 2015), http://hdl.handle.net/11299/174097; Lisa Calahan and Carol Kussmann, *Electronic Records Task Force Phase 2 Final Report* (University of Minnesota, August 2017), http://hdl.handle.net/11299/189543.

7. Marc Hudson, "Detroit's Broadband Infrastructure, Connectivity and Adoption Issues" (PowerPoint presentation, FCC, 2015), http://transition.fcc.gov/c2h/10282015/marc-hudson-presentation-10282015.pdf ; Karl Vick, "The Digital Divide: A Quarter of the Nation Is without Broadband," *Time*, March 30, 2017, http://time.com/4718032/the-digital-divide/.

8. Kit Hughes, "Appraisal as Cartography: Cultural Studies in the Archives" *American Archivist* 77 (Spring/Summer 2014): 290.

9. Angelika Menne-Haritz, "Appraisal or Documentation: Can We Appraise Archives by Selecting Content?" *American Archivist* 57 (Summer 1994): 541.

10. Richard Brown and Daniel Caron, "Appraising Content for Value in the New World: Establishing Expedient Documentary Presence," *American Archivist* 76 (Spring/Summer 2013): 138, 149.

11. Ibid., 154.

12. Erway, "Walk before You Can Run"; Erway, "Walk This Way."

13. AIMS, *AIMS Born-Digital Collections*.

14. Laura Carroll, Erika Farr, Peter Hornsby, and Ben Ranker, "A Comprehensive Approach to Born-Digital Archives," *Archivaria* 72 (Fall 2011): 61–92.

15. Robert Sink, "Appraisal: The Process of Choice," *American Archivist* 53 (Summer, 1990): 452.

16. Geof Huth, "Appraising Digital Records," in *Appraisal and Acquisition Strategies*, eds. Michael J. Shallcross and Christopher J. Prom (Chicago: Society of American Archivists, 2016), 10–66.

17. Gabriela Redwine, Megan Barnard, Kate Donovan, Erika Farr, Michael Forstrom, Will Hansen, Jeremy Leighton John, Nancy Kuhl, Seth Shaw, and Susan Thomas, *Born Digital: Guidance for Donors, Dealers, and Archival Repositories* (Washington, DC: Council on Library and Information Resources, 2013): 17, https://www.clir.org/wp-content/uploads/sites/9/pub159.pdf.

18. Brown and Caron, "Appraising Content for Value in the New World."

19. Sink, "Appraisal," 456.

20. Mark A. Greene, "MPLP: It's Not Just for Processing Anymore," *American Archivist* 73 (Spring/Summer 2010): 175–203.

21. Cyndi Shein, "From Accession to Access: A Born-Digital Materials Case Study," *Journal of Western Archives* 5 (2014): 4.

22. Ibid., 5.

Chapter Two

Description and Delivery

Dorothy Waugh

As archives acquire increasing numbers of born-digital materials, the need for responsive access strategies becomes more urgent. This chapter examines the challenges involved in describing and delivering born-digital content and takes as its basis the core archival principle that archives be used. Many of the experiences described are from the Stuart A. Rose Manuscript, Archives, and Rare Book Library at Emory University in Atlanta, Georgia (Rose Library).

In 1956, T. R. Schellenberg declared that "the end of all archival effort is to preserve valuable records and make them available for use."[1] Given the many complexities of born-digital materials, Schellenberg's emphasis on use serves as a valuable end goal. This goal of use guides archivists as they devise strategies for managing and, in particular, facilitating access to born-digital materials.

That archival materials should be used may seem like a rather obvious point to make in a chapter focused on description and access, but a focus on this end goal helps archivists simplify the overwhelming challenges associated with born-digital materials. A lack of IT support and infrastructure, limited staffing and time, gaps in the tools required to perform essential tasks (such as descriptive metadata extraction or the redaction of confidential information), and a need for best practices concerning policy and workflow are some of the major obstacles hindering the provision of access to born-digital material.[2] Archivists have been slow to address these challenges, focusing more on the tasks related to the acquisition and preservation of born-digital archival materials. These are important topics, but their prioritization has left something of a gap in the literature on description and delivery of electronic material. This has begun to be remedied in recent years, as a number of case studies, reports, and presentations at professional conferences have focused on describing and accessing digital materials.[3]

Even so, addressing the description and delivery of born-digital archival materials can seem daunting. Efforts aimed at devising strategies raise a series of questions. First, how can archival programs adapt existing descriptive principles and practice to meet the needs of digital objects? Next, where can archives make access available? Finally, what sorts of delivery methods are possible within the constraints of the archives' time, funding, and technical infrastructure? Answers to these questions provide a starting point for delivering access to electronic material found in existing and incoming donations to archives. To remember Schellenberg is perhaps the best advice for archivists navigating these questions and to focus on the importance of use and the experiences of other archives programs. As Cyndi Shein, assistant archivist at the J. Paul Getty Trust Institutional Records and Archives, advises, "We needed to think big (consider scalable, extensible models for the future), but start small (do something now)."[4]

HOW DO WE FACILITATE USE?

Meaningful description is crucial for materials residing in special collections libraries and archives where access is frequently restricted and typically must occur on site. As a result, descriptive records are often the first point of contact for researchers wanting to know whether the material is relevant to their work. Traditionally, the finding aid has performed this role. Collections are described at the aggregate level based on provenance, with description moving from the general to the specific depending on what level of detail resources allow. The More Product, Less Process (MPLP) method, introduced by Mark Greene and Dennis Meissner in 2005, encourages archivists to reduce backlog by "creat[ing] a baseline level of access to all collection material."[5] Such a task demands that description is limited to only what is necessary. Daniel Santamaria at Princeton University refers to the functional requirements for bibliographic records (FRBR) developed by the International Federation of Library Associations and Institutions (IFLA) to define what this might include. Description, according to FRBR, should enable researchers to find, identify, select, and obtain relevant material. Santamaria argues that "archivists should strive to do just enough to create finding aids or other descriptive records and systems that allow users to perform each of these tasks."[6]

Faced with limited resources, such an approach certainly prioritizes use, but to what extent can it be applied to born-digital materials? The MPLP model argues that the creation of description should be an iterative process beginning at least as early as appraisal. However, this can be challenging when dealing with born-digital materials that require intermediary technologies in order to be rendered and viewed. At the Rose Library, it has often regrettably been the case that digital media arrives with little information about its content (and there is often very little can be gleaned from even the most thorough examination of the case of a disk or drive). In such situations, archivists at the Rose Library were hard pressed to provide useful description without first doing some additional processing work (e.g., capturing and mounting a disk image). This highlights the importance of early intervention with donors and ensuring that this scenario occurs less frequently. When possible, speaking with donors at the acquisition stage provides an opportunity to gather at least summary information about digital content, which can be repurposed as high-level description preprocessing.

At the Rose Library, where baseline finding aids are created for unprocessed collections during accessioning, researchers are often given access to boxes of papers organized just as they were received. For born-digital materials, however, description does not necessarily equate access. Some level of processing is required to make material, often stored on obsolete media using obsolete file formats, accessible. To date, the interpretation of MPLP for born-digital materials at the Rose Library has involved a brief description of what is included at the collection level alongside language that instructs interested researchers to contact an archivist if they wish to view the materials. These instructions include the proviso that some processing will be required before allowing access, so researchers should not expect materials to be available immediately. Archivists at the Rose Library also advise that, in some cases, collection restrictions, copyright limitations, personal or private content, or technical complications might prevent access altogether.

This processing-on-demand model is not ideal. To date, collection-level description has been limited to physical description of the media, and this lack of information might make potential researchers reluctant to contact archivists at the Rose Library, especially if they do not have experience working with born-digital (or simply archival) material. Nevertheless, collection-level description establishes a baseline level of access.

AGGREGATE-LEVEL VERSUS ITEM-LEVEL DESCRIPTION

Archivists at both the Rose Library and elsewhere have struggled with questions about balancing limited resources with the need for adequate description of digital collections. Some have suggested focusing more on the metadata associated with born-digital objects. From a preservation and technical perspective, the capture of metadata relating to both the digital object and the environment in which it was created and stored is essential. John Langdon, who notes that existing archival standards cannot accommodate all of this required metadata, suggests that alternative standards (e.g., PREMIS and METS) might supersede traditional description.[7]

Digital management tools, such as DSpace or CONTENTdm, are typically designed to accommodate item-level description that facilitates granular search and discovery for researchers. In this model, there is a one-to-one relationship between each digital object and corresponding metadata record. It is still unclear how this model corresponds with traditional archival description, which describes collections at the aggregate level and prioritizes contextualization.[8] The Digital Public Library of America (DPLA) addresses this question in a 2016 report. The report acknowledges that institutions are looking for ways in which to "translate their archival description practice into the world of digital repositories."[9] The authors propose an initial solution whereby records contain enhanced collection information and finding aids can be accessed from the DPLA interface in order to better expose contextual information.[10]

Jane Zhang and Dayne Mauney define DPLA's approach as a segregated model of representation in which emphasis is placed on the discovery of digital objects through item-level metadata with links directing researchers to additional contextual information as needed. The danger of this approach, they argue, is that such contextual information may be lost or ignored.[11] Alternatively, many institutions currently making born-digital material available online do so using what Zhang and Mauney call an "embedded model" of representation, whereby researchers access digital objects through links embedded in the finding aid.[12] Unlike the segregated model, this approach foregrounds context, although possibly at the expense of online search and discovery.[13]

Zhang and Mauney also define a third model of representation, the parallel model, which attempts to unite a context-based and item-centric approach to description without favoring either. They cite the Washington State Digital

Archives as an example, in which a single interface offers researchers the opportunity to both perform metadata-based search functions and browse contextual collection information that more closely resembles a traditional finding aid.[14] This, according to Zhang and Mauney, lets researchers simultaneously discover relevant materials by taking advantage of two supplementary systems. This is a major step forward in the description of digital material and they believe that the next step is to integrate these two systems.[15]

APPLYING DESCRIPTIVE STANDARDS

Since the 1990s, content and structural standards have helped archivists create consistent and reusable description that supports interoperability across institutions. The ability to reuse descriptive data is especially valuable in connection to born-digital materials. The consistent use of standards to encode and transmit current descriptive data allows for greater levels of computer processing, which in turn may simplify attempts to repurpose that data in future systems.[16]

In recent years, studies have focused on which existing standards can best accommodate born-digital material. Widely used content standards, such as DACS (Describing Archives: A Content Standard) and ISAD(G) (General International Standard Archival Description), are designed to be format neutral, and an increasing number of archivists are using these standards to describe born-digital material. In 2016, the Descriptive Standards Roundtable in the UK published a report examining the ISAD(G) framework. The report recommends how the standard might be applied in this context. The assessment focuses both on the need to reconcile meaningful description with limited manual effort and on the challenges inherent in doing so. For example, auto-populating the title field with original file names could make the description process more efficient but might also result in meaningless and unhelpful titles. The authors recommend using original file names, arguing that to manually create meaningful titles would require too much time and effort and could result in inconsistent naming conventions. They suggest that a mandatory scope and content note at the collection or series level might help address remaining concerns. As a possible new direction for description, the authors of the report ask whether crowdsourcing might be used to supplement description when metadata extracted from the files for the sake of efficiency might be misleading (e.g., researchers may be able to supply correct dates if file metadata had changed as a result of migration).[17] Throughout the report, the authors emphasize the importance of transparency in describing born-digital material, particularly with reference to instances when a machine is responsible for the description as opposed to a human.

Despite such efforts, some archivists doubt the suitability of existing standards to address the challenges of born-digital material. They argue that the use of standards in archival description has been beneficial, but it has also encouraged a kind of "groupthink, . . . rendering it harder, if not impossible to conceptualise alternative ways of seeing, or to explore alternative or supplementary models."[18] The need to address description of born-digital materials presents an opportunity to reevaluate current practices and their underlying archival principles.

American archival practice is based on the principles of provenance and original order. Provenance in particular—which emphasizes the origin or source of records as a key organizing principle—has driven the development of the traditional finding aid and approaches to description. As the inclusion of born-digital materials in archival collections increasingly becomes the norm, archivists have questioned whether these core principles remain relevant. Some have argued that these principles help archivists develop strategies for dealing with born-digital material.[19] Other archivists, however, have argued that the nature of born-digital archives exposes both the technical and ideological limitations of these principles.

From a technical perspective, Jefferson Bailey suggests that the physical arrangement of data as inscribed on digital media is reason enough to question the applicability of these guiding archival principles. Referring to original order, Bailey notes that unlike an analog object, a digital object is composed of bits of data randomly distributed across multiple tracks and sectors of a hard drive or disk depending on where storage space was available. Bits belonging to a single digital object are reconstructed each time the object is accessed and rendered at the file level. In the process, however, the file is "altered in minute ways (for instance, a file's 'last-opened' date) and [will] thus be composed of a new order as new bits are assigned to other available areas of the disk."[20] Consequently, at the level of physical inscription at least, the order of bits that make up a file shifts regularly as they are accessed and interpreted. In terms of provenance, too, traces of physical data created and stored by previous users of the media can coexist alongside newer data. This leaves what Bailey calls "a trail of ownership . . . extend[ing] beyond the object, creator or fonds."[21]

Others, like Bailey, have also argued that the principle of provenance is poorly suited to address the challenges of born-digital material. Jarrett Drake notes that increasingly popular applications designed to support the collaborative creation and management of files, such as Google Drive, Dropbox, and Box, are complicating notions of ownership and a single fonds.[22] This is not necessarily a new problem, as the application of provenance to archival collections has long forced archivists to make difficult decisions about analog records for which there is evidence of shared ownership or multiple creators. Nonetheless, the ubiquity of tools like Google Drive has highlighted this issue.

Social context and perspective influences what archives collect. Archivists must consider the extent to which description imposes a worldview. Jarrett Drake writes about the role archival description and its reliance on provenance has played in privileging certain perspectives over others.[23] Similarly, Richard Cox suggests that archival finding aids can be viewed as structures serving to legitimize social and political viewpoints.[24]

Finding aids have long served as the predominant form of description for archival collections. Over the past two decades, archivists have questioned how well-suited the finding aid is to describing digital material. In an article from 1995, David Wallace argues that the ability to capture detailed metadata about digital files renders the finding aid redundant as a tool for description.[25] Since then, many have suggested that single, linear, fonds-based narratives provided by finding aids are ill equipped to deal with the technical complexities of digital data, which is increasingly distributed across different platforms and models of ownership.

In their 2015 article, Sarah Higgins, Christopher Hilton, and Lyn Dafis maintain that traditional finding aids are emblematic of an era more comfortable with paper records than digital files. They argue that ISAD(G) developed out of the now-outdated assumption that these documents would be presented to researchers for passive consumption as opposed to more interactive engagement.[26] Similarly, John Langdon argues that the availability of online description and digital content complicates the assumption that researchers will continue to engage with whole finding aids as a means of discovery. Instead, online search functionality increases the likelihood that researchers will be delivered directly to "individual, decontextualized entries," thus limiting the value of a finding aid's hierarchical approach to description.[27]

New technology offers different options for adapting archival descriptive standards to digital materials. The possibilities afforded by linked open data and the Semantic Web, for example, have been widely discussed in recent years and could present a viable alternative to the static and hierarchically structured finding aids that have been the mainstay of archival description for so long. In contrast, linked data is built upon a network of modular records. For example, each record might represent a person, a place, or an archival object and could be connected through a series of links with other modular records to which it has a relationship. When made available online, data structured in this way is easily shared across systems for increased discovery and use.[28]

In September 2016, the Expert Group on Archival Description (EGAD) of the International Council on Archives published a draft of a new standard, *Records in Contexts: A Conceptual Model for Archival Description* (RiC-CM). The group echoes many of the criticisms outlined above, arguing that current practices fail to "reflect the social and material complexity of the origins of [archival] records."[29] In response, EGAD proposes a new standard built upon linked open data technology to provide a multidimensional, as opposed to hierarchical, approach to description.[30]

WHERE DOES USE OCCUR?

Today's library users expect that all information should or could be available online. While this assumption is often incorrect for analog materials, it seems somewhat less unreasonable when the records in question are born-digital to begin with. Nevertheless, many institutions limit access to born-digital holdings to their reading room, where researchers must view digital content at secure, standalone workstations. This is, for the most part, true at the Rose Library, where access is confined to the reading room due to donor restrictions, donor and third-party privacy concerns, and copyright restrictions. Similar reasons are given at the University of Hull, Duke University, Penn State University, North Carolina State University, and the University of Virginia, all of which use reading room workstations to provide controlled access to the bulk of their processed born-digital collections.[31]

Reading-room-only access to digital materials is not ideal, for both researchers and archivists. At the Rose Library, the workstations require constant upkeep. Reading room laptops provide access to digitized still images, born-digital and digitized audiovisual recordings, and processed born-digital manuscript collections. The collections are accessed through different applications (some of which require an internet connection) and require security settings that prevent sharing or download. The biggest challenge for archivists has been mandatory updates of each software application, which often violate existing security settings. Thus, archivists must reconfigure settings on a fairly regular basis, resulting in confused reading room staff and hasty documentation.

In spite of the drawbacks, controlled reading room access through workstations allows researchers to consult the digital materials. This option may be as simple as a directory of processed born-digital files stored locally on a desktop and available for researchers to browse. Such a setup offers a low barrier to entry for institutions with limited resources that just want to achieve the end goal and make material available for use.

Despite the popularity of this approach, archivists are aware that researchers would be better served (and higher in number) with online access to digital content. At Princeton University's Seeley G. Mudd Manuscript Library, unrestricted material can be accessed directly from the finding aid.[32] As another example of this more open framework, the Rose Library in collaboration with the Emory Center for Digital Scholarship created an Omeka website on which researchers can view materials from one of the library's unrestricted collection.[33]

Other institutions are building access systems that allow for remote access to born-digital materials with restrictions. Michelle Light writes about the implementation of a virtual reading room at the University of California, Irvine. Light and her colleagues recognized the demand for online access and designed a system that requires researchers to register and agree to the same set of policies as would apply if they had visited the actual reading room. Once this step is complete, online researchers can access files through an instance of DSpace. As Light explains, this compromise "mitigated the risks involved in providing this kind of access to personal, archival materials with privacy and copyright issues by limiting the number of qualified users."[34] Archivists at the University of Georgia's Richard B. Russell Library for Political Research and Studies took a similar approach. Virtual researchers request access to digital material via the finding aid, and once access has been approved, relevant files are delivered to a Google Drive account, and the researcher is given viewing permissions.[35]

In both instances, archivists used existing reading room policies to guide and justify implementation of online access models. At the University of

California, Irvine, the same user agreements and procedures governing how archival materials are used inside the reading room were required of remote researchers, which shifted the onus of responsibility for use to the researcher. Light argues that this application of established reading room policy to the virtual reading room environment enabled her to reconcile this new approach to access with the terms laid out in the donors' gift agreements.[36] Similarly, archivists at the University of Georgia changed their virtual reading room policies to reflect the use of digital cameras in the physical reading room. Because the policy established that the fair-use provision of copyright law permits photography of archival materials on site, Adriane Hanson and her colleagues used the same justification to allow remote researchers to download copies of files from the virtual reading room.[37]

While both of these cases provide very positive examples of how remote access can be achieved in spite of various restrictions, the ability to implement similar models depends on the extent to which institutions are comfortable in taking risks. If institutional support is lacking to make original materials available online, online access to surrogate information may prove a tenable alternative. As an example, archivists at Stanford University developed ePADD.[38] Designed to help archives manage the acquisition and delivery of collections of email, ePADD uses named-entity recognition (NER) tools to extract defined entities, such as personal names and geographic locations, from an email corpus. These can be displayed in graphs to give a sense of how frequently a particular entity appears in a collection. Also, remote researchers can access what ePADD's developers call "a redacted email archive," in which all content other than the selected entities is blocked from view.[39] Such an approach blurs the lines between online access and online description (after all, the entities are a part of the digital object itself) by allowing access to some content alongside the redaction of other material. This approach is based on the idea that the extraction of entities, such as the titles of works and personal names, might prove a valuable resource to researchers of an author's personal papers in lieu of the records themselves.

HOW DOES USE OCCUR?

There is a well-documented need for additional research into users of born-digital archival materials.[40] Unlike a book or file of papers, digital objects must be interpreted and rendered by some compatible configuration of hardware and software in order to be viewed. There are typically multiple options when it comes to selecting a particular configuration of hardware and software, each with its own set of advantages and disadvantages. Each choice can alter the characteristics of a digital object and will have a direct effect on what researchers eventually see and interact with. The needs of the researchers are a vital consideration when designing an access approach, and every archives program has different groups of researchers wanting different things. Some researchers are interested in the content of digital files, while others, particularly those interested in the personal papers of writers and artists, are seeking evidence of how a creative work might be the product of a particular technology or digital environment.

Emulation

The director of the Folger Shakespeare Library, Michael Witmore, recently described a project in which conservation staff at the library submitted samples of dust taken from books in their care for analysis at the National Institutes of Health. As a result, scientists have been able to identify full DNA profiles for two individuals, perhaps early modern readers.[41] Putting all ethical questions aside for one moment, this extraordinary example demonstrates just how difficult it is to predict how future researchers might study digital collections. As this example shows, the content of a book or archival record, though often conceptualized as the thing itself, could very well play a secondary role in future research. Instead, the physical materiality of an item or the environment in which it was created might be of primary interest to researchers. As an archivist responsible for born-digital material, this raises the question as to how to provide access that will, in so far as is possible, permit an unknown number of potential use cases. One possibility might be to deliver born-digital material within an emulated environment.

Emulation allows a disk image to be mounted using legacy operating systems or software running on a modern computer. This can be particularly helpful in the following use cases:

- Use case 1: The quality or format of the data in question makes other access options impossible. For example, obsolete file formats might prohibit migration to a modern alternative.
- Use case 2: The interactive or performative nature of the data requires that researchers engage with it in its original environment. This is sometimes the case for computer games, digital artworks, or hypertext fiction.

- Use case 3: The quality or research value of the data is judged to warrant access methods that provide the fullest possible context and a view of the original creation environment.

Though widely discussed as a method for providing access, there are few actual instances of emulation in use. At the New York Public Library (NYPL), researchers can interact with computer games received as part of the Timothy Leary papers and made available through emulation. At New York University (NYU), archivists have used emulation to provide access to a collection of complex digital artworks from the Jeremy Blake papers. Both of these examples demonstrate the value of emulation as articulated in use cases 1 and 2. The formatting of the Timothy Leary games in particular could not be interpreted by any of the available forensics tools, making emulation the only viable option for access.[42] Similarly, archivists at Yale University Library have identified a number of use cases involving interactive artworks and legacy applications in which access via emulation appears to be the only current solution.[43]

At the Rose Library, researchers can access an emulated version of Salman Rushdie's Performa 5400 computer. Writing shortly after their work on the project was complete, the Emory team explained their rationale for choosing emulation:

> Emory wants researchers to log in to a digital space that will provide a view into Rushdie's computer exactly as he saw it while researching and writing. Just as researchers of nineteenth-century fiction are interested in book covers and bindings, current and future scholars will be interested in the digital environment that supported Rushdie's literary production.[44]

In this instance, emulation was not used out of technical necessity but in order to support scholarship focused on material evidence of textual and creative production within a digital environment. This is an example of use case 3. Advocates for this kind of approach urge archivists to consider capturing disk images of born-digital media as standard practice.[45] In terms of access, the creation of disk images facilitates the reconstruction of a complete digital environment through system emulation, as was done at Emory. Even if resources do not allow for such work to be undertaken immediately, the capture and preservation of disk images at least leaves this option open should it be judged a valuable use of resources at a future time.

The few examples of institutions using emulation as an access point demonstrate the difficulties associated with this approach. From a technical standpoint, emulation can be challenging. In their 2016 essay, Dianne Dietrich, Julia Kim, Morgan McKeehan, and Alison Rhonemus, note that "in most known cases, skilled teams of archivists and technologists had to invest enormous amounts of time, effort, and resources to work with emulation."[46] This was certainly true at Emory, where the Performa 5400 is tellingly still the only one of Rushdie's four computers that is available. The work involved in building the emulation and, in particular, creating a redacted copy of the disk image that could be loaded into it ultimately proved too manual of a process to be sustainable. Archivists at Emory still stand behind the principles that led to emulation initially, and those experiences to date have only confirmed that additional work is needed in order to transition this approach from the realm of a one-off project to a program that is scalable and sustainable.

At the University of Freiburg in Germany, researchers are building a framework designed to support just such a move. Emulation as a Service (EaaS) provides access to emulation components (for example, specific emulators and copies of legacy operating systems) from a web browser, allowing researchers to customize an environment compatible with their data.[47] This model provides convenient access to the necessary components for emulation but relieves collecting institutions with limited resources of the responsibility for managing them. This does not eliminate the need to create a redacted copy of the disk image, which can be an incredibly time- and labor-intensive process, but tools under development as part of the BitCurator Access project may soon offer a far less manual solution.[48]

Writing about test cases using EaaS at Yale University Library, Euan Cochrane notes that software licensing agreements are not yet clear on the legal implications of using copies of legacy software in order to support emulation. Cochrane reports that at Yale further pursuit of emulation as an access point is on hold until clarification can be reached between their general counsel and their software vendors. He explains that continued dialogue between software vendors and the broader archival profession is crucial if archivists are to put services in place that will allow ongoing preservation and access for at-risk digital content. Happily, such work is underway. The Software Preservation Network (SPN) works to foster discussion and collaboration among archivists and institutions responsible for the ongoing stewardship of software and software-dependent objects. Similarly, a Code of

Best Practices in Fair Use for Software Preservation, recently published by the Association of Research Libraries (ARL) in affiliation with SPN, takes important first steps in addressing the legality of preserving legacy software in order to support continued access to digital material.[49]

Migration

Not only can emulation be a very time- and labor-intensive process, but also it can be entirely inappropriate depending on the collection in question. At the Rose Library, archivists assess collections against a set of criteria in order to determine both the appropriate level of processing and the method of access most likely to be effective.[50] While the infrastructure and resources needed to support additional emulation access points are not currently available at Emory, this approach identifies good candidates for emulation.

As part of the evaluation, archivists look at the extent to which a collection captures a broad spectrum of the donor's digital life, both in terms of the comprehensiveness of content and the number of years covered. They also try to anticipate whether a collection might receive particularly high levels of use. This is especially useful for identifying digital content that might fall into the category of use case 3. As an example of this assessment and use case, archivists at the Rose Library selected the Salman Rushdie computers for emulation. The viability of data is also a consideration. Cases like the Timothy Leary papers at NYPL might well leave no option but emulation.

In many cases, however, other less resource intensive options might be more achievable and more appropriate. Judged by the same criteria, a collection of floppy disks provides a less comprehensive set of data than does a complete computing environment. Unless obsolete or especially complex file formats require emulation due to technical necessity or the need for a specific user experience, it would likely be a wholly unsuitable approach.

Recent practice at the Rose Library has been to migrate copies of born-digital files to well-documented, well-supported, and, where possible, open-source formats for access. The Sustainability of Digital Formats website of the Library of Congress is one of a number of helpful resources that provides file format recommendations.[51] The migration of files can often be performed in batch, making it a convenient and efficient approach to access. However, while not as technically challenging as emulation, migration can be time consuming, especially when dealing with old or obscure file formats. The Rose Library recently acquired a number of files created using an early version of the screenwriting software Final Draft. Without a copy of the Final

Draft application, migration of the files involved a painstaking, multistep process using an alternative (and less costly) compatible software to export files to PDF one by one.

Of course, the migration of data from one file type to another can alter metadata and the formatting of content. The dates associated with a new file generated as a result of migration, for example, will obviously not match the original. At the Rose Library, archivists have addressed this issue in several ways, depending on a collection's level of use. For low-use or relatively small collections, the finding aid's scope and content note documents file dates that have changed as a result of migration and provides a date range for the files in question. For a larger collection or one that receives higher levels of use, the original file metadata generated in the process of extracting individual files from a disk image to populate a spreadsheet can be made available to researchers.

In addition to file metadata, the look and feel of content rendered using a different file format can also be altered. In 2014, the Rose Library acquired files from a poet who kept multiple versions of Microsoft Word on his computer because the act of reformatting existing files so they would remain compatible with newer versions of the software changed the very consciously organized way in which he had laid out the text of his poems on the page. In using migration as a means to provide access, archivists must be cognizant of the changes that this process sometimes creates and the extent to which those changes can affect the interpretation and use of a digital object. This is particularly important in light of evidence suggesting that researchers perhaps assume that objects are, by virtue of the fact that they are delivered by archival institutions, inherently trustworthy and unchanged. [52]

In its report on the application of ISAD(G) to born-digital materials, the Descriptive Standards Roundtable of the Archives and Records Association of the UK and Ireland repeatedly emphasized the need for transparency in how descriptive data has been generated. [53] Archival description should clearly articulate what steps have been taken in processing a collection of files and preparing them for access when those steps may have affected how content is later interpreted by researchers. This argument is by no means applicable only to born-digital material. Many in the archival profession have advocated for increased levels of transparency in all archival description, challenging the traditionally held notion that processing can be a neutral and objective act. [54] That digital data must be translated and rendered for use by some combination of hardware and software, however, and that the selection and configuration of said hardware and software is typically performed by an archivist serves as an explicit call for increased transparency in all communication with researchers, especially descriptive records. This is particularly important in cases in which digital content is made available online, thus decreasing the likelihood that researchers will interact with an archivist.[55]

Deliver Files in Their Original Format

In some cases, files that have been created recently with commonly used applications may be easily accessed in their original format using modern computing equipment. Similarly, a file viewer tool like Avantstar's Quick View Plus might be able to display older file formats without the need for migration. There are certainly advantages to both approaches, most notably that they demand little in the way of resources and let archivists get born-digital content into the hands of researchers quickly. Furthermore, viewing a file using its native application ensures that its significant properties (i.e., its look and feel) are preserved. At the same time, this approach offers a fairly short-term solution. As files age, they will inevitably grow outdated and will eventually lose compatibility with modern systems. The alternative solution of periodic migration will become necessary, and the longer an archivist waits to migrate the content, the more technically challenging it may become. Tools like Quick View Plus, though incredibly useful, are also risky as a long-term solution. More obscure file formats may not be supported by the application. Further, the proprietary nature of the software limits the extent to which archivists can depend on its continued availability.[56]

For some institutions, the provision of meaningful access means not only access to the files themselves but also access to the original hardware and media. For example, the Maryland Institute for Technology in the Humanities (MITH) emphasizes the physical objects upon which data was stored and how this hardware contributed to an understanding of the collection as a whole. For the Deena Larson collection, archivists at MITH displayed a handmade "cozy" that Larsen crafted for her Mac Classic computers, which, during public installations of her work, would be paired with an antique wooden school desk at which researchers would sit to explore works of electronic literature. Larsen, they argued, had "therefore imagined a full ergonomics for the end-user's encounter with her work, and designed a hybrid digital and physical space to support its presentation."[57] During an interview in 2012, Matthew Kirschenbaum explained that researchers at MITH have access to Larsen's original diskettes and computers.[58] This approach requires added support from staff, plus the ongoing care and upkeep of legacy hardware that an institution like MITH is perhaps singularly capable of providing. Where such levels of access are not possible, archivists can include photographs of particularly noteworthy pieces of media in descriptive records.

Researcher Responses

There have been few studies examining how researchers respond to current tools and methods of access for digital collections. Thus, archivists have relied on anecdotal evidence or assumptions about what characteristics of born-digital objects are most valued by researchers. Whether the material is analog or digital, archivists agree that content alone fails to provide researchers with sufficient understanding of a collection as a whole. Contextual information plays a crucial role in helping researchers make sense of the materials they encounter. Any resulting impulse to preserve as much of the look and feel of born-digital materials, however, has to be balanced with the availability of staff time and resources. Consequently, taking the time to understand as much as possible about the community of researchers before embarking on a particular access strategy is crucial.[59]

Dianne Dietrich, Julia Kim, Morgan McKeehan, and Alison Rhonemus note the extent to which emulation especially lends itself to particular research topics. They use Timothy Leary's computer games as an example, observing that researchers working "on the technical specifications or . . . writing a book-length work on Leary's work processes . . . would explore the emulator more fully," while those more interested in the theory behind the games have little interest in playing them.[60] Similar trends occurred at Emory, where Rushdie scholars whose research interests focus primarily on the analysis of content are likely to access migrated copies of files via a searchable, browsable database, while access to the emulation is valued by scholars interested in computer history and how Rushdie's creative process was affected by his use of technology.

Emulation often means interaction with unfamiliar environments and applications. In these cases, it is unclear to what extent facilitating access should require that archives staff provide additional training and documentation for researchers. Many archivists have compared such a scenario to researchers accessing materials in a foreign language.[61] Just as the onus is typically on the researcher to have the requisite skills to translate a language, they argue that the onus should also be on the researcher to understand and navigate the technologies in question. Though certainly a useful comparison to keep in mind as archivists prepare born-digital material for access, such an argument may create a prioritized group of scholars trained in computer science and history. The fact that content exists digitally is a question of format and, as such, transcends boundaries of specific scholarly disciplines. Valuable research material is likely to exist digitally for researchers with any number of interests, which means that archivists must encourage and facilitate use across a wide user base.

The few existing studies on researcher interaction with born-digital material have identified that ease of use is the most important factor. In a study at NYU's Fales Library and Special Collections, Julia Kim notes that participants "found the emulation's authentically slow-processing speed and instability impediment enough to prefer contemporary computing system access."[62] Other studies generated similar feedback, with the observation that "stability, speed, and familiarity were much more important to researchers than authenticity and fidelity."[63] In their 2006 study, Margaret Hedstrom, Christopher Lee, Judith Olson, and Clifford Lampe report that "subjects weighed ease of use, their familiarity with current software applications and the speed of interaction more heavily than the experience of using the original on an obsolete platform."[64] That being said, their study confirms the value of contextual information to researchers, stressing in particular "the context in which the objects were originally created and used, information about the purpose and audience for the materials, and information about the original computing environment."[65]

LEVERAGING THE BORN-DIGITAL FORMAT FOR ENHANCED USE

In a conversation with a researcher at the Rose Library, an archivist asked what additional tools and processes could be made available in order to enhance access. The researcher responded, saying that the ability to apply analytical software to born-digital materials is ultimately what distinguishes a born-digital object from microfilm. Though concerns about donor and third-party privacy are certainly valid, those issues should not prevent archivists from leveraging, wherever possible, the unique characteristics of the born-digital format in order to support innovative and informative methods of discovery and access.

Tools developed for the digital humanities let archivists take advantage of the structure and attributes particular to digital data in order to develop new research methods and increase the scalability of their work. The development of archives-specific software designed to support such uses is already well underway, with tools like ePADD incorporating NER technology in order to create graphs and the "redacted email archive" approach described earlier. Natural language processing (NLP) tools can also be used to identify patterns and themes running across born-digital collections, which, even after many hours of painstaking close reading, is likely not possible but for the born-digital format. Muse, a research tool developed at Stanford, applies NLP to track how mood is represented throughout an email corpus.[66] BitCurator, too, recently embarked on a project that will apply existing NLP software libraries to born-digital materials in order to extract entities and identify thematic groupings.[67] The process of identifying thematic groupings within a collection, or topic modeling, has the potential to greatly enhance archival description by providing an overview of what a collection is about. This offers one way to respond to criticism that archivists have often focused too heavily "on what collections are made up of (*Ofness*)" in spite of studies reporting that "many users prefer to learn what collections are about (*Aboutness*)."[68] Writing about topic modeling, Trevor Owens acknowledges that the tools in question do not always perform with total accuracy. Nevertheless, he encourages archivists to approach such tools not in pursuit of perfection but rather in order to provide adequate descriptive signposts that act as a useful supplement to existing descriptive tools.[69]

In instances where access to collections is unrestricted, enabling the application of digital humanities methods and tools should be uncomplicated. Although such instances are rare, the Rose Library recently received permission to make a small collection of born digital material available online and has since explored ways in which analytical software can be applied to open up new avenues of research. The Turner Cassity Born-Digital Collection, built in collaboration with the Emory Center for Digital Scholarship, uses NER technology to extract geographical place names from the digital files of poet Turner Cassity. The results are then mapped to provide an alternative point of access for researchers. The extraction of file dates also enabled the creation of an interactive timeline. These uses provided examples of ways in which researchers might apply digital humanities methods in order to recontextualize collection material, but the Rose Library also chose to make the data downloadable as a text file so as to support additional researcher-driven analysis using whatever tools are available.[70]

Of course, donor restrictions and privacy concerns often prevent such levels of access and frustrate researchers who want to take advantage of powerful research tools. Given the important ethical and legal obligations of any archives program, finding a good compromise has proven difficult. At the Rose Library, a pilot project developed as part of the instructional program has provided insight into how digital humanities tools could be used within the constraints of the reading room. The project required undergraduate students to use the text analysis software Voyant to apply distant reading methods to a corpus of born-digital poetry only available at dedicated reading room laptops.[71] In addition to increasing awareness and use of Emory's born-digital collections by faculty and students, this project showcased some of the possibilities for using digital humanities tools and methods to access digital archives. Further, the project increased staff's engagement with born-digital collections and demonstrated potential approaches to the use of digital collections in the reading room. At the same time, the pilot project raised challenging questions about the level of technical support that should be expected from reading room staff and what training and documentation they needed. The project also demonstrated limitations as to the number and types of tools that could be accommodated within the constraints of the reading room.

As noted earlier, research interests will often dictate the level of access to born-digital collections. Matthew Kirschenbaum, whose interests focus on the materiality of digital media, developed a wish list for archives that included access to disk images when available and forensic tools with which to view them.[72] Although this would obviously provide a wealth of information about the material in question, the provision of access to digital data at the bit level significantly increases the risk that private or sensitive information is exposed. It is tempting to argue that this is not unlike providing access to unprocessed analog collections, a practice upheld at many institutions, including the Rose Library, but the presence of deleted data makes such a comparison somewhat precarious. Proactive and candid conversation with donors, in addition to the inclusion of language in donor agreements that explicitly addresses levels of access, will help remove any question as to what is permitted even if it does not fully satisfy the requests of researchers. When access to the disk image is not an option, archivists may be able to find ways to integrate some of the output from digital forensic tools into descriptive records. Similarly, the application of digital humanities tools to search metadata or finding aids, as opposed to actual archival content, might offer a way to take advantage of these powerful tools without compromising the rights and privacy of donors.

Issues related to privacy and copyright are not the only obstacles to these types of enhanced access. Staff time and technical expertise is needed to implement such strategies. Reflecting on how an MPLP approach might be applied to born-digital processing and access, Kathleen O'Neill suggests that institutions consider partnering with researchers who have the skills necessary to enhance discovery and access. [73]

Partnerships between the Rose Library and the Emory Center for Digital Scholarship have resulted in projects that deliver original research and showcase what is possible when digital humanities methods are applied to archival collections. Perhaps archivists and researchers could design an archives-specific environment, developed along the lines of BitCurator, that compiles a suite of digital humanities tools with user-friendly graphic interfaces. That environment could be accessible through reading room workstations or possibly even a secure online environment. The development of new tools to support enhanced use requires a great deal of time and effort, but the precedent for open-source and collaborative software emerging out of the archives community demonstrates a willingness to overcome these challenges and meet the needs of researchers.

USE IS USE IS USE IS USE IS USE IS USE IS USE

Archivists have a variety of tools and options at their disposal to better enable use of born-digital collections. Resources, on the other hand, are too often stretched. Despite the limitations, archivists must focus on the established principle that researchers value "access by any means" over no access at all. [74] This principle must be an explicit call to action for archivists: whatever we do in terms of facilitating use of born-digital collections, we must do something now. Just like analog collections, no single approach to description and access to digital material will satisfy every researcher or accommodate the idiosyncrasies of every collection. Promoting and emphasizing use of born-digital materials is the goal, even if the approach taken is good enough as opposed to perfect. To reach that goal, archivists can move forward with a few simple approaches.

Know the Constraints

Given the nature of archival collections and available resources, there will always be limits. As new approaches to description and access emerge, archivists must balance the needs of researchers with what is possible. Often, specific models of description and access must be adapted or created to meet institutional demands. A careful assessment of perceived constraints may also reveal places where, in fact, restrictions can be lifted or loosened. For example, archivists revoked the Rose Library policy that prohibited copies of born-digital materials for researchers in response to a corresponding policy that permitted copies of analog collections.

Communicate with Donors

Whenever possible, archivists must engage in early and frequent communication with donors. The details of these conversations contribute significantly to the decisions made during each stage of born-digital workflows. To help ease the anxiety understandably induced as donors prepare to transfer their computers and other digital data to an archives program, archivists must clearly explain what types of policies and access guidelines will be used to mediate use of digital collections. Such conversations can help reassure donors as to the research value of their materials and what will and will not be accessible to researchers. For example, archivists at the Rose Library recently showed a donor how to use a text analysis tool to provide enhanced access to their born-digital materials. As a result, the donor was far more receptive to such possibilities in the classroom and reading room. Regular communication with donors and clearly articulated expectations in deeds of gift help to eliminate ambiguity on how digital collections are described, discovered, and used.

Be Transparent with Researchers

The tools that provide description and delivery of born-digital collections will inevitably play some role in shaping how a researcher approaches a collection. Increased transparency as to what steps archivists take in order to create descriptive records and prepare digital objects for access creates better-informed researchers. Sharing the methodology and best practices used to guide description and delivery helps them understand how to assess the collection, which ultimately informs the ways in which collections are understood and interpreted.

Contribute to the Professional Dialogue

There is no single approach to the description and access of born-digital material. Nonetheless, archivists are devising effective strategies to facilitate use. There is much to be learned from sharing these stories and acknowledging both the successes and the inevitable bumps in the road. As approaches enabling use continue to emerge, the collective experiences of archivists—shared formally and informally at conferences, workshops, in the professional literature, on blogs, and through online forums—create an invaluable body of knowledge. From these lessons, archivists are empowered to create best practices, navigate challenges, and guide the ongoing development of relevant and responsive tools and services for describing and accessing digital archives.

NOTES

1. Theodore R. Schellenberg, *Modern Archives: Principles and Techniques* (Chicago: University of Chicago Press, 1956), 224.

2. Rachel Appel, Alison Clemens, Wendy Hagenmaier, and Jessica Meyerson, *Born-Digital Access in Archival Repositories: Mapping the Current Landscape Preliminary Report*, August 2015, https://docs.google.com/document/d/15v3Z6fFNydrXcGfGWXA4xzyWlivirf UXhHoqgVDBtUg/edit?usp=sharing.

3. Laura Carroll, Erika Farr, Peter Hornsby, and Ben Ranker, "A Comprehensive Approach to Born-Digital Archives," *Archivaria* 72 (Fall 2011): 61–92; Catherine Stollar Peters, "When Not All Papers are Paper: A Case Study in Digital Archivy," *Provenance: Journal of the Society of Georgia Archivists* 24 (January 2006): 22–34; Michael Forstrom, "Managing Electronic Records in Manuscript Collections: A Case Study from the Beinecke Rare Book and Manuscript Library," *American Archivist* 72 (Fall/Winter 2009): 460–77; Laura Wilsey, Rebecca Skirvin, Peter Chan, and Glynn Edwards, "Capturing and Processing Born-Digital Files in the STOP AIDS Project Records: A Case Study," *Journal of Western Archives* 4 (2013): 1–22, http://digitalcommons.usu.edu/westernarchives/vol4/iss1/1; Society of American Archivists Electronic Records Section, "Born-Digital Access Blog Series," *bloggERS!* (blog), https://saaers.wordpress.com/tag/born-digital-access-blog-series/; Society of American Archivists Reference, Outreach, and Access Section, "Access to Electronic Records Working Group," http://www2.archivists.org/groups/reference-access-and-outreach-section/access-to-electronic-records-working-group.

4. Cyndi Shein, "From Accession to Access: A Born-Digital Materials Case Study," *Journal of Western Archives* 5 (2014): 8–9, http://digitalcommons.usu.edu/westernarchives/vol5/iss1/1.

5. Daniel A. Santamaria, *Extensible Processing for Archives and Special Collections: Reducing Processing Backlogs* (Chicago: American Library Association, 2015), quote 16; Mark Greene and Dennis Meissner, "More Product, Less Process: Revamping Traditional Archival Processing," *American Archivist* 68 (2005): 208–63.

6. Santamaria, *Extensible Processing*, quote 35.

7. John Langdon, "Describing the Digital: The Archival Cataloguing of Born-Digital Personal Papers," *Archives and Records* 37, no. 1 (2016): 39, https://doi.org/10.1080/23257962.2016.1139494.

8. Jane Zhang and Dayne Mauney, "When Archival Description Meets Digital Object Metadata: A Typological Study of Digital Archival Representation," *American Archivist* 76 (Spring/Summer 2013): 174–95.

9. The DPLA Archival Description Working Group, *Aggregating and Representing Collections in the Digital Public Library of America*, November 2016, 4, https://docs.google.com/document/d/16r_px4GajLIOZMlyXyN0pJFfWpstJIKxHF3brgM4YOo/edit.

10. Ibid., 35.

11. Zhang and Mauney, "Archival Description," 189.

12. "Tiger Hockey Email Newsletters," Princeton University Library Finding Aids, http://arks.princeton.edu/ark:/88435/q524jn84d; "Warren Petoskey Papers," University of Michigan, Bentley Historical Library Finding Aids, http://quod.lib.umich.edu/b/bhlead/umich-bhl-2016048.

13. Zhang and Mauney, "Archival Description," 189.

14. Washington State Archives—Digital Archives, http://digitalarchives.wa.gov.

15. Zhang and Mauney, "Archival Description," 189–90.

16. Jenn Riley and Kelcy Shepherd, "A Brave New World: Archivists and Sharable Descriptive Metadata," *American Archivist* 72 (Spring/Summer 2009): 104.

17. Descriptive Standards Roundtable, *Best Guess Guidelines for Cataloguing Born Digital Material*, 2016, http://www.archives.org.uk/images/Data_Standards/Best_Guess_Guidelines_v1.0_160325.pdf.

18. Sarah Higgins, Christopher Hilton, and Lyn Dafis, *Archives Context and Discovery: Rethinking Arrangement and Description for the Digital Age*, 2015, 4, http://www.girona.cat/web/ica2014/ponents/textos/id174.pdf.

19. J. Gordon Daines III, "Processing Digital Records and Manuscripts," in *Archival Arrangement and Description*, eds. Christopher J. Prom and Thomas J. Frusciano (Chicago: Society of American Archivists, 2013), 99.

20. Jefferson Bailey, "Disrespect Des Fonds: Rethinking Arrangement and Description in Born-Digital Archives," *Archive Journal* (June 2013): 6, http://www.archivejournal.net/issue/3/archives-remixed/disrespect-des-fonds-rethinking-arrangement-and-description-in-born-digital-archives/.

21. Ibid., 7.

22. Jarrett M. Drake, "RadTech Meets RadArch: Towards a New Principle for Archives and Archival Description," *On Archivy* (blog), April 2016, https://medium.com/on-archivy/radtech-meets-radarch-towards-a-new-principle-for-archives-and-archival-description-568f133e4325.

23. Ibid.

24. Richard J. Cox, "Revisiting the Archival Finding Aid," *Journal of Archival Organization* 5, no. 4 (2008): 18–19.

25. David A. Wallace, "Managing the Present: Metadata as Archival Description," *Archivaria* 39 (Spring 1995): 11–21, http://archivaria.ca/index.php/archivaria/article/view/12064.

26. Higgins, Hilton, and Dafis, *Archives Context and Discovery*, 5.

27. Langdon, "Describing the Digital," 46.

28. Santamaria, *Extensible Processing*, 81.

29. Experts Group on Archival Description, *Records in Contexts: A Conceptual Model for Archival Description* (Consultation Draft v0.1), August 2016, 5, http://www.ica.org/en/egad-ric-conceptual-model.

30. Ibid., 10.

31. AIMS Work Group, *AIMS Born-Digital Collections: An Inter-institutional Model for Stewardship*, (University of Virginia Libraries, January 2012), 85, https://dcs.library.virginia.edu/files/2013/02/AIMS_final_text.pdf; Matthew Farrell, "A Multi-Faceted Challenge: Breakouts on Access at the BitCurator User Forum," *bloggERS!* (blog), February 4, 2016, https://saaers.wordpress.com/2016/02/04/a-multi-faceted-challenge-breakouts-on-access-at-the-bitcurator-user-forum/.

32. Rossy Mendez, "Ensuring Born-Digital Access at the Seeley G. Mudd Manuscript Library," *bloggERS!* (blog), February 2016, https://saaers.wordpress.com/2016/02/09/ensuring-born-digital-access-at-the-seeley-g-mudd-manuscript-library/.

33. The Turner Cassity Born-Digital Collection, http://cassity.digitalscholarship.emory.edu.

34. Michelle Light, "Managing Risk with a Virtual Reading Room: Two Born Digital Projects," in *Reference and Access: Innovative Practices for Archives and Special Collections*, ed. Kate Theimer (Lanham, MD: Rowman & Littlefield, 2014), 17.

35. Adriane Hanson, "Access to Born-Digital Archives at the Russell Library," *bloggERS!* (blog), January 2016, https://saaers.wordpress.com/2016/01/20/access-to-born-digital-archives-at-the-russell-library/.

36. Light, "Virtual Reading Room," 24.

37. Hanson, "Access to Born-Digital Archives."

38. ePADD, http://epadd.stanford.edu.

39. Josh Schneider, "Viewing Email through a New Lens: Screening, Managing, and Providing Access to Historical Email Using ePADD," *bloggERS!* (blog), January 2016, https://saaers.wordpress.com/2016/01/12/viewing-email-through-a-new-lens-screening-managing-and-providing-access-to-historical-email-using-epadd/.

40. Higgins, Hilton, and Dafis, *Archives Context and Discovery*; Margaret L. Hedstrom, Christopher Lee, Judith Olson, and Clifford Lampe, "'The Old Version Flickers More': Digital Preservation from the User's Perspective," *American Archivist* 69 (Spring/Summer 2006): 159–87; Wendy Hagenmaier, "When It Comes to Born-Digital, How Well Do We Know Our Users?" *bloggERS!* (blog), January 2016, https://saaers.wordpress.com/2016/01/26/when-it-comes-to-born-digital-how-well-do-we-know-our-users/.

41. Michael Witmore, "The Wonder of Will" (lecture, Emory University, Atlanta, December 5, 2016).

42. Dianne Dietrich, Julia Kim, Morgan McKeehan, and Alison Rhonemus, "How to Party Like It's 1999: Emulation for Everyone," *Code4Lib* 32 (April 25, 2016): section title, http://journal.code4lib.org/articles/11386.

43. Euan Cochrane, "Emulation as a Service (EaaS) at Yale University Library," *The Signal* (blog), August 2014, https://blogs.loc.gov/thesignal/2014/08/emulation-as-a-service-eaas-at-yale-university-library/.

44. Carroll et al., "A Comprehensive Approach," 83–84.

45. Matthew G. Kirschenbaum, Erika L. Farr, Kari M. Kraus, Naomi Nelson, Catherine Stollar Peters, Gabriela Redwine, and Doug Reside, "Digital Materiality: Preserving Access to Computers as Complete Environments," *California Digital Library* (October 5, 2009): 111–12, http://escholarship.org/uc/item/7d3465vg.

46. Dietrich et al., "Party Like It's 1999," Background.

47. bwFLA, "bwFLA— Emulation as a Service," http://eaas.uni-freiburg.de.

48. BitCurator, "BitCurator Access," January 2018, https://bitcurator.net/bitcurator-access/.

49. Cochrane, "Emulation as a Service"; The Software Preservation Network, http://www.softwarepreservationnetwork.org/; The Association of Research Libraries, Code for Best Practices in Fair Use for Software Preservation, September 2018, http://www.arl.org/storage/documents/publications/2018.09.24_softwarepreservationcode.pdf.

50. Dorothy Waugh, Elizabeth Russey Roke, and Erika Farr, "Flexible Processing and Diverse Collections: A Tiered Approach to Delivering Born Digital Archives," *Archives and Records* 37, no. 1 (2016): 3–19.

51. Caroline R. Arms, Carl Fleischhauer, and Kate Murray, "Sustainability of Digital Formats: Planning for Library of Congress Collections," March 2017, http://www.digitalpreservation.gov/formats/index.shtml.

52. Hedstrom et al., "The Old Version Flickers More," 184.

53. Descriptive Standards Roundtable, *Best Guess Guidelines*.

54. Jennifer Douglas, "Toward More Honest Description," *American Archivist* 79 (Spring/Summer 2016): 26–55; Maureen Callahan, "The Value of Archival Description, Considered," *Chaos → Order: Four Archivists' Battles with Masses of Legacy Description* (blog), April 2014, https://icantiemyownshoes.wordpress.com/2014/04/04/the-value-of-archival-description-considered/.

55. Geoffrey Yeo, "Trust and Context in Cyberspace," *Archives and Records* 34, no. 2 (2013): 218.

56. Forstrom, "Managing Electronic Records," 467.

57. Kirschenbaum et al., "Digital Materiality," 109.

58. Martin J. Gengenbach, "'The Way We Do It Here': Mapping Digital Forensics Workflows in Collecting Institutions" (master's thesis, University of North Carolina, Chapel Hill, 2012), 50.

59. Hedstrom et al., "The Old Version Flickers More," 159–87.

60. Dietrich et al., "Party Like It's 1999," Step 3.

61. Ibid.

62. Julia Kim, "Researcher Interactions with Born-Digital: Out of the Frying Pan and into the Fire," *bloggERS!* (blog), January 2016, https://saaers.wordpress.com/2016/01/28/researcher-interactions-with-born-digital-out-of-the-frying-pan-and-into-the-reading-room/.

63. Dietrich et al., "Party Like It's 1999," step 3.

64. Hedstrom et al., "The Old Version Flickers More," 186.

65. Ibid., 187.

66. Muse, https://mobisocial.stanford.edu/muse/.

67. BitCurator, "BitCurator NLP," February 2018, https://bitcurator.net/bitcurator-nlp/.

68. Jennifer Schaffner, *The Metadata Is the Interface: Better Description of Archives and Special Collections, Synthesized from User Studies* (Dublin, OH: OCLC Research, 2009), 6, https://www.oclc.org/content/dam/research/publications/library/2009/2009-06.pdf.

69. Trevor Owens, "Mecha-archivists: Envisioning the Role of Software in the Future of Archives," *Trevor Owens* (blog), May 2014, http://www.trevorowens.org/2014/05/mecha-archivists-envisioning-the-role-of-software-in-the-future-of-archives/.

70. The Turner Cassity Born-Digital Collection.

71. Voyant Tools Documentation, http://docs.voyant-tools.org.

72. Matthew Kirschenbaum, "Researching the Literary History of Word Processing: Lessons Learned" (presentation at CurateGear 2016: Enabling the Curation of Digital Collection, University of North Carolina, Chapel Hill, January 14, 2016).

73. Kathleen O'Neill, "Born Digital Minimum Processing and Access," *The Signal* (blog), September 2012, https://blogs.loc.gov/thesignal/2012/09/born-digital-minimum-processing-and-access/.

74. Kim, "Researcher Interactions."

Chapter Three

Digital Preservation

Bertram Lyons

When archivists develop preservation strategies for paper-based materials, the underlying chemistry of the physical materials is an essential consideration. Paper is an organic compound, made of cellulose fibers or, sometimes, a mix of cellulose and lignin fibers. Cellulose is a polysaccharide of carbon, hydrogen, and oxygen atoms, $C_6H_{10}O_5$. Cellulose is hydrophilic (attracted to water) and not hydrophobic (repelled from water). Additionally, cellulose is hydrolytic: not only is cellulose attracted to water, but also when in contact with water, the molecular bonds will begin to breakdown. This is called "hydrolysis," and it occurs with direct contact with water and with exposure to moisture (humidity) in the air.[1]

Because of this understanding of the behavior of the molecules that constitute paper materials, archivists design preventive preservation techniques to prolong the life of these materials and to minimize undesired changes to them overtime. To preserve paper and other analog items, archivists store them in protective boxes in dry locations away from water sources. Of course, there are other characteristics of cellulosic materials that we use to infer preservation strategies for paper (e.g., low light exposure, low acidity exposure). The point is that archivists must understand the construction of materials to design preservation strategies that will work. This same level of understanding can be applied to digital file-based materials that have become common donations to archives programs.

As archivists, if we are going to be able to take care of digital collections into the future, we must understand the basic building blocks of digital collections and design repositories to store the material. Certainly, we must understand the physicality of hard drives, digital tape, SSD technology, optical media, and other storage devices for digital information. But to preserve the digital content, archivists must embrace the concept of "the chemistry of digital preservation." That would be the knowledge that digital files are constructed of bits and bytes, are guided by format specifications, and are stored in file systems. To know files, we must know how they are constructed. We must be able to dissect them. We must understand how they decompose, how they are kept alive, and how to correct them if they are broken. And from this knowledge, we will be better equipped to design preservation strategies for our digital collections.

Even though archivists think of preservation activities as something that occurs after a donation is complete, with digital content, the idea of preservation must begin before collections are received or in many cases before they have been created. In addition, digital preservation is an ongoing process that ensures security and authenticity of the original digital material. A preservation system that handles ingest of content, maintenance, security, and provides access is an essential part of managing digital archives.

Preservation of digital content is a central part of the long-term management of archival collections. This chapter is focused on how archivists can prepare for the digital preservation challenges of the next decade. It starts with an overview of the structures of digital information and then highlights the important components of building and administering a digital preservation repository for archival content. The chapter provides the basic strategies and standards for starting a digital preservation program and communicating that concept to donors and concludes with future directions for this growing subfield of archival work.

BUILDING BLOCKS OF DIGITAL CONTENT

Bits

It all starts with a bit. A bit is a binary digit: a 1 or a 0. Binary itself is not an electronic thing. Binary is a counting system, a positional notation system, like our more commonly known decimal counting system, but instead of ten characters used to represent values, binary only has two characters: 0 and 1. This means that we open new positions much faster when we count, and the value of each new position increases by a factor of two. In computing, bits are used to store values.

Sometimes the value stored is a single value; sometimes bits are grouped into sets of eight (bytes) or sixteen (words) or thirty-two (double words) to store larger values.[2]

Bytes

A byte is a grouping of eight bits that is often used to store information in computing. Because a byte is an eight-bit binary number, it can contain any value from 0 to 255. Eight binary digits together can express a total of 256 values. When we put multiple bytes together, we can express even more information. A word is typically two bytes, a sixteen-bit value. Sixteen binary digits together can express any value from 0 to 65,535, a total of 65,536 possible values. There are other variations to the rules on bytes, but the main concept is that bits, bytes, and combinations of bytes form the basic building blocks of digital files.

For example:

Binary	Decimal
0	0
1	1
10	2
11	3
100	4
101	5
110	6
111	7
1000	8
1001	9

The following represents a value of ten in binary:

1 0 1 0

In decimal this is the equivalent of:

(8)	(4)	(2)	(1)
1	0	1	0

8 + 0 + 2 + 0 = **10**

Figure 3.1. Counting to ten in binary

Files

A digital file is a string of bytes from the first byte to the last byte. And it must be addressable (i.e., indexed and findable) by a file system so that it is clear where the string of bytes is stored on the physical storage device. One of the most basic file types is a simple text file made up of ASCII characters. This file has no true format short of the knowledge that the bytes in the file represent ASCII characters. In figure 3.2, the string of characters in the gray-outlined box is a hexadecimal representation of the bytes that make up a single file.

Hexadecimal is another positional counting system, like decimal and binary. It has sixteen unique characters that can be used to count: 0, 1, 2, 3, 4, 5, 6, 7, 8, 9, a, b, c, d, e, f. So each new position is a factor of sixteen, instead of ten (decimal) or two (binary). Hexadecimal is a shorthand way to represent bytes (eight bits) because (as mentioned above) a byte can represent 256 values, and a two-character hexadecimal value can represent up to 256 values too. So we can save space and represent bytes as two-digit hexadecimal values: from 00 to ff. The string of values in the box below represents the twelve bytes of the file: file.txt. These are all the bytes in the file. In this case, they are read from left to right. If the file is opened on a computer, it appears as follows.

Figure 3.3 reads, "Short file," and it is a .txt file. If you were to use the ASCII chart to translate the hexadecimal byte values listed, you would see that they translate exactly to "Short file." There are other variations of course, but this is the basic model of how files work.

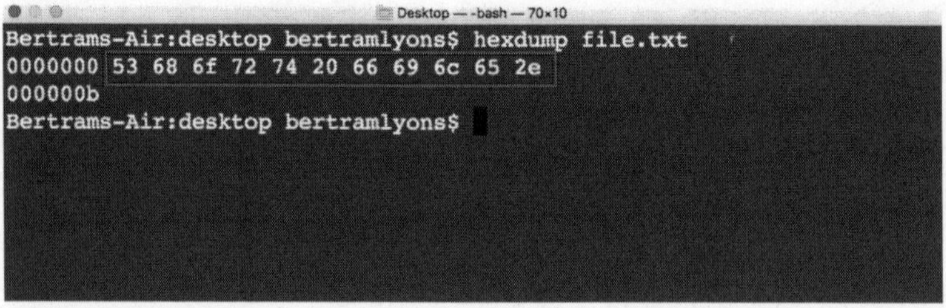

Figure 3.2.   Bytes in a file

● ○ ● ☐ file.txt ⌄

Short file.

Figure 3.3. Actual Contents of the file in figure 3.2

Formats

Different formats make it possible to encode more complex information and to use files in the context of certain software. A format is a recipe for constructing a specific type of file. The format specification defines how bytes are interpreted throughout the file, how they are grouped, what they represent at various locations in the file, and how the values are interpreted to communicate the intended encoded information. The formats are the compounds of digital preservation. There are rules for their construction, and certain molecules (bytes) and atoms (bits) are used in unique ways depending on the format specification.

In the previous file example, there was nothing to the file but the content of the file itself. With a photograph as the example, the content would be the image itself. The captured color and brightness information that can be translated to a recognizable image for a human to see and understand is part of that content. Software makes it possible to view this image and evaluate the color and brightness characteristics of the pixels. With context, the user can understand what is in the image and learn from it. The information contained within the file represents the encoded information that the file was intended to transmit.

Complex formats require more structural information within the bytes (and support more embedded information) to allow a software program to properly decode the image data so that it is understandable to a human in the way it was intended. For the digital image example, this information may include color space, height, width, bits per sample, or date created. The format specification for each file stipulates how and where this information is encoded (or declared) within the file and how the bytes are used to store this information as numeric values.

File Systems

To write files to a storage medium so that they persist over time, archivists and records creators need a way to access and manage those files. This is

```
0000000  42 4d 2a b7 0f 00 00 00 00 00 8a 00 00 00 7c 00
         magic #   file size (bytes)    reserved    offset to img data   DIB ...
0000010  00 00 77 02 00 00 98 01 00 00 01 00 20 00 03 00
         ... header size  height (pixels)   width (pixels)  planes  bits/pix  compression
0000020  00 00 a0 b6 0f 00 00 00 00 00 00 00 00 00 00 00
                   image size (bytes)
0000030  00 00 00 00 00 00 00 00 ff 00 00 ff 00 00 ff 00

0000040  00 00 00 00 00 ff 42 47 52 73 80 c2 f5 28 60 b8
```

Figure 3.4. Excerpt of BMP File

done using file systems such as Windows NTFS, Mac HFS+, or the ISO 9660 optical media file system. As mentioned earlier, files must be addressable. To keep track of where files are stored on digital storage media, file systems are used to index files, track permissions, document dates of modification and creation, remember storage locations, and support findability of files by users and computers. At any given time, a file is known by a file system, and this system stores information about the file that the file itself is unaware of (e.g., filename). Most files do not know their names. The file system forms the context in which a file's provenance is known. A common concern for archivists responsible for the care of digital files is the preservation of the create, modify, and access dates (sometimes known as m/a/c dates, also known as stat metadata) for the files in their custody. There are a lot of moving parts related to the preservation of this information (and the solutions are different in different situations).

Metadata

Metadata is the information about a digital file that allows users to understand, use, manage, and preserve it. Without it, we would not know about the file (e.g., the title, who created it, and on what date), what the file is (e.g., the wrapper or codec in use, data rate, pixel dimensions, and duration), how it relates to other files (e.g., part one of three), and how it has been monitored (e.g., fixity checks) over its lifetime. Without the appropriate metadata, a file becomes inaccessible and unusable—ultimately losing its value.

Metadata is produced at various times during a file's lifespan. Descriptive metadata is the information about a file or files that enables identification and discovery. It includes the title, creator, date of creation, and keywords that document the subject of the file's content. Structural metadata is the information that designates how a set of files relate to one another, such as songs on a CD, or how the parts of a single file are structured. Technical metadata captures the essence of a digital file—the technical information that describes how a file functions and enables a computer to understand it at the bit level. Administrative metadata includes information about how to manage a digital file and track its process history. This ranges from rights metadata (which indicates who owns or holds copyright for a file and how it can be used and accessed) to source and preservation metadata. [3]

While all forms of metadata are important to provide long-term access to digital collections, preservation metadata ensures that digital content can be authenticated over time. Preservation metadata is the information necessary to support the long-term accessibility and usability of an object. It tracks the processes that are necessary to manage a file in a digital environment over time, including monitoring fixity (and performing any repairs that are a result of fixity checks), auditing logs to identify who has interacted with an object and when, obsolescence monitoring information, and provenance information to support the authenticity of an object. Examples of preservation metadata include checksums, storage locations, and the recording of process activities and dates (e.g., when a file is moved from one location to another and the date that the move occurred).

The most common metadata standards for digital preservation are METS and PREMIS. The METS (Metadata Encoding and Transmission Standard) schema is a standard for encoding descriptive, administrative, and structural metadata regarding objects within a digital library, expressed using XML. METS provides an XML document format for encoding metadata necessary for both management of digital library objects within a repository and the exchange of such objects between repositories (or between repositories and their users). The PREMIS (Preservation Metadata: Implementation Strategies) Data Dictionary for Preservation Metadata is the international standard for metadata to support the preservation of digital objects and ensure their long-term usability. PREMIS is a comprehensive, practical resource for implementing preservation metadata in digital archiving systems. [4]

ARCHIVISTS AND DIGITAL PRESERVATION

To manage and preserve digital content, archivists must understand its nature at a detailed level. Archivists have much to learn from computer scientists in this domain. If archivists know their collections at the elementary levels, they will be better equipped to care for these collections, to design preventive preservation techniques, to perform conservation treatments when necessary, and to ensure the long-term accessibility of records in the face of continued technological obsolescence and change. Historically, archivists have understood digital preservation from an organizational perspective. Any choices about digital preservation occur within the context of policies, staffing, and budgets of archives programs.

At its most simple definition, "digital preservation is the active management of digital content over time to ensure ongoing access."[5] It is an integral part of a larger process of curation, which consists of a set of activities that take place across the content lifecycle: selection and appraisal, description, ongoing care and management, long-term access, and/or deaccessioning/disposal. Without some level of digital preservation activities, digital assets and their associated content are at risk, either through the failure of physical media, human error, format obsolescence, or an absence of necessary metadata.

The technological systems that make it possible for us to create, share, store, and access digital information are in a state of constant change. This change takes place at all levels, including physical hardware, software, storage media, storage file system formats, file formats, and information exchange standards. Such changes, also, are almost never parallel—a storage system may need to be replaced even if the file format is stable. Likewise, a file format may need to be migrated to a newer version, while storage remains unchanged. Understanding this abstraction between the various layers of digital technology helps archivists manage their collections effectively.

The fundamental requirements of digital preservation are threefold: (1) maintain the quantity and order of bits in each of the digital files (the data object), (2) maintain the content of each file so that it is accessible and understandable by maintaining the necessary instructions for how to interpret the stored bits (representation information), and (3) preserve the bits and the content (the information object) for as long as required by the archives program. This last requirement demands more than a technological solution. Digital collections require holistic management to ensure their long-term preservation and access, and organizational factors are crucial. Incorporating the organization's goals and objectives into the preservation plan is essential to ensuring support for a sustainable digital preservation program. Without high-level organizational buy-in, ongoing support for staff, funding, hardware, software, and storage are not guaranteed. Digital preservation, then, includes planning to establish policies and standards-based practice so that archivists understand their roles and so that technology can be utilized effectively for an institution's digital collections. [6]

Communicating with Donors

When archivists acquire physical collections from donors, they typically seek the original materials themselves and not copies; additionally, archivists prefer that donors provide some context about the origin, function, and organization of the materials being acquired. These priorities should not change for digital donations, although archivists are faced with the task of applying new methodologies to account for the inherent differences between digital and physical sources of information.

One difference archivists face with digital donations is that the movement of digital files always creates a new copy. Establishing authenticity of a digital object requires first creating a calculated checksum (e.g., using an MD5 or SHA algorithm) of the sequence of bytes that constitute the file in the stored location where it is first encountered by an archivist. This value can then be stored, and each time the file is copied to a new storage location, a new checksum (using the same algorithm used originally) can be created. This new checksum can be compared to the originally created algorithm. If they match, then it can be verified that the file has not changed or been altered during the copy process. Maintaining this chain of custody for digital files from as early in the donation process as possible is the only way for archives to be able to verify to future researchers that they in fact are accessing an "original" copy of the digital record.

When communicating with donors, archivists should help donors understand the importance of providing archivists access to the files being donated on the original storage locations if possible. This will help archivists establish the provenance and chain of custody early in the process of acquisition. It is always possible that a file is altered or corrupted when it is copied to a new location for delivery to the archives. Without checksums that were created before files were delivered, archivists will never be able to verify for a researcher whether the file was originally corrupted or whether the corruption happened during acquisition. These simple risks can have a tremendous effect on archival collections if archivists do not work closely with donors to practice safe digital acquisition methodologies. [7]

During this process of establishing provenance, archivists can also attempt to preserve the create and modification dates that are associated with the digital files being acquired. As noted previously, digital files are stored within file systems that are responsible for maintaining an inventory of where the files are stored within a physical storage device, what they are called, what permissions are associated with access to them, when they were created in the file system, when they were last modified in the file system, and sometimes when they were last accessed. Different file systems are employed by different operating systems and on different storage media. Each file system type has a distinct manner of storing this metadata about the files being managed in the system. To maintain this useful metadata, some archivists create disk images of the original storage media, which essentially freezes the files and file system metadata in place and allows a user to access the entire package at a later date. [8]

Other approaches to extract file system information for future use by archives include the use of command line directory listing programs (e.g., "ls" on a Mac or Unix-based operating system or "dir" on a Windows operating system). These programs are standard on almost all computers and can be used to access information in the local file systems and to write the information to a simple text file that can be saved and stored by the archives for use during accessioning, processing, and collections management. [9]

A rarely discussed yet essential component of digital preservation practice is the concept of representation information. For example, if I gave you a sheet of paper with a sequence of 0s and 1s on it, with no further information, you would not find that record to be very valuable for your use. However, if I gave you a decoder so that you could identify what the sequence of numbers was meant to represent (e.g., the text of my first poem), then you would place greater value on the piece of paper and the information it contained. Plus, you would be able to access the poem and read its contents. The decoder, in this case, was the necessary representation information that you needed to turn the indecipherable numbers into information. Because of the nature of digital information, quality representation information is central to our ability to have meaningful access to the information contained within digital files today and into the future. When communicating with donors, it is essential that archivists understand any limitations that might exist to being able to access and interpret digital files that are being donated. Limiting factors could include proprietary file formats, ambiguously named files, or access keys for encrypted or locked content, among others. If archivists miss the opportunity to acquire necessary representation information from donors, it could turn out that an archives program finds itself storing only sequences of 0s and 1s that have lost all informational meaning.

Another conversation that archivists conduct with donors is related to privacy and security for the donor and others documented within the donors' collections. This conversation should also include conversations about personally identifiable information (PII), passwords, and other sensitive information that may be included within a donor's digital materials. Often when files are deleted from digital storage media, the files persist on the storage media and only the file system index is adjusted. If a donor gifts a hard drive or other storage device (or if the archivist creates a disk image of a donor's storage device), then there is a chance that previously deleted files, or remnants of them, will be included in the donation. It is important for archivists to discuss this with donors during acquisition and to understand the wishes of the donor regarding previously deleted information that may be discovered within the donation. By informing the donor of these possibilities, and by documenting the donor's wishes, an archives program can develop a fair and ethical plan for acquiring only the information that a donor would like to donate and not put the privacy or security of the donor or others in jeopardy.

Risk Management

At its core, digital preservation is risk management. The nature of risks is varied and may be human generated, mechanical, or natural. The human risks to technology may be ones of omission (e.g., file formats are not selected for migration, metadata is not captured), they may be nefarious (e.g., viruses, cyber attacks), or they may be accidental (e.g., deletions, misfiling, or misnaming files). Organizational risks include insufficient planning and policies, which lead to a loss of or lack of sustainable funding to support trained staff and/or appropriate technologies. Risks may also be mechanical, such as when files unknowingly change at the bit level or media and storage fail. Risks may also come from nature (e.g., floods and fires can destroy electronic media on which files are stored).[10]

Over time, risks shift based on the organization, its resources, and industry-wide technical changes. As risks evolve, how archivists identify, respond to, and monitor them must change, too. Successful preservation strategies must be flexible, yet cautious, to be able to react to risk effectively.

Standards and Guidelines

Many industries employ standards to make certain they comply with accepted practice, ensure the safety of their customers and employees and provide a foundation upon which new technologies can be built. There are two international standards documents that have served as the cornerstone for the management of digital collections. These standards guide institutions in the development of sustainable preservation programs and serve as checks and balances for institutions offering preservation management technologies. In addition, groups like the National Digital Stewardship Alliance (NDSA) have created tools and published guidelines for digital preservation.

OAIS Reference Model, ISO 14721:2012

The first standard, ISO 14721:2012, is focused on space data and information transfer systems. The Open Archival Information System (OAIS) reference model is based on this standard. The OAIS reference model is a conceptual framework for an archival system dedicated to preserving and maintaining access to digital assets over the long term. It is not meant to be prescriptive but rather provide guidance about best practice for building a sustainable preservation environment.[11]

The OAIS framework takes into account producers (creators) of content (and their embodiment as file-based assets and data that will be preserved); the system (technology, workflows) in which the content is preserved; the administration, management, and preservation planning structure that administers the program; and the consumers (users) that will use the content at some point in the future. This preservation environment conceives of three types of information packages: submission information packages (SIPs), created in preparation for ingest (accessioning) into the system; archival information packages (AIPs), the data that is managed and stored over time, which may include the SIP contents and additional data created by the system; and dissemination information packages (DIPs), the data made sharable for users of the content, typically a subset of the AIP. As the ovals in figure 3.5 indicate, content is packaged in different formats throughout its lifecycle.

The value of OAIS is that it provides a model for functions that should occur in a preservation environment and the types of data that must be managed over time. It is an example of how to take a holistic approach to digital preservation. The model factors into the technological requirements and the organizational resources and staffing needed to make it successful.

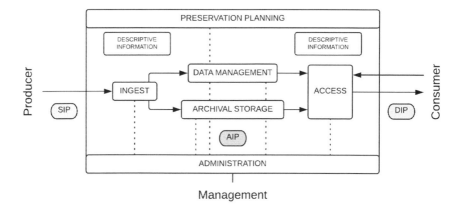

Figure 3.5. OAIS reference model

Trustworthy Digital Repositories, ISO 16363:2012

ISO 16363 is the international standard that outlines what a trustworthy digital repository (TDR) should be. It includes categories of metrics that identify the individual components that together comprise the system. A trustworthy digital repository is measured by three core qualities. First, it operates within context to understand and respond to threats to its systems. Second, a TDR ensures the content is understandable and preserved in a form that is findable, accessible, and interpretable by the designated communities a repository supports. Finally, the repository is accountable to stakeholders, which include the producers of the data deposited and the designated communities who will access and use the data. The OAIS framework is the basis for the TDR. The expectation is that any TDR will reflect the various components of the OAIS model, including a robust submission and ingest process, archival storage and data management system, and access components. A digital object in ISO 16363 is referred to as "information packages" (as it is in the OAIS standard), and other vocabulary from OAIS carries over as well. [12]

While the standard was developed to provide a framework for certifying a digital preservation program as "trustworthy," the reality is that most institutions will probably not attain actual certification. Instead, many organizations use the standard's metrics to guide development and growth of their digital archives program and to focus energy and resources on areas for improvement. ISO 16363 defines 109 metrics and sub-metrics in three overarching areas of compliance: organizational infrastructure, digital object management, and infrastructure and security risk management.

Compliance with the 109 metrics of ISO 16363 is not a means to an end. The requirements of the standard form a holistic view of the digital preservation and access repository, encompassing policy, documentation, staff, fiscal obligations, and workflows necessary to ensure long-term persistence of the digital resources managed by the system. These elements of a digital repository are determined in response to one another, creating an evolving entity that adjusts to the changing factors of its environment to ensure the content it supports remains useful over time.

As figure 3.6 indicates, any repository must approach preservation as a dynamic and coordinated system. The environment must have policies and procedures that ensure the capture of essential information for preservation and ongoing maintenance of the information's authenticity and accessibility. These processes are specified and assigned in procedural documentation and agreements between the repository and its stakeholders. The outcomes of these efforts are further documented in procedural logs that serve as evidence of the repository's success and inform future preservation planning as the repository changes over time as technology changes.

Levels of Digital Preservation (LoDP)

To aid the development of digital preservation strategies, the National Digital Stewardship Alliance created the Levels of Digital Preservation (LoDP). These guidelines are a tiered set of recommendations for archives programs beginning to think about digital preservation and those with established programs ready to take the next step to enhanced services. The focus of LoDP is on the content in digital collections and the infrastructures in place to manage them. It addresses technology rather than the overall readiness of programs. [13]

The LoDP matrix provides a categorical approach for analyzing digital preservation activities from a grassroots perspective. Focusing on tangible activities of digital preservation systems, the LoDP matrix covers five functional areas of digital preservation systems. These areas include: storage and geographic location, file fixity and data integration, information security, metadata, and file formats. Each functional area is gauged against a set of criteria that help an institution identify its own level of digital preservation readiness. [14] As figure 3.7 indicates, the four levels are progressive with the first level as the building blocks for the digital preservation program.

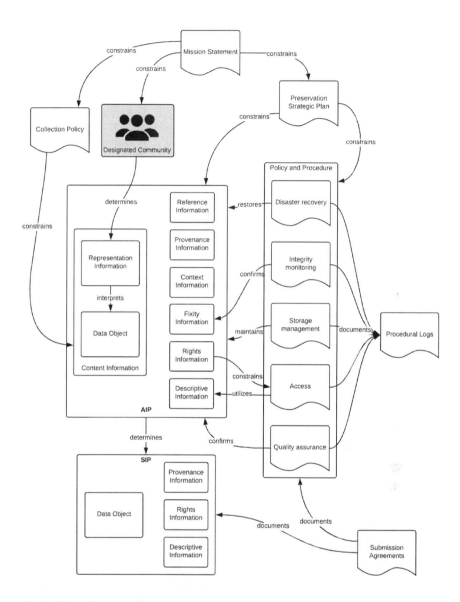

Figure 3.6. Preservation repository ecosystem

The LoDP approach offers digital preservation programs the flexibility to prioritize the needs of an organization. It also allows an archives program to create preservation goals for the short term and long term. The move toward a programmatic solution should be continuous, fluid, and flexible—with the

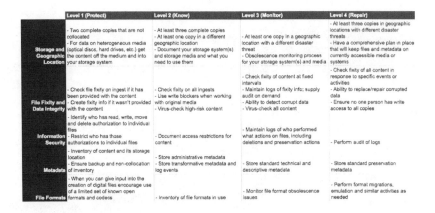

	Level 1 (Protect)	Level 2 (Know)	Level 3 (Monitor)	Level 4 (Repair)
Storage and Geographic Location	- Two complete copies that are not collocated - For data on heterogeneous media (optical discs, hard drives, etc.) get the content off the medium and into your storage system	- At least three complete copies - At least one copy in a different geographic location - Document your storage system(s) and storage media and what you need to use them	- At least one copy in a geographic location with a different disaster threat - Obsolescence monitoring process for your storage system(s) and media	- At least three copies in geographic locations with different disaster threats - Have a comprehensive plan in place that will keep files and metadata on currently accessible media or systems
File Fixity and Data Integrity	- Check file fixity on ingest if it has been provided with the content - Create fixity info if it wasn't provided with the content	- Check fixity on all ingests - Use write blockers when working with original media - Virus-check high-risk content	- Check fixity of content at fixed intervals - Maintain logs of fixity info; supply audit on demand - Ability to detect corrupt data - Virus-check all content	- Check fixity of all content in response to specific events or activities - Ability to replace/repair corrupted data - Ensure no one person has write access to all copies
Information Security	- Identify who has read, write, move and delete authorization to individual files - Restrict who has those authorizations to individual files	- Document access restrictions for content	- Maintain logs of who performed what actions on files, including deletions and preservation actions	- Perform audit of logs
Metadata	- Inventory of content and its storage location - Ensure backup and non-collocation of inventory	- Store administrative metadata - Store transformative metadata and log events	- Store standard technical and descriptive metadata	- Store standard preservation metadata
File Formats	- When you can give input into the creation of digital files encourage use of a limited set of known open formats and codecs	- Inventory of file formats in use	- Monitor file format obsolescence issues	- Perform format migrations, emulation and similar activities as needed

Figure 3.7.   NDSA levels of digital preservation

understanding that a preservation program is being built that can withstand the organizational changes that happen around them.

Strategies and Tools

Disparate Locations

Maintaining multiple copies of digital content in disparate geographic locations is a fundamental practice of preservation, whether in the physical domain (more than one library may preserve copies of the same film) or in the digital domain (the same audio files stored on servers in Chicago and Denver). It also means ensuring that digital content is stored on different types of media—for example, spinning disk and data tape.

In the digital realm, the ideal number of copies to maintain of your digital content is three: stored in different geographic locations, on different types of media, and maintained in such a way that the copies are always the same.[15] This approach ensures that if something happens to one copy in one location or on one type of media, at least two other unchanged copies of the digital content persist, and the third copy can be recreated to recomplete the set of three. This practice is also referred to as "replication." All digital content that is of primary importance for long-term preservation should be replicated as described above.

Backup Copies of Digital Content

Backing up digital content on a regular basis is a standard practice for individual computer users and large organizations with complex technical infrastructure. Active data backups involve copying actively used files, often on a daily basis, for the purpose of short-term retention while the files are in use. These backups might be saved for a week or a month, but after a period of time, they are overwritten by new backups.

Backup copies are different from replication copies. Those procedures focus on a given storage location, and they focus on keeping snapshots of active content (content that is being changed regularly) in case someone makes a change he or she did not intend to make and wants to restore the previous content or if something unforeseen goes wrong and the storage location needs to be restored to a previous point in time. Together, backup and replication strategies serve to ensure that no needed content is lost and that there are always extra copies available in case of an emergency.

File Fixity and Data Integrity

In the context of digital preservation, fixity describes the unchanged state or "fixed-ness" of a digital file. Monitoring fixity can identify if a file has changed for any number of reasons, such as human error, hardware failure, or bit rot (the slow deterioration of data—literally the physical entropy of the 1s and 0s on the underlying storage medium). Archivists monitor files for changes to the bits with short alphanumeric strings that reflect the uniqueness of every digital file. These strings are called "checksums" (or "hashes") and are generated by a program that uses a particular algorithm (e.g., MD5 or SHA256) to read the 0s and 1s of a file and create a unique string of characters to represent them. The string becomes that file's signature and can be repeatedly recalculated as long as the bits do not change. If a file is changed, even in seemingly insignificant ways, a completely different checksum will be produced by the checksum generator.[16]

Checksums are valuable for many different reasons. They can be used to authenticate a file: if a file is an original document from a donor, it can be authenticated by first creating a checksum signature from the file and then running the checksum program against a copy of the file later to be sure that the signature has not changed (and is therefore an authentic copy of the file) or has changed and is therefore inauthentic. One of the greatest values of checksums is their use in monitoring file fixity. While different files have

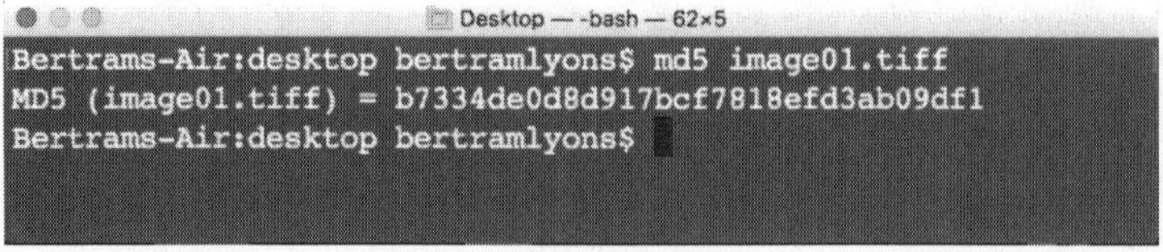

Figure 3.8.   A checksum and its associated File

different checksum signatures, exact copies of files will have the same signature. As long as a file does not change, it will always have the same checksum signature as other identical copies. This means that files can be monitored for change using a tool that checks fixity on an ongoing basis and repairs files when checksums do not match by replacing them with another unchanged copy of that file. Monitoring fixity over time (e.g., once every month, six months, a year) allows archivists to identify changes and replace erroneous files with an unchanged copy. Checksums can also be used as an inventory to monitor file attendance or identify if a file is new (the checksum signature has never been produced before), removed (a checksum is missing from a list), or moved (the checksum appears with files in another location).

Some institutions have sophisticated systems and workflows that can automate the monitoring of fixity and file attendance in their digital collections, but others rely on open-source tools, such as Fixity.[17] This simple application enables automated checksum production and file attendance monitoring and reporting. Fixity scans a folder or directory, creating a manifest of the files, including their file paths and checksums. It then monitors file integrity through generation and validation of checksums and file attendance by monitoring and reporting on new, missing, moved, and renamed files. Finally, Fixity emails a report to the user, documenting flagged items along with the reason for a flag.

Planning for Obsolescence

Managing digital content requires a great deal of long-range planning. A fundamental practice of digital preservation is monitoring file formats and media to ensure they remain usable and not obsolete. Obsolescence can happen at the file or program level (e.g., RealMedia, WordStar) or with the media on which the file is stored (e.g., Zip drives). When this happens, the digital content becomes unreadable or inaccessible. Before obsolescence happens, archivists can transition digital content to current storage options or more stable formats. Keeping track of changes in technology, called "obsolescence monitoring," involves maintaining awareness of file formats, software, and systems that are ubiquitous and those that are specialized. Paired with proactive planning, transitioning to more stable systems minimizes the chances that digital content becomes obsolete.[18]

The goal of digital preservation is the ongoing accessibility of and access to digital content. The media on which digital files are stored will become obsolete or unstable with age—usually with more frequency than file formats—and the files on such media will need to move to new and current digital storage media. Even hard drives, which many people think of as long-term storage solutions, have a life span of less than ten years.[19] The good news is that obsolescence tends to happen slowly. Routinely reviewing files, conferring with colleagues, and learning about industry-standard formats in use are some of the best strategies for ongoing obsolescence monitoring.

Refreshing and Migrating Data

Refreshing is one method to overcome obsolescence. Refreshing refers to the approach of transferring digital files from one media, server, or system to another. This may consist of moving files from an aging server to a new one or shifting metadata from an obsolete database to a more widely used system. The challenge of this approach is to make sure that all information is transferred without loss and that the integrity of the content is verified after the fact. Error checking includes running fixity checks on files moved from one server to another to look for changes to files or missing content. The technology determines how often refreshing needs to occur. For example, data on spinning disk hard drives should be refreshed at least every three to five years.[20]

Migration is another approach to keeping files from becoming inaccessible. This process refers to the transfer of the content and metadata from one format into another. Migration is necessary when the format and software used to read the format become less ubiquitous and are on the verge of becoming obsolete. Because obsolescence can happen at many levels (file format, content management system, and storage media), migration plans must consider the hardware, software, and databases associated with the files.[21]

STARTING A DIGITAL PRESERVATION PROGRAM

Establishing a digital preservation program is often a modular process that evolves over time as needs change and resources become available. For most institutions, implementation of a complete set of digital preservation policies can take several years. Building momentum and creating awareness are initial steps, which will ultimately lead to the adoption of policies, committed financial support, and deployment of technologies. The larger goal is to add necessary components that lead to a trustworthy digital environment for managing collections. With continued evolution and improvement, the adoption of these plans, policies, and services will support the goal of long-term preservation and access to digital collections.

Develop a Plan

A preservation strategy begins with a brief written statement. First, project leaders identify the general and specific needs for the care of the collections. Factors to consider include the organizational commitment to the preservation of and continued access to digital collections, the authenticity of digital collections, environmental controls on the physical media on which digital collections are held, monitoring collections and addressing errors or changes as necessary, and migrating digital collections from obsolete software and hardware. This information helps project leaders establish priorities and secure the necessary resources to get the project underway.[22]

Digital preservation plans communicate needs and objectives in a few short paragraphs. Many institutions make their digital preservation plans available online, and each is unique to its organization, structure, and goals. These plans can be invaluable resources for other archives programs just establishing digital preservation priorities.

Organizational Infrastructure

A key facet of a sustainable preservation environment is an organizational infrastructure that supports it. Organizational infrastructure is one of the main components of a trustworthy digital repository.[23] This includes all the elements that any program needs to address digital preservation requirements, including planning, policies, funding, procedures, stakeholders, and decision makers.[24] Documentation of the available resources, decisions, policies, and commitments are imperative. Further, project leaders must document the status of digital collections that they want to preserve.

Software and Information Technology

Navigating the wide variety of options when it comes to software technologies for handling an organization's digital object and metadata requirements can be a significant effort. There is no easy answer to the question, "Which system should I use?" In all cases, whether an organization is looking to build, adopt, or a buy a digital preservation system, the first step is to evaluate what functions and features are needed and to document this information as a set of requirements for the organization. Business requirements define overarching needs of the institution and goals for the new technology. Functional requirements express characteristics and functions of a system designed to meet the needs of the organization in the context of the business requirements. Nonfunctional requirements include those related to technology and expectations for technology support, training, documentation, and maintenance. Together, these sets of requirements can be used to evaluate whether a particular software product or solution is right for the organization.

For example, if an organization did not have web archiving as a requirement, then certainly a solution such as Archive-It would not be included in the list of possible systems to adopt. Each technical system or product will have features and services that it provides and these can be aligned with an organization's requirements to determine how good the fit will be.

Security

It is necessary for an organization to control which users are accessing and manipulating data in a digital preservation environment. Some users may have access to view files, while others may have controls over where files reside, their formats, and who can access them. Creating, assigning, logging, and managing permissions and restrictions are crucial in mitigating the risk of intentional or unintentional data corruption and misuse of content. Many preservation management systems make permissions management easy. When data management happens manually or outside of a management system, IT staff can often set access permissions on directories on networked servers, which creates secure spaces to store digital collections. Systems administrators should have full access to the collection so that if the digital content needs to move, migrate, or be monitored for fixity, there are no restrictions for them to do so.

As with all digital preservation activities, it is important to document decisions about permissions, especially the levels of access for each person. Logging access and internal actions taken on digital collections is equally important. Logs (or audit trails) enable digital collections administrators to audit actions taken and track back changes to a user and date, which can be valuable when trying to understand when and where errors have occurred. Many preservation management systems automate this documentation.

Every organization needs to be concerned about how to protect its assets from external threats. This is particularly important for storage devices (like servers) that are connected via networks and to the internet. Controlling access to these devices via good password and username practice is imperative. The threats of viruses or other corrupting malware are just as dangerous to a preservation system. Virus scanning should be performed on all incoming files from donors or other units within an organization. This process must be completed before the new material is ingested into the preservation system. Once the content is reviewed and added to the system, there can be routine virus scanning of all content in the digital preservation environment.[25]

Storage

In the digital environment, how digital content is stored is paramount. Best practices and standards suggest that digital content be stored on "active" servers that are backed up and managed with preservation in mind. On the contrary, storage on fixed devices, such as optical media (e.g., DVDs) or external hard drives that are not monitored or backed up, is not a recommended approach.

At a high level, storage options can be either locally managed by the organization or through a vendor with a cloud-based service. There are associated costs to managing the servers and media on which digital content is stored. Staffing, facilities, and ongoing management of and upgrades to technology must all be factored into the costs of maintaining storage locally. It is valuable for digital collections managers to develop strong relationships with the IT staff that manage storage at their institution so that they can work together to build the best storage environment possible for the digital content they wish to preserve over time.

Cloud storage is a service model in which digital content is maintained, managed, backed up remotely, and made available to users over the internet. Examples of cloud storage include Amazon S3, Amazon Glacier, and Microsoft Azure. Cloud providers offer different services, features, and performance levels based on costs and the intended market. A few considerations when assessing cloud storage options include access time, where geographically the data will be stored, security of the system, disaster recovery mechanisms, and how to remove data.[26]

The architecture of storage options affects decision making. Online, nearline, and offline represent the different types of storage architectures. These terms speak to the ease and immediacy with which data can be accessed and the varying costs and scalability of storage. An online system means that the data is immediately available to users on a storage system. Servers that host an institution's networked drives are examples of online storage systems. It is the fastest but most expensive storage option. Nearline systems make digital content available to users with some lag time. It is automated and networked, usually accessing a magnetic tape library. This tends to be an option for larger institutions with the resources to diversify their storage architectures. Finally, offline options store digital content on media that requires a human to connect it to a computer to access the data on it. Offline storage, often based on a magnetic tape system, is often used to back up digital content for long periods of time. It is cost effective but also takes time to access because it is not connected to a network. For digital preservation, offline storage is often used for the third-copy backup (or disaster recovery copy) of digital content.

The cost of storage systems is important but not the only consideration. Decisions about what type of storage works best for an institution's needs are influenced by such factors as the level of reliability or "uptime" required to access the material, the number and types of users that need access to the content, the types and amount of digital content, the amount of redundancy in collections, and expected growth of new content. Based on an institution's requirements, technical infrastructure, and resources, both cloud and local storage options may be utilized. Many institutions have a hybrid solution of on-premises and cloud storage architecture. Cloud storage vendors have options for both online and nearline storage that, together with local storage, may provide an institution with a redundant and secure approach to managing its digital content. No matter what storage systems are in place, the preservation of digital content depends on having frequent backups resulting in as many as three copies of each file.[27]

NEXT STEPS

Digital preservation encompasses more than the systems and hardware infrastructure supporting functions and procedures. Central to successful digital preservation is a well-equipped and well-managed operational environment. Funding, staffing, and management resources must be optimized to ensure the long-term sustainability and functionality of a digital preservation environment. The inclusion of an entire section in ISO 16363 addressing organizational infrastructure is a testament to the importance of these factors when developing and maintaining a digital repository. Without a strong organizational foundation and support, the repository cannot remain viable over time.

Approaching digital preservation as a whole is intimidating and overwhelming. Prioritizing approaches based on a written digital preservation plan makes decisions about incoming digital content much easier. Instead of thinking about the "foreverness" of digital preservation, archivists should consider it in five-year increments. The aphorism "perfect is the enemy of good" is a useful way of thinking about prioritizing and phasing digital preservation activities. Doing something now—for example, creating an inventory of collections, developing a collection policy, or making a backup copy of digital content—is better than waiting for the perfect technology solution and resources and organizational framework to support it. Being flexible, putting what you know into practice, and taking a proactive approach today will establish a foundation that makes implementation and adoption of new technologies and programmatic preservation strategies easier in the future.

As we look to the future of digital archives and digital information, we can be assured that the landscape will change continuously. Storage media will evolve; computing systems and software will too. Access and inventory platforms will come and go. Archivists will be best served by focusing on maintaining a fundamental understanding of digital information; developing strong and collaborative relationships with information technology colleagues; ensuring programmatic (not project-based) funding for digital preservation staff, services, and technology systems; and creating agile and feasible acquisition procedures to engage donors within their personal computing environments to ensure the digital collections of the future are significant, accurate, and an inclusive representation of what the archives program collects.

NOTES

1. Bertram Lyons, "What Is the Chemistry of Digital Preservation," *AVP* (blog), February 18, 2016, https://www.weareavp.com/what-is-the-chemistry-of-digital-preservation/.

2. Ashley Taylor, instructor, CS101—Introduction to Computing Principles, "Bits and Bytes," 2018, https://web.stanford.edu/class/cs101/bits-bytes.html.

3. The Digital Curation Centre in Edinburgh provides a useful overview of metadata with regard to digital files. "What Are Metadata Standards," February 2007, http://www.dcc.ac.uk/resources/briefing-papers/standards-watch-papers/what-are-metadata-standards.

4. The writ-large standard concept for preservation metadata for digital objects is articulated within PREMIS. The PREMIS Data Dictionary for Preservation Metadata is the international standard for metadata to support the preservation of digital objects and ensure their long-term usability. Developed by an international team of experts, PREMIS is implemented in digital preservation projects around the world, and support for PREMIS is incorporated into a number of commercial and open-source digital preservation tools and systems. PREMIS, "Preservation Metadata Maintenance Activity," June 22, 2018, http://www.loc.gov/standards/premis/; METS, Metadata Encoding and Transmission Standard, August 18, 2017, available at http://www.loc.gov/standards/mets/mets-home.html.

5. "Digital Preservation," Library of Congress, http://www.digitalpreservation.gov/about/.

6. A foundational resource for understanding digital preservation from an organizational and technical perspective is Anne R. Kenney and Nancy Y. McGovern, "The Five Organizational Stages of Digital Preservation," in *Digital Libraries: A Vision for the Twenty-First Century; A Festschrift in Honor of Wendy Lougee on the Occasion of Her Departure from the University of Michigan*, eds. Patricia Hodges, Maria Bonn, Mark Sandler, and John Price Wilkin, (Ann Arbor: University of Michigan Library, 2003), https://quod.lib.umich.edu/cgi/t/text/text-idx?c=spobooks;idno=bbv9812.0001.001;rgn=div1;view=text;cc=spobooks;node=bbv9812.0001.001%3A11.

7. There are many useful resources that provide guidance on careful handling of digital files for archivists, including Ricky Erway, *Walk This Way: Detailed Steps for Transferring Born-Digital Content from Media You Can Read In-House* (Dublin, OH: OCLC Research, 2013), https://www.oclc.org/content/dam/research/publications/library/2013/2013-02.pdf; Gabriela Redwine, Megan Barnard, Kate Donovan, Erika Farr, Michael Forstrom, Will Hansen, Jeremy Leighton John, Nancy Kuhl, Seth Shaw, and Susan Thomas, *Born Digital: Guidance for Donors, Dealers, and Archival Repositories* (Washington, DC: Council on Library and Information Resources, 2013), https://www.clir.org/wp-content/uploads/sites/9/pub159.pdf.

8. See the work of the BitCurator Community for examples of this practice. BitCurator, April 17, 2018, https://bitcurator.net/.

9. For example, the open-source tool Exactly creates file system exports and stores the information as a text file for all files included in a packaging process. This information is gathered from the original file system before files are copied. Exactly, 2018, https://www.weareavp.com/products/exactly/.

10. A good place to start regarding risk assessment for digital preservation is Sally Vermaaten, "Identifying Threats to Successful Digital Preservation: The SPOT Model for Risk Assess-

ment," *D-Lib Magazine* 18 (September/October 2012), http://www.dlib.org/dlib/september12/vermaaten/09vermaaten.html.

11. Often referred to as OAIS, ISO 14721 sets the foundation for digital preservation systems. Available formally from ISO at https://www.iso.org/standard/57284.html. Previous versions can be accessed for free at https://public.ccsds.org/pubs/650x0m2.pdf.

12. Often referred to as the TDR specification, ISO 16363 defines functional metrics that can be tested and measured to identify whether a digital preservation system is trustworthy or not. The metrics are helpful for organizations looking to benchmark their efforts and identify gaps in their own systems. Available formally from ISO at https://www.iso.org/standard/56510.html. Previous versions can be accessed for free at https://public.ccsds.org/pubs/652x0m1.pdf.

13. Megan Phillips, "The NDSA Levels of Digital Preservation: An Explanation and Uses," Proceedings of the Archiving (IS&T) Conference, April 2013, http://ndsa.org/documents/NDSA_Levels_Archiving_2013.pdf.

14. Ibid.

15. Ibid.

16. The Digital Preservation Coalition offers a brief introduction to fixity and checksums and pointers to more information. "Fixity and Checksums," https://www.dpconline.org/handbook/technical-solutions-and-tools/fixity-and-checksums.

17. "Fixity," AVP, http://www.avpreserve.com/tools/fixity/.

18. For example, principle 9 in *Yale University Library's Digital Preservation Policy Framework* ensures that such monitoring is central to Yale's ongoing success with digital preservation practices. *Yale University Library's Digital Preservation Policy Framework*, November 2014, https://web.library.yale.edu/sites/default/files/files/YUL%20Digital%20Preservation%20Policy%20Framework%20V1%200.pdf.

19. Brian Beach, "How Long Do Disk Drives Last?" *BackBlaze* (blog), November 12, 2013, https://www.backblaze.com/blog/how-long-do-disk-drives-last/.

20. David Rosenthal, developer of LOCKSS and digital preservation expert at Stanford University Libraries, provides continued review and analysis of digital storage media longevity and costs on his blog. *DSHR's Blog* (blog), https://blog.dshr.org/search/label/storage%20media.

21. The Digital Preservation Coalition offers high-level commentary on preservation strategies, including migration. "Preservation Action," https://dpconline.org/handbook/organisational-activities/preservation-action.

22. Liz Bishoff, "Digital Preservation Plan: Ensuring Long-Term Access and Authenticity of Digital Collections," *Information Standards Quarterly* 22 (Spring 2010): 20–25.

23. Consultative Committee for Space Data Systems, *Audit and Certification of Trustworthy Digital Repositories* (Washington, DC: CCSDS, 2011), section 3, https://public.ccsds.org/pubs/652x0m1.pdf.

24. Digital Preservation Management: Implementing Short-Term Strategies for Long-Term Projects, http://www.dpworkshop.org/dpm-eng/program/index.html.

25. Every effort should be made to ensure that virus scan libraries are kept up to date with any virus scanning software employed by the organization. Many organizations in the digital preservation community use open-source virus scanning software, such as ClamAV, available at https://www.clamav.net/.

26. For up-to-date reviews of cloud service providers from the perspective of digital preservation, see AVP's "Cloud Storage Vendor Profiles," https://www.weareavp.com/cloud-storage-vendor-profiles/.

27. Popularized by the American Society of Media Photographers, the 3-2-1 rule is a good rule of thumb for determining digital preservation storage copy needs: http://www.indiepreserves.info/preservation-tips-blog/the-3-2-1-rule; http://dpbestflow.org/node/262.

Chapter Four

Digital Forensics and Curation

Martin Gengenbach

Over the past decade, there has been a rapid expansion of collecting digital archives in cultural heritage institutions.[1] While incoming acquisitions or transfers are more likely to include born-digital content, the devices on which these digital materials were stored during their active life—floppy disks, magnetic hard drives, optical discs, and other media carriers—may be less accessible to the contemporary user. For many organizations, the challenges posed by these legacy digital materials have precluded the provision of access: if there is not an available computer that can read a floppy disk, then there is no way to access the files on that disk. For this reason, in conjunction with the recent growth in digital collecting, researchers and practitioners in cultural heritage fields have pursued new tools and strategies to make this legacy digital information more accessible. One such strategy is the application of digital forensics approaches to acquire, analyze, preserve, and provide access to digital information.

Digital forensics is a practical field born out of the criminal investigative community, characterized by "the use of scientifically derived and proven methods toward the preservation, collection, validation, identification, analysis, interpretation, documentation and presentation of digital evidence derived from digital sources."[2] Digital forensics is a set of processes and guiding principles that facilitate the acquisition and analysis of digital materials while preventing or minimizing their alteration. The technologies used in forensic analysis also generate documentation of the activities taken by the investigator in their identification and acquisition of items of interest. The tools, processes, and principles of digital forensics ensure that digital evidence acquired in criminal investigations meets the legal requirements for their presentation in court. The methods employed by digital forensics practitioners also align with many archival best practices, including respect for provenance and chain of custody, original order, and the integrity and authenticity of digital materials.[3]

As applied in the archival field, digital forensics is a relatively recent development. Interest in digital forensics has grown rapidly, with archives programs offering training related to data recovery and an increasing number of practitioners using digital forensics tools and methods in their home institutions. Despite public pronouncements of a "digital dark age," there is a growing community dedicated to the preservation of digital content from legacy storage media. In a 2016 survey of cultural heritage workers managing the intake of digital materials into their collections, Jody DeRidder notes that over half of respondents have the technical capability to manage legacy media such as 5.25-inch floppy disks (52 percent), Zip disks (74 percent), and 3.5-inch floppy disks (90 percent).[4] These figures reflect the growth of digital forensic acquisition activities in collecting institutions.

The adoption of digital forensics tools and techniques presents an exciting opportunity for the management of digital archives in cultural heritage organizations. Digital forensics is particularly geared toward the acquisition of born-digital content and the documentation of actions taken upon that content through its management and curation. This chapter will provide a broad overview of digital forensics and its applications in the curation of digital archives. It explores how digital forensics is uniquely suited to the collection of certain types of born-digital materials, how digital forensics tools assist in the communication of complex digital preservation ideas to donors, and how curatorial decisions are reflected through digital forensic analysis and reporting.

DIGITAL FORENSICS AND ARCHIVES

Digital forensic investigation is comparable to a physical crime scene investigation in which the investigator tries to capture and understand evidence of a crime or activity from the physical environment in which the crime took place.[5] In the digital realm, this environment is created by the computer's software and hardware. There is often a conception of ephemerality to digital materials, reinforced by the seeming fragility of digital media carriers and the frequency with which files may seem to vanish from a user's computer screen. But at its most fundamental level, a file is a series of physical signals on a physical storage device, which are then interpreted through layers of computer hardware and software to reproduce the digital object that is seen and manipulated by the user.[6]

The job of the forensic investigator is to preserve, analyze, and present the evidence of activities that transpired in that environment through its residual digital and physical signals. This evidence is used by the investigator to construct hypotheses about events that may have occurred—whether a computer was used to create a document, share a picture or video, send an email, or visit a website. Investigators attempt to preserve as much information as they can from that digital environment so they have more evidence to support their hypotheses and more ways to independently verify their conclusions.[7] Investigators also take steps to prevent any change or alteration to that environment as a result of their work, just as forensic investigators would wear masks and gloves when exploring a crime scene. The resulting digital evidence can be presented in court as authentic because the rigorous and well-documented processes used to collect and understand that evidence serve as a chain of custody.[8]

There are important parallels between how criminal forensic investigators collect and analyze a subject's computer and how cultural heritage professionals approach the acquisition and curation of digital content.[9] The 2010 CLIR report *Digital Forensics and Born-Digital Content in Collecting Institutions* notes that throughout their research, the project participants "were struck again and again by the extent of the crossover between the archivist's world and that of the modern forensic investigator."[10] Similar to law enforcement scenarios, archivists seek to acquire evidence of activities in a digital environment (e.g., documents, emails, photos, videos) and to understand the context of their creation and use. Archivists also have an interest in demonstrating that their work has not inadvertently or irreversibly changed the content that they are trying to capture, which reflects fundamental archival concepts like original order and chain of custody.[11] While a criminal investigator may look for evidence of a computer crime (e.g., stolen credit card information, social security numbers), archivists also look for the same kind of sensitive information so that it may be redacted or restricted per donor agreements, organizational policies, or legal requirements.[12] To that end, archivists may use digital forensics tools to explore the contents of a hard drive or floppy disk, identifying and highlighting sensitive information. While the ultimate goal of each professional investigation may differ, the alignment in the principles and practices can be an important driver in creation of digital forensics workflows in cultural heritage institutions—identifiable examples help to enable their implementation in a different context.

Archivists have long understood the challenges of long-term preservation of digital information. The potential loss of information, whether through technical obsolescence or digital decay, is perhaps the most common issue of managing electronic collections. Throughout the life cycle of electronic materials, archivists must document the chain of custody in such cases in which actions need to be taken to "refresh" physical hardware or to migrate digital content to new formats so as to continue to make digital content available. The central component of long-term sustainability for electronic materials is the reliability and authenticity of digital content—whether it is what it purports to be and is trustworthy as a record of the evidence it documents. [13]

Archival practitioners have explored the use of digital forensics from a variety of perspectives with respect to these challenges. In a 2008 article, Jeremy Leighton John highlights the use of computer forensics, ancestral computing, and machine learning for capturing, accessing, and analyzing legacy digital information. [14] Matthew Kirschenbaum worked with archivists from a number of different institutions to process the legacy computer and media collections of literary figures. [15] Luciana Duranti and others probed the intellectual alignment between digital forensics and diplomatics. [16] These authors helped introduce the field of digital forensics to libraries, archives, and museums. By demonstrating the alignment of the technologies and methodologies of digital forensics for use in archival settings, these early works provided a foundation for subsequent practical application.

The following sections outline how to establish a digital forensics program integrated with other acquisitions activities in an organization, focusing on tools, workflows, and the documentation necessary to get a program started. It concludes with a discussion of the ways in which the information resulting from digital forensic acquisition may bring new considerations into the donor engagement strategy of an organization. It also points to how digital forensic tools and workflows can be used to document donor interactions and curatorial decisions, both of which affect the provision of long-term access to digital collections.

TOOLS

One of the more challenging hurdles to launching a digital forensics program is building or purchasing a workstation for conducting acquisition and analysis. Beyond issues of cost, common questions such as "Do I need to buy a purpose-built machine?" and "What type of peripherals do I need to get?" often paralyze a new practitioner. Thankfully, there are a wealth of recommendations from researchers and archivists about the components necessary to get a workstation up and running. The basic elements are the computer itself, the peripherals, and the software necessary to conduct forensic acquisition and analysis. [17]

When it comes to the computer itself, a few considerations to take into account are the CPU or processing power, the available RAM (random access memory) that can be devoted to processing tasks, and the overall storage capacity that will be available to store and process materials on the workstation. This workstation does not need to be expensive to be well suited to its task. There are a number of case studies that emphasize ways to maximize performance at minimal expense while still meeting the basic requirements for a forensic acquisition station. [18] Others document where institutions have opted for a commercial digital forensic acquisition workstation (a forensic recovery of evidence device or FRED), which frequently come preloaded with a variety of cables and adapters to facilitate connectivity to legacy media devices. [19] Broadly speaking, the workstation should have sufficient CPU power to run the programs that will be used to conduct digital forensic acquisition and analysis. Many of the software applications used by digital forensic practitioners include minimum hardware requirements so that practitioners can get a better sense of the type of computer they will need. [20]

RAM is storage that can be utilized by the CPU to assist in processing data and is an important part of a digital forensics workstation. [21] RAM must be allocated to run software applications that process data, from virtual machines to granular indexing. It is for this reason that most workstation guides recommend a significantly greater amount of RAM than is commonly found on a modern workstation—and the more, the better. [22] Beyond CPU and RAM, the machine should have sufficient storage to hold and work with the expected quantity of content that will be acquired and processed. This is of particular concern for digital forensic practitioners, as forensic disk images may require large storage footprints. Archivists must first assess the anticipated size and quantity of digital content that is to be acquired and then make decisions about the storage space for a forensic workstation.

In addition to the basic specifications of the digital processing workstation, there are other factors to consider, such as the types and formats of digital information that will be acquired and analyzed on the workstation. Existing literature provides a great deal of insight into the necessary components to be able to access information from a range of different environments, but the guiding principle should always be an assessment of an organization's own needs and an understanding of its own collections.[23] The history of modern computing is rife with competing standards, proprietary systems, and challenges in interoperability. Will the organization acquire content from removable media like floppy disks, Zip disks, or other now-obsolete storage media? One of the most useful online sites for an archivist wanting to build his or her own workstation may be eBay.com, where any number of obscure legacy hardware components may be found.

In addition to the workstation and hardware peripherals, there is also the technical issue of having the correct adapters and cables that make it possible to connect to and interact with the devices themselves.[24] One complicating factor is that modern computers do not necessarily have the proper software drivers to allow communication with legacy media devices. Even if a 5.25-inch floppy drive could be connected to a computer, it may not be recognizable as such. For this reason, many workstations will need a floppy drive controller, a separate piece of hardware that facilitates communication between the computer and the drive. While there are a number available, one of the more frequently used in archives and special collections with digital forensics programs is the KryoFlux.[25] This device facilitates interaction with both 3.5- and 5.25-inch floppy disk drives, provides a variety of different formatting options (for use with different computing environments and operating systems), and has a robust community of users online.[26] Archivists who use KryoFlux for their forensic services have recently completed an instruction manual for the tool that is specifically geared toward its use in libraries, archives, and museums. This type of cultural-heritage-specific documentation is invaluable for those just starting a digital forensics program.[27]

To successfully create a forensic disk image, archivists use a variety of different tools, including special software and hardware to access and image the target device. Special care should be taken not to alter the contents of the target device. As a caveat, turning on a computer to access its files initiates a set of internal, automatic operations that may inadvertently erase information about its users, recently accessed files, or other potentially important contextual metadata.[28] For this reason, when capturing information from a media carrier, digital forensics practitioners recommend removing the hard drive and accessing the content through a dedicated workstation while using a write blocker. A write blocker is a hardware device or software designed to prevent any "write" commands from being executed onto the target device while still allowing the "read" commands that enable rendering and interaction with the content on the device. Write blockers generally come in two flavors: either hardware-based physical gateways between a target device and the host workstation used to capture its contents or software-based programs that preemptively interrupt the host workstation's outgoing "write" commands.

Finally, implementation of a digital forensics workstation requires a range of software tools capable of rendering, analyzing, or otherwise interpreting and presenting the content of the forensic disk image captured from the target media. Commercial digital forensics workstations frequently come bundled with licensed, commercial digital forensics software systems, while the investigator on a shoestring budget might utilize open-source applications.[29] In either case, these digital forensics tools provide highly granular indexing and searching capabilities with a wide array of tools to analyze and render digital content in disk images. With few exceptions, these tools have been developed for the purpose of criminal investigation.[30]

Over the past five years, the BitCurator project has cultivated a community of users around a suite of open-source digital forensics tools specifically geared toward use in archives, libraries, and museums. Funded by a grant from the Andrew W. Mellon Foundation and collaboratively led by the School for Information and Library Science at the University of North Carolina at Chapel Hill (SILS-UNC) and the Maryland Institute for Technology in the Humanities (MITH), the BitCurator project developed a Linux environment for a suite of free and open-source tools for acquiring and working with digital content from removable media.[31] This suite of applications includes tools for acquiring, analyzing, interpreting, and presenting digital content extracted from forensic disk images. Its creators have also documented how disk images can be managed as a part of archival electronic records workflows, which provides additional value for the cultural heritage community.[32]

WORKFLOWS

Equally important to the selection and procurement of a digital forensics workstation is the way in which that workstation will be employed to facilitate digital acquisitions. For organizations implementing digital forensics workflows into their acquisitions processes, the workflow will function as a means of establishing the format and packaging of a digital submission headed for preservation storage. Acquisition workflows must also be able to incorporate analysis, reporting, and rendering capabilities, enabling archivists and curators to work with donors to establish the terms and any restrictions of a donation. For this reason, digital forensics workflows must be flexible and must facilitate these interactions with donors to clearly address any concerns that may come up throughout the donation process. Along with the growing number of case studies documenting digital forensics approaches in cultural heritage settings, there are a number of published workflows that illustrate the sequence of events from acquisition to the final "put" into storage. Because digital forensics workflows are closely tied to the donor's context and digital preservation capacity of a particular institution, this chapter focuses only on the workflow at the time of initial capture and analysis of a digital acquisition.[33]

One fundamental component in a digital forensic workflow is the initial capture—the creation of a copy of the target media or device.[34] This copy goes far beyond the simple and familiar "drag-n-drop" activity on a graphical desktop. Through the creation of a forensic disk image, the investigator captures a bit-level copy of the entire physical surface of the target media. This bit-level copy contains all of the information that was present on the disk or device—it is "a 'snapshot' of the medium's content, including all allocated files, file names, and other metadata information associated with the disk volume."[35] The disk image can be used to document file integrity and chain of custody for any files exported from the target media and to demonstrate the authenticity of that digital content. This low-level copy also facilitates further analysis without the risk of loss.

There are a number of tools that are used to create disk images. Within the BitCurator environment, these tools may be bundled into a single interface; disk imaging tools are also individually available for installation within Unix/Linux or Windows environments.[36] As an output of these imaging tools, disk images also come in a variety of different formats. These formats range from a simple, uncompressed sector-level copy created using the Linux command "dd" that would generate a 1 TB file for a 1 TB drive to forensic disk image formats (e.g., AFF and E01) that incorporate robust acquisition metadata and segmented compression to minimize the storage footprint of a disk image while allowing for the contents of that image to be accessible.[37] The KryoFlux device generates a "stream file," a proprietary format that "divorces the understanding of the content fully from the stabilization of the content."[38] In practice, this allows archivists to conduct capture and interpretation or analysis of a target media as separate activities, which may be helpful for modular workflows that do not necessarily need to take place in immediate sequential order (e.g., large collections of floppy disks in which imaging may be one step followed by processing at a later date). Like other aspects of a digital forensics program, the choice of which type and format of disk image to generate and whether to maintain those disk images as long-term preservation objects should be based on an assessment of institutional needs and capacity.

The creation of a disk image allows a great deal of flexibility around subsequent curatorial activity. This curatorial activity is part of the analysis stage, the second part of the workflow, which most often occurs after the capture of the information. In some cases, analysis may not take place until long after the initial capture of digital materials. Other times, analysis occurs during negotiations with the donor to determine what materials are in or out of scope, or if private or sensitive information such as credit card or social security numbers are present in the collection. Forensic analysis may also uncover email addresses, website URLs, or keywords that may be considered by the donor to be personal information that he or she would rather not include as part of the donation. Simply put, the analytical tools available through forensic investigation allow a highly granular level of access to information in a digital donation that may yield unexpected results.

To understand how such a forensic analysis workflow might operate, archivists must remember that a forensic disk image contains sector-by-sector information from a storage or media device. Forensic workflows utilize this low-level capture to identify information outside of the commonly understood parts of a digital donation, such as the files and folders with which most donors generally interact. Within the BitCurator suite, a tool called bulk_extractor scans the disk image at this low level for "features"—patterns and other indicators that may suggest information that may be important to the archivist conducting analysis. Such features might include email domains, social security numbers, credit card numbers, telephone numbers, and website URLs, among a number of other filters.[39] BitCurator takes this output and combines it with the output of another tool, fiwalk.[40] This tool generates "an XML file detailing file system hierarchy within a disk image, including files and folders, deleted materials, and information in slack space."[41] The result is a map of sorts, containing granular technical metadata about the disk image and informational content pulled from the bulk_extractor results that may indicate the presence of sensitive information not only in files and folders but also in unexpected places (e.g., deleted file fragments that may not have been erased following the user's deletion of the file) or the slack space that is left when a file is not completely overwritten.[42]

This acquisition workflow is not specific to using the BitCurator tool suite. Workflows may take a variety of different forms, depending upon the context of the institution in which they are implemented. In their 2013 article, "Capturing and Processing Born-Digital Files in the Stop AIDS Project: A Case Study," Laura Wilsey, Rebecca Skirvin, Peter Chan, and Glynn Edwards introduce a similar workflow using commercial forensic analysis software and hardware (FTK and FRED) to conduct imaging and analysis.[43] Similarly, Greg Wiedeman outlines how digital forensics tools can be used to generate contextual metadata during accession without creation of a disk image and what costs and benefits there are to this approach for collecting institutional records in a university setting.[44] Archivists at the University of Albany also developed their own software application, built on digital forensics tools, to enable to collection of file system information for Windows machines.[45] These examples demonstrate the variability—by necessity—of digital forensic workflows and the importance of institutional context.

Along with workflow variability, digital forensic practitioners face other challenges. Articles such as Dorothy Waugh's "A Dogged Pursuit: Capturing Forensic Images of 3.5" Floppy Disks," A. L. Carson's "#digitalarchivesfail: Well, That Didn't Work," and Alice Prael and Amy Wickner's "Getting to Know FRED" describe the many technical roadblocks—some complex, some mundane—that may impede or delay digital forensics implementation.[46] Similarly, Julia Kim discusses working with forensic disk images from acquisition to access, imaging large, multiterabyte hard drives. She notes the necessary investment of time when working with contemporary born-digital collections.[47] In recent work at Yale University, Alice Prael presented some of the complexities in working with optical media and posed the question whether forensic disk images provide the best capture mechanism.[48] The complexities of working with digital forensic acquisitions—or any digital content for that matter—requires a degree of flexibility and adaptation.

It is important, however, to understand that flexibility may come at a price. Even when capture is successful, there may be many challenges when working with legacy content that affects how researchers interpret and use the collection. In "Invisible Defaults and Perceived Limitations: Processing the Juan Gelman Files," Elvia Arroyo-Ramirez explains how actions that may make digital materials computationally "easier" to manage, such as the removal or automatic "cleaning" of diacritic characters from a Spanish-language collection, may obscure meaning in that collection by altering its "cultural and political integrity." Arroyo-Ramirez writes, "We need to reflect, think critically and conscientiously of how our own perceptions of what is possible are so influenced by the invisible defaults we all operate on as citizens working in and alongside industries that are dominated by cisgendered, heterosexual, English-speaking, white, men."[49] As archivists move ahead with establishing digital forensics programs, they must keep in mind the limitations of tools, how their institution operates, and the cultural contexts in which the digital archives were created.

DOCUMENTATION

Organizational documentation plays a significant role in establishing a program that will provide long-term value to archival donors, researchers, and practitioners. The decision to collect digital content using digital forensic tools and processes affects organizational documentation at multiple levels. At the collection policy level, the program must make clear the collection scope of digital information. Second, at the level of donor agreement and deed of gift, the organization and the donor agree upon what is being donated and, perhaps just as importantly, what is not. Finally, at the process documentation level, an organization articulates how it uses tools and technologies to acquire and analyze digital donations via standardized, repeatable processes. Taken together, this documentation provides transparency to donors, researchers, and other stakeholders.

Collection Policies as Institutional Policies

A collection development policy is "used to select materials that the repository will acquire, typically identifying the scope of creators, subjects, formats, and other characteristics that influence the selection process."[50] Collection development policies commonly include information about the subjects, geographical areas, time periods, and physical formats collected by a particular institution. This policy should state how and when, in alignment with an organization's mission, an organization will acquire and preserve content. It should also describe what materials are not collected. For digital content, a collection policy may require amendments or additions. Such changes may include information on what, if any, content types or formats are excluded, whether the organization will collect hardware in addition to digital content, and whether or not the digital content collected will be unique.[51] The AIMS Work Group notes that a collection policy should set the organization's position on a range of digital stewardship issues: "This will ensure that it is effective in guiding discussions and decisions relating to specific donations and individual accessions during collection development activities."[52]

The information listed above does not need to be contained in a collection development policy specifically. Instead, the collection policy should be considered part of an ecosystem of documentation intended to facilitate the acquisition of digital content from donors. The collection policy may be less granular, while other documentation such as donor agreements and deeds of gift may provide additional specificity. To this end, Aaron D. Purcell notes that a strong collection policy should be "short, clear, and publicly available."[53] Erin Faulder advocates for a collection policy that is "format neutral and focus[ed] on specific topics or subject matter . . . as archives are usually interested in records as evidence of key functions or activities, regardless of format."[54] In the 2012 AIMS Report, the authors suggest a collaborative method of collection development incorporating the curator and donor and technical support and subject matter expertise from archival staff with born-digital experience.[55] For any type of organization, it is important that the collection development policy include some articulation of a review cycle as the policy will likely change as the organization encounters new donations that require policy revisions.[56]

Clarity of Donor Agreements

While a collection development policy articulates an organization's overall goals and objectives with regard to its collections, a donor agreement documents a specific donation of content to the archives and the responsibilities and obligations of both donor and recipient institution with regard to the content to be donated. More simply, "the point is to clearly state who is donating, what they are donating, and to whom they are donating."[57] While archival organizations have a wealth of knowledge and experience in crafting donor agreements for physical materials, digital content may pose unexpected challenges to standard donor agreement language.

Even if a donor agreement has language to address digital content, it may not be sufficient to address the granular information recovered through digital forensic investigation. Because decisions made during the acquisition of born-digital material will have repercussions throughout the subsequent archival workflows and affect the ultimate utility and use of the materials in the future, specific policies must address the potential outcomes of digital forensics capture. Such clarity and discussions build trust between the donor and the archives program. It also helps archivists respond confidently to any questions that come up related to the forensic acquisition or processing of digital content.[58]

In 2012, Matthew Farrell surveyed collecting repositories and their deeds of gift. His research concludes that while an organization's deeds of gift may discuss digital content, they do not necessarily address them in the level of detail necessary to meet the challenges confronted in working with forensically acquired materials. Farrell notes that "less than one-third of repositories address digital material at all and fewer single out issues related to born-digital objects in their deeds of gift."[59] This ambiguity may lead organizations to be more reticent in pursuing forensic acquisition of digital content, despite the wealth of additional information a forensically captured environment may provide. Thus, while a growing number of organizations are beginning to explore the use of digital forensic tools and technologies, there are fewer examples that demonstrate how organizations are revisiting donor agreements, informed by the technical capabilities these tools can bring to bear. Christopher A. Lee notes the importance of crafting donor agreements that account for digital forensics practices when eliciting the "curatorial intent" of donors. He raises important questions about "what properties of materials an archivist should be sure to reproduce over time, even if technology changes, and what forms of access to the materials the archivist should allow."[60]

Specificity and transparency are central to defining the terms and conditions of a donation of forensically acquired materials. An excellent summary of the types of information to include in donor agreements is found in the CLIR report *Born Digital: Guidance for Donors, Dealers, and Archival Repositories*. Among the recommendations that are included for repositories managing digital acquisition activities, there are many that are relevant to digital forensic capture, including whether there has ever been legally protected information on the target device and the importance of archivists properly communicating information to donors about the types of digital content that are accessible through digital forensics.[61]

Process Documentation

Finally, it is important for organizations that utilize digital forensic tools in acquiring digital content to have clearly documented processes and procedures that ensure acquisition processes occur in a standard and repeatable manner. In the 2010 CLIR report, *Digital Forensics and Born-Digital Content in Cultural Heritage Collections*, the authors explain: "To foster and maintain mutually beneficial working relationships with data creators, archival repositories that accept born-digital materials and use forensic methods to preserve them must make their methodologies transparent and, when possible, must work with creators to ensure that they understand what they are transferring and how it may be used."[62] Given the complexities of working with collections acquired through forensics processes, however, it may be necessary to expand the importance of process documentation into a more responsive framework for managing failures and exceptions in digital forensic analysis. Indeed, Arroyo-Ramirez notes that "with more archivists processing a diverse array of born-digital material, we recognize the need for a flexible workflow that is best suited as *guidelines* to consider rather than a hard-lined set of instructions."[63] Individual collections may have processing requirements that are unique to those collections, and as such, process documentation must strike a balance between transparency to donors and flexibility for practitioners. This further emphasizes the need for donor agreements to spell out explicitly the terms of acquisition.

DONORS, ARCHIVES, AND FORENSICS

The relationship between donors and archives is complex and does not end when the donor delivers his or her materials to the archives.[64] The use of digital forensics tools and processes in acquiring digital content compounds this complexity, as the types of information found on a forensic disk image may not be known or anticipated by the donor. For this reason, it is imperative for archivists to inform donors of the types and forms of information that may be discovered through forensic investigation. In *Digital Forensics and Born-Digital Content in Cultural Heritage Collections*, the authors note that new and adapted skills will be necessary for cultural heritage workers who work with donors. They explain that "among the skills to foster will be even closer working relationships with data creators and depositors."[65]

Simplify the Language and Terms

Today's archivists must understand the importance of forensics and also the tools and the technology. Then archivists need to be prepared to communicate that information to donors and records creators. Many digital forensics tools used in archival environments still contain concepts and terms that reflect their origins in the law enforcement community and the context of criminal investigation. Tools that describe forensic analysis as an "investigation" label the user of digital forensics tools as the "investigator" and target donated digital materials as "evidence." These terms unintentionally reinforce a perspective in which archivists are actively searching for evidence of wrongdoing. An alternative approach reframes the relationship as a partnership in which donors and archivists explore digital material with the shared goal to provide access and protect privacy.

Following forensic analysis, donors must be confident and comfortable that their information is not being inadvertently released against their wishes. On this issue, Jeremy Leighton John explains: "A primary purpose of the archival application of forensics is in fact to protect the privacy of originators and third parties."[66] The donor or depositor of the content can provide additional context associated with the materials. With the possibility of passwords, encryption, or other security mechanisms that limit access to content, without donor assistance, significant quantities of information could be unavailable. Similarly, the FIDO project (Forensic Investigation of Digital Objects) recommends short, helpful guidelines for archivists and donors on what characteristics of forensic objects to consider in the donation of born-digital materials.[67] Further, the AIMS Work Group suggests questions for donors to help archivists determine whether existing collections contain private or sensitive information.[68]

Properly framed, digital forensic analysis is the process through which archivists identify and then redact, restrict, or remove sensitive personal information in alignment with the terms of a donor agreement or legal obligation. There are efforts in the digital forensics archival community to develop tools that support this approach. The BitCurator project creates archivist-friendly tools for digital forensic acquisition and analysis and continues to develop functionality intended to help identify and redact information from disk images. [69] Redaction at the forensic level ensures that there is no possibility for inadvertent disclosure, as information has been identified and scrubbed at the lowest available level of interaction.

Empathy and Appraisal

Digital forensics tools may retrieve highly personal or sensitive information, including website history, deleted files, and other content that would be unanticipated by donors and potentially unintended for transfer. [70] A constant theme of the existing literature on digital donations is that the point of acquisition is not the end of the relationship between archives and donors. Rather, it is a starting point for ongoing communication regarding the nature of the content identified through analysis of the donation. At the same time, digital forensics raises additional questions about existing collections when the donors are no longer available. Because many collections containing legacy digital content may have been acquired years or decades past, archivists must determine the nature of their obligation to the donor after the donor has passed away and whether to make a new point of contact with the donor's family or executor. Further, archivists must understand their role in digital forensic analysis when there are no living links to the donor.

These scenarios are certainly common when dealing with analog donations, but when forensic tools uncover previously inaccessible material, archivists must face the challenge of reengaging with donors or the last point of contact. While deeds of gift are legal documents for digital donations, archivists should also be empathic in their decision making. In "From Human Rights to Feminist Ethics: Radical Empathy in the Archives," Michelle Caswell and Marika Cifor demonstrate how shifting from a rights-based conception of archival custody to a perspective that identifies and affirms the archivist as caregiver affects the decisions made in the appraisal and analysis of archival content surfaced through forensic investigation. [71] This new role of archivists as advisors, as seen with the rise of community archives managed by non-archivists, may mean that digital forensics acquisition becomes a service: decisions about access and redactions rest with the creators or the keepers of the material, not the archivists.

Digital forensics complicates the acquisition of archival material in multiple ways, including the relationship between the archivist and the record creator and the relationship between the archivist and the records themselves.

After the deed of gift is finalized or the records transferred, archivists often encounter digital content of a sensitive nature that was not identified through the initial acquisitions survey. This may be the case for the metadata, file fragments, and other digital artifacts present on the drive discovered through analysis of a forensic disk image. As another example, file slack may be encountered in older computer media whose operating systems did not zero out the unused sectors when a file was written to a cluster. In some cases that may result in access to previously deleted content that had not been replaced with the newly written file. Some operating systems would overwrite the remaining drive sectors but would use leftover fragments of data from the CPU cache. Modern machines generally overwrite the remaining sectors with zeroes, but older hardware containing digital content may not. [72]

THE LONG VIEW OF FORENSICS

Digital forensics has the potential to change the way that archivists work with digital archives and the creators of digital material. Use of these new tools affects the process of a donation, the flow of communication and nego-tiation, the terms of the donation, and most importantly the long-term rela-tionship between the donor and the archives. To build successful archives programs, archivists must include digital forensics as part of their core skill set and take an active role in adapting tools and methods from the law enforcement community for use by cultural heritage professionals.

Digital forensics also changes the role of archivists when working with donors and records creators. When accepting donations of digital materials to archives, archivists must communicate to donors how the collection will be accessed and what will and will not be available. This careful balance of privacy and access may change as new tools and technologies facilitate ac-cess to previously irretrievable digital content from past donations. As archi-vists take on the role of advisors, they must reframe their perspective from that of the legal terms of the donation into a relational framework, making decisions about curation that reflect an archivist-as-caregiver relationship.

No matter where and how digital collections are made available for public use, archivists have a long-term responsibility to work with donors and records creators. This means that long after the legal obligations were satis-fied through the formal acquisition of archival materials and receipt of signed donor agreements, archivists maintain their program's commitments to the donors and the digital materials themselves. The advancement of digital fo-

rensic tools to provide new ways of retrieving and searching digital content
will only deepen the relationship between archives and donors.

NOTES

1. The general term "cultural heritage institutions" includes libraries, archives, museums, galleries, and other organizations dedicated to the preservation, management, and use of cultural and historical artifacts in physical and digital form.

2. Digital Forensic Research Workshop, *A Road Map for Digital Forensic Research* (Utica, NY: Digital Forensic Research Workshop, 2001), 16, http://dfrws.org/sites/default/files/session-files/a_road_map_for_digital_forensic_research.pdf.

3. Matthew Kirschenbaum, Richard Ovendon, Gabriela Redwine, and Rachel Donahue, *Digital Forensics and Born-Digital Content in Cultural Heritage Collections* (Washington, DC: Council on Library and Information Resources, 2010), 2, https://www.clir.org/pubs/reports/reports/pub149/pub149.pdf.

4. Pallab Ghosh, "Google's Vint Cerf Warns of 'Digital Dark Age,'" *BBC News*, https://www.bbc.com/news/science-environment-31450389; Jody DeRidder and Alissa Matheny Helms, "Intake of Digital Content: Survey Results from the Field," *D-Lib Magazine* 22 (November/December 2016), http://www.dlib.org/dlib/november16/deridder/11deridder.html.

5. Brian Carrier and Eugene H. Spafford, "Getting Physical with the Digital Investigation Process," *International Journal of Digital Evidence* 2 (Fall 2003): 1–2, http://citeseerx.ist.psu.edu/viewdoc/summary?doi=10.1.1.156.9541.

6. Christopher A. Lee, *I, Digital: Personal Collections in the Digital Era* (Chicago: Society of American Archivists, 2011), 5.

7. Dan Farmer and Wietse Venema, *Forensic Discovery* (Upper Saddle, NJ: Addison-Wesley, 2005), 10.

8. Brian Carrier, *File System Forensic Analysis* (Indianapolis: Addison-Wesley Professional, 2005) 4–7.

9. Christopher A. Lee, Kam Woods, Matthew Kirschenbaum, and Alexandra Chassanoff, *From Bitstreams to Heritage: Putting Digital Forensics into Practice in Collecting Institutions* (Chapel Hill, NC: BitCurator, 2013), http://hdl.handle.net/1903/14736.

10. Kirschenbaum et. al., *Digital Forensics*, 7.

11. *A Glossary of Archival and Records Terminology*, Society of American Archivists, s.v. "Chain of Custody" and "Original Order," https://www2.archivists.org/glossary.

12. Digital forensics is thus part of a much larger digital investigative ecosystem. EDRM at Duke Law, "Electronic Discovery Reference Model," https://www.edrm.net/frameworks-and-standards/edrm-model/.

13. Donald Waters and John Garrett, *Preserving Digital Information: Report of the Task Force on Archiving Digital Information* (Washington, DC: Council on Library and Information Resources, 1996), https://www.clir.org/wp-content/uploads/sites/6/2016/09/pub63watersgarrett.pdf; Seamus Ross and Ann Gow, *Digital Archeology: Rescuing Neglected and Damaged Data Resources* (Glasgow, Scotland: Humanities Advanced Technology and Information Institute, University of Glasgow, 1999), http://www.ukoln.ac.uk/services/elib/papers/supporting/pdf/p2.pdf; Jeff Rothenberg, "Ensuring the Longevity of Digital Documents," *Scientific American* 272 (January 1995): 24–29; Luciana Duranti, "Reliability and Authenticity: The Concepts and Their Implications," *Archivaria* 39 (Spring 1995): 5–10, https://archivaria.ca/index.php/archivaria/article/view/12063/13035; Charles T. Cullen, Peter B. Hirtle, David Levy, Clifford

A. Lynch, and Jeff Rothenberg, *Authenticity in a Digital Environment* (Washington, DC: Council on Library and Information Resources, 2005), https://www.clir.org/pubs/reports/pub92/.

14. Jeremy Leighton John, "Adapting Existing Technologies for Digital Archiving Personal Lives: Digital Forensics, Ancestral Computing, and Evolutionary Perspectives and Tools," (London: iPRES, 2008), https://pdfs.semanticscholar.org/c94b/65fcee685cfdf39da6db461f25 bbb7894b43.pdf?_ga=2.259437320.303660665.1518447367-1688519077.1518447367.

15. Matthew G. Kirschenbaum, Erika Farr, Kari M. Kraus, Naomi L. Nelson, Catherine Stollar Peters, Gabriela Redwine, and Doug Reside, *Approaches to Managing and Collecting Born-Digital Literary Materials for Scholarly Use: White Paper to the NEH Office of Digital Humanities Level 1 Digital Humanities Start-Up Grant* (College Park: University of Maryland, 2009), https://securegrants.neh.gov/publicquery/main.aspx?f=1&gn=HD-50346-08.

16. Luciana Duranti, "From Digital Diplomatics to Digital Records Forensics," *Archivaria* 68 (Fall 2009): 39–66, https://archivaria.ca/index.php/archivaria/article/view/13229/14548.

17. Ben Goldman, "Outfitting a Born-Digital Archives Program," *Practical Technology for Archives* 2 (June 2014), https://practicaltechnologyforarchives.org/issue2_goldman/; Porter Olsen, "Building a Digital Curation Workstation with BitCurator (Update)," 2013, https://bitcurator.net/2013/08/02/building-a-digital-curation-workstation-with-bitcurator-update/.

18. John Durno and Jerry Trofimchuck, "Digital Forensics on a Shoestring: A Case Study from the University of Victoria," *Code4Lib Journal* 27 (January 2015), http://journal.code4lib.org/articles/10279.

19. Laura Wilsey, Rebecca Skirvin, Peter Chan, and Glynn Edwards, "Capturing and Processing Born-Digital Files in the STOP AIDS Project Records: A Case Study," *Journal of Western Archives* 4 (2013): 1–22, http://digitalcommons.usu.edu/westernarchives/vol4/iss1/.

20. BitCurator, "BitCurator Quick Start Guide" (Chapel Hill, NC: BitCurator, 2017), slide 6, https://wiki.bitcurator.net/downloads/BitCurator-Quickstart.pdf; Justin Johns, "Forensic Toolkit 5.6: System Specification Guide," 2017, https://support.accessdata.com/hc/en-us/articles/202905229-System-Specification-Guide-FTK.

21. Computer Hope, s.v. "RAM," 2018, https://www.computerhope.com/jargon/r/ram.htm.

22. Ben Goldman recommended 16 GB of RAM for a machine intended to work with multi-gigabyte or terabyte sized collections. Goldman, "Outfitting a Born-Digital Archives Program."

23. Dorothy Waugh, "A Dogged Pursuit: Capturing Forensic Images of 3.5" Floppy Disks," *Practical Technology for Archives* 2 (June 2014), https://practicaltechnologyforarchives.org/issue2_waugh/; Alice Prael and Amy Wickner, "Getting to Know FRED: Introducing Workflows for Born-Digital Content," *Practical Technology for Archives* 4 (May 2015), https://practicaltechnologyforarchives.org/issue4_prael_wickner/.

24. A. L. Carson, "#digitalarchivesfail: Well, That Didn't Work," Society of American Archivists Electronic Records Section, *bloggERS!* (blog), https://saaers.wordpress.com/2017/03/07/digitalarchivesfail-well-that-didnt-work/.

25. KryoFlux, https://kryoflux.com/.

26. KryoFlux Support Forums, https://forum.kryoflux.com/.

27. Jennifer Allen, Elvia Arroyo-Ramirez, Kelly Bolding, Faith Charlton, Patricia Ciccone, Yvonne Eadon, Matthew Farrell, Allison Hughes, Victoria Maches, Shira Peltzman, Alice Prael, Scott Reed, and Dorothy Waugh, *The Archivist's Guide to KryoFlux*, 40, https://docs.google.com/document/d/1LViSnYpvr2jf1TrCh6ELuL-FWo14ICw-WZeb8j5GGpU/edit. As of the time of this writing the long-term location for this resource is forthcoming.

28. Farmer and Venema, *Forensic Discovery*, 5–6.

29. Examples of licensed tools include FTK and Encase. Examples of free suites of tools include CAINE (Computer-Aided-Investigative-Environment) and Autopsy.

30. Simson L. Garfinkel, "The Expanding World of Digital Forensics," *;login: The Usenix Magazine* 40 (December 2015): 12–16, https://www.usenix.org/system/files/login/articles/login_dec15_03_garfinkel.pdf.

31. "BitCurator Project," BitCurator, https://bitcurator.net/.

32. Kam Woods, Christopher A. Lee, and Simson L. Garfinkel, "Extending Digital Repository Architectures to Support Disk Image Preservation and Access," in *JCDL '11: Proceedings of the 11th Annual International ACM/IEEE Joint Conference on Digital Libraries* (New York: ACM Press, 2011), 57–66, https://ils.unc.edu/callee/p57-woods.pdf.

33. Martin J. Gengenbach, "'The Way We Do It Here': Mapping Digital Forensics Workflows in Collection Institutions" (master's thesis, University of North Carolina, Chapel Hill, 2012).

34. This capture stage may include other information capture strategies, such as documenting and photographing the media prior to attempting forensic capture of the data itself. Wilsey et al., "Capturing and Processing."

35. Woods, Lee, and Garfinkel, "Extending Digital Repository Architectures," 58.

36. Examples of disk imaging tools include Guymager, http://guymager.sourceforge.net/; FTK Imager, http://accessdata.com/product-download/ftk-imager-version-3.4.2; dd, http://pubs.opengroup.org/onlinepubs/9699919799/utilities/dd.html.

37. There are also logical disk image formats. They contain only information that is available through the file system, which would not contain the same amount or kinds of information present in a forensic disk image. Simson L. Garfinkel, David J. Malan, Karl-Alexander Dubec, Christopher C. Stevens, and Cecile Pham, "Advanced Forensic Format: An Open, Extensible Format for Disk Imaging," in *Advances in Digital Forensics II: FIP International Conference on Digital Forensics, National Center for Forensic Science, Orlando, Florida, January 29–February 1, 2006*, eds. Martin Olivier and Sujeet Shenoi (New York: Springer, 2006), 17–31.

38. Stream files are larger than a regular disk image for an equivalent-sized media, and stream files themselves are not necessarily recommended for long-term preservation storage. Allen et al., *The Archivist's Guide to KryoFlux*, 40.

39. A full list of filters is available at http://www.forensicswiki.org/wiki/Bulk_extractor. It is also possible to generate a "stop list" containing specific user-submitted words that may be input to bulk_extractor for identification. This can be helpful for domain-specific searches (such as health or financial information) that are specific to an industry or field of study.

40. More information on BitCurator DFXML workflows is available at "Generating DFXML Output," BitCurator, https://confluence.educopia.org/display/BC/Generate+Filesystem+Metadata+as+DFXML.

41. "Workflow Overview," BitCurator, https://confluence.educopia.org/display/BC/Workflow+Overview.

42. "Slack," Forensics wiki, http://forensicswiki.org/wiki/Slack; Simson L. Garfinkel and Abhi Shelat, "Remembrance of Data Passed," *Data Forensics* 1 (January/February 2003): 17–27, https://simson.net/clips/academic/2003.IEEE.DiskDriveForensics.pdf.

43. Wilsey et al., "Capturing and Processing," 5–10.

44. Gregory Wiedeman. "Practical Digital Forensics at Accession for Born-Digital Institutional Records," *Code4Lib Journal* 31 (January 2016), http://journal.code4lib.org/articles/11239.

45. "ANTS: Archival Network Transfer System," M. E. Grenander Department of Special Collections and Archives, University of Albany, http://library.albany.edu/archive/UniversityArchives/ANTS.

46. Waugh, "A Dogged Pursuit;" Carson, "#digitalarchivesfail;" Prael and Wickner, "Getting to Know FRED"; Gloria Gonzalez, "The Top Ten Things I Don't Let Stop Me from Getting Things Done (with Digital Archives)," (presentation, Society of American Archivists Annual Meeting, August 2014, Washington, DC), http://gloriagonzalez.org/2014/08/14/top10things/; John Durno, "Digital Archaeology and/or Forensics: Working with Floppy Disks from the 1980s," *Code4Lib Journal* 34 (October 2016), available at http://journal.code4lib.org/articles/11986.

47. Julia Kim, "Creating Workflows for Born-Digital Collections: An NDSR Project Update," *The Signal* (blog), March 2015, https://blogs.loc.gov/thesignal/2015/03/creating-workflows-for-born-digital-collections-an-ndsr-project-update/.

48. Alice Prael, "To Image or Copy—The Compact Disc Digital Audio Dilemma," *Saving Digital Stuff* (blog), December 2016, http://campuspress.yale.edu/borndigital/2016/12/20/to-image-or-copy-the-compact-disc-digital-audio-dilemma/.

49. Elvia Arroyo-Ramirez, "Invisible Defaults and Perceived Limitations: Processing the Juan Gelman Files," *On Archivy* (blog), October 2016, https://medium.com/on-archivy/invisible-defaults-and-perceived-limitations-processing-the-juan-gelman-files-4187fdd36759.

50. *A Glossary of Archival and Records Terminology*, Society of American Archivists, s.v. "Collection Development," https://www2.archivists.org/glossary/terms/c/collection-development.

51. Megan Barnard and Gabriela Redwine, "Collecting Digital Manuscripts and Archives," in *Appraisal and Acquisition Strategies*, eds. Michael J. Shallcross and Christopher J. Prom (Chicago: Society of American Archivists, 2016), 78–79.

52. AIMS Work Group, *AIMS Born-Digital Collections: An Inter-institutional Model for Stewardship* (University of Virginia Libraries, 2012), 6, https://dcs.library.virginia.edu/files/2013/02/AIMS_final_text.pdf.

53. Aaron D. Purcell, *Donors and Archives: A Guidebook for Successful Programs* (Lanham, MD: Rowman & Littlefield, 2015), 9.

54. Erin Faulder, "Accessioning Digital Archives," in *Appraisal and Acquisition Strategies*, eds. Michael J. Shallcross and Christopher J. Prom (Chicago: Society of American Archivists, 2016), 138.

55. AIMS, *AIMS Born-Digital Collections*, 4.

56. Barnard and Redwine, "Collecting Digital," 78.

57. Purcell, *Donors and Archives*, 18.

58. AIMS, *AIMS Born-Digital Collections*, 10–11.

59. Matthew J. Farrell, "Born-Digital Objects in the Deeds of Gift of Collecting Repositories: A Latent Content Analysis (master's thesis, University of North Carolina, Chapel Hill, 2012), 33, https://cdr.lib.unc.edu/indexablecontent/uuid:385c4fd9-a403-4ba3-85ac-2ea128400ddb.

60. Christopher A. Lee, "Donor Agreements," in *Digital Forensics and Born-Digital Content in Cultural Heritage Collections*, by Matthew Kirschenbaum, Richard Ovendon, Gabriela Redwine, and Rachel Donahue (Washington, DC: Council on Library and Information Resources, 2010), 57, https://www.clir.org/pubs/reports/reports/pub149/pub149.pdf.

61. Gabriela Redwine, Megan Barnard, Kate Donovan, Erika Farr, Michael Forstrom, Will Hansen, Jeremy Leighton John, Nancy Kuhl, Seth Straw, and Susan Thomas, *Born Digital: Guidance for Donors, Dealers, and Archival Repositories* (Washington, DC: Council on Library and Information Resources, 2013), 6, 10, 14–15, 18, https://www.clir.org/wp-content/uploads/sites/6/pub159.pdf.

62. Kirschenbaum et al., *Digital Forensics*, 56.

63. Arroyo-Ramirez, "Invisible Defaults."

64. Purcell, *Donors and Archives*, 99–115.

65. Kirschenbaum et al., *Digital Forensics*, 51.

66. Jeremy Leighton John, *Digital Forensics and Preservation* (York, England: Digital Preservation Coalition, 2012), 33, http://www.dpconline.org/docs/technology-watch-reports/810-dpctw12-03-pdf/file.

67. Gareth Knight, "The Forensic Curator: Digital Forensics as a Solution to Addressing the Curatorial Challenges Posed by Personal Digital Archives," *International Journal of Digital Curation* 7 (December 2012): 40–63, http://www.ijdc.net/article/view/218/287.

68. AIMS, *AIMS Born-Digital Collections*, 10–11.

69. Christopher A. Lee and Kam Woods, "BitCurator: Redacting and Providing Access to Data from Disk Images," (Digital Forensics Workshop, Philadelphia, 2015), slides 85–91, http://docplayer.net/51544475-Bitcurator-redacting-and-providing-access-to-data-from-disk-images.html.

70. Kirschenbaum et al., *Digital Forensics*, 49–59.

71. Michelle Caswell and Marika Cifor, "From Human Rights to Feminist Ethics: Radical Empathy in Archives," *Archivaria* 81 (Spring 2016): 35–36, https://archivaria.ca/index.php/archivaria/article/view/13557.

72. *Glossary of Computer Forensics Terms*, Computer Forensics e-Discovery Litigation Support Services, s.v. "File Slack," (Lafayette, LA: PC Recovery Digital Forensics, 2018), available at, http://www.pcrforensics.com/index.php?option=com_glossary&letter=F&id=154.

Chapter Five

Contracts, Intellectual Property, and Privacy

Heather Briston

The donor relationship is one of the most important interactions for archivists and special collections librarians. It is through these relationships that archives programs build collections, financial resources, and advocacy groups. Along with the stewardship investment in building the relationship, the key documentation of the relationship is the legal agreements and discussion of legal issues that underlie a donation of materials to a repository.

For archivists in any type of program, there is always a moment of trepidation when presenting a donor with a deed of gift. For archivists, few who are trained lawyers and very few who are the legal representatives for their institution, sharing a deed of gift means that questions will follow, many of which cannot be answered quickly or easily. For donors, reviewing a deed of gift form often creates anxiety because it is a very legal-looking document. At this stage of the donation process, archivists find themselves thrust into a world where a certain level of facility and knowledge of the legal issues involved in these transactions is both needed and expected. Archivists have an institutional responsibility to forge donor agreements that support the mission of their program. At that same time, archivists have a professional responsibility to share information with donors and to advise them on the choices for making a gift that fulfills their goals.

Digital donations are teeming with issues of intellectual property management, most commonly, copyright but also the rights embodied in trademarks and patents. This chapter reviews the legal issues involved in donating materials and addresses common questions and concerns that archivists face during donations of digital content.[1] It focuses on those areas where the legal issues and considerations change when the format of materials moves from analog to digital. As with many intersections of the law and archives, it is often that the law was written at a time when digital materials were not considered or did not exist. This chapter focuses on those gray areas in which the digital format affects the decisions made by archivists and informs potential concerns of the donors.

The existing literature on the intersection of law and archives is small, especially related to digital material. Peter B. Hirtle, Emily Hudson, and Andrew T. Kenyon's *Copyright and Cultural Institutions: Guidelines for Digitization for U.S. Libraries, Archives, and Museums*, focuses on copyright and the access and duplication issues regarding archival documents. Menzi L. Behrnd-Klodt's *Navigating Legal Issues in Archives* takes a more general view of all of the legal issues facing archives.[2] The 2015 edited book of modules, *Rights in the Digital Era*, discusses the legal issues related to donations with some discussion of digital content.[3] This chapter builds on these works by bringing together the current state of the law and archival practice related to digital archives.

The structure of this chapter roughly follows the structure of the most common deed of gift forms used in archival repositories across the country.[4] This arrangement makes it possible for readers to go to the point in the chapter in which their questions arise. In addition, this structure mirrors the conversations that occur with donors regarding the donation of a collection and the range of legal considerations involved over the course of the transaction.

TRANSFER OF OWNERSHIP AND CONTRACT LAW

The legal foundation of a donation of any materials, regardless of format, is the document that transfers ownership of the materials that are the subject of the gift. The legal instrument is often referred to as a deed of gift. It operates as a recital of the agreements between two or more parties regarding the transfer of materials, contractually binding those parties. Archivists experience a range of donor interactions. Some negotiations extend over years, while other donations occur suddenly with a drop-off of material and a quick signature to a standard form. Archivists also have a lot of experience with how deeds have evolved over time, from those that were a single page of general language, where it is unclear what rights or sometimes even what materials were transferred to the archives, to extraordinarily detailed agreements that were negotiated by lawyers and uniquely crafted for the gift at hand. It is good practice for a repository to regularly review its deed templates, especially with specific consideration of digital donations.

The most important role of a deed of gift is to transfer the ownership of the material to the repository. Without a transfer of ownership, either because of an invalid, poorly worded, or nonexistent deed, the repository does not own the materials. Thus, another party owns the material, and that lawful owner can, at any time, demand the return of his or her property. All archivists know of horror stories of repositories that held collections for years, processed it, cataloged it, made it available for research only to have the legal owner appear and successfully demand to have the collection returned and, in some cases, transferred to a different repository. At the same time, archivists provide access to collections for which there is no deed of gift. What are the options? Some repositories search for owners to complete deeds of gift or use other existing documentation in their files to demonstrate the owner's intention to donate. Many states have an abandoned property law, which, while often onerous, may also be an option.[5] For some collections, it becomes a balance of risking investing resources versus the need to care for holdings in the repository.

Every archival repository needs to have a deed of gift that incorporates clauses that address the donation, preparation, and access to born-digital materials. It should be used for all current donations, whether they contain born-digital materials or not because this obviates the need for a separate deed in the future and a simple addendum can be used for any new additions regardless of format. As a final resort, if it is impossible to persuade a donor to sign an updated deed for a born-digital new addition, a codicil that references the previous deed but incorporates the specific born-digital clauses could be used. The archives program should ensure that all of the born-digital clauses are copied verbatim from the general deed of gift to guarantee that there is no confusion and to standardize treatment of all born-digital materials.

With ownership, the repository can invest in the preservation of the materials. This is particularly important for digital materials, as the preservation work is intensive and ongoing, and should begin at the moment of ingest. Thus, if possible, the deed of gift should be completed prior to accession or ingest and, at the very least, simultaneously. Unfortunately, the more time that elapses after the transfer of materials the harder it can be to complete the deed of gift. Very simply, the impetus for donors recedes once they have found a home for their materials and from their perspective their work is done. A deed of gift first defines the transfer of ownership; equally important is the warranty and authority of the parties that they have the right to make the agreement.

The "warranty and authority" portion of the deed is the heart of the document because the agreement is only valid between parties that have the right to lawfully enter into that contract.[6] This can be a tricky part of the agreement for archivists, who are often uncomfortable having conversations regarding inheritance or requesting access to a will or other documentation after an individual's passing. All the more reason why, when possible, even for gifts eventually transferred by will, archivists should complete as much of the agreement with the living donor when possible, creating documents that outline the wishes of the donor and make arrangements clear to any heirs. This clarity is also important because once an individual has died, his or her estate, particularly the residual, can be divided into a number of different pieces. If a donation is fractionally owned, such as in the case of siblings, it is important that all sign the deed or that there is documentation signed by all of the heirs that designates a single representative. While it may be awkward, particularly for those collections that are particularly important, valuable, or contentious, it is advised to require a valid agreement among donors with fractional ownership to ensure that the archives program has full clear title to the materials prior to accepting and investing in the gift. This is also the case for an individual donating material on behalf of an organization. There must be clear documentation or a resolution that states that the individual has a right to enter into the donor agreement. On the other hand, it is also important that leaders of the archives program are clear on who can sign deeds of gift on behalf of the organization. This is particularly important to clarify because in the case of high-value gifts, normal practice is that only certain positions within the repository or organization can sign those agreements.

In exchange for the gift of materials, archivists make certain promises on behalf of the organization. These promises include outlining the activities that archivists will take with the materials in support of the mission of that organization, including processing the collection and preserving the materials so that they are accessible over time. These clauses may or may not include specific references to actions taken on behalf of digital materials. Sometimes repositories use specific language regarding digital donations in the deed of gift to lead the conversation with the donor about the process. For example, if an archives program has a policy of retaining imaged hardware, it would be important to include it at this point. This is also the portion of the deed of gift in which future access and use of the gift is outlined. It should be clear to the donor in the agreement that the collections will be made accessible according to the mission of the archives program and within the guidelines of use and access. While it may seem like an easy assumption, archivists encounter donors who are surprised to learn that public research really means that the general public will have access to conduct research in their papers.

This is also the section in the deed of gift in which donors and archivists should articulate any temporary access restrictions. Many archivists have heard of, or inherited, collections that have unworkable restrictions or restrictions that clash with the mission or spirit of the archives program. It is an accepted ethical standard of the profession that current deeds of gift that include restrictions have restrictions that are narrowly defined and limited in duration.[7] This practice is ethical and makes collections much easier to manage. Any collection, or portion of a collection, managed outside of the primary workflow of the repository is at risk from accidental violations of the terms of the deed of gift.

Restrictions articulated by the donor take two different forms. In one example, the donor writes out his or her wishes and shares his or her terms with the archives program within space provided in the deed of gift form. For archivists, it is important that the donor's stated restrictions align with the goals and needs of the repository prior to signing the deed. The second example, which is preferred and supports better legal clarity, involves the creation of terms after negotiation between the archivists and the donor. This language is added to the deed of gift by the archivists, normally in conjunction with the clause articulating the repository's responsibilities for access. Any restrictions, special donor requests, and the details of any subsequent negotiations must be documented. Final deeds should not contain holographic notations from the donor. Once the terms are finalized, the written "meeting of the minds" documentation is included in the collection file.

A common restriction involves closing personal materials. The key is to have "personal material" clearly defined as a part of the deed of gift or documented along with the gift, even if it seems like a straightforward designation. Since this restriction is a part of a signed contract, archivists must have clear direction from the donor as to what in his or her mind constitutes "personal material." This is also an opportunity to manage expectations with donors, as complex restrictions often delay processing and access. Added restrictions may also require the institution and perhaps its legal department to reexamine acceptance of the gift given the effect of restrictions. Ultimately, once the deed of gift is signed, it is an enforceable legal contract between the donor and the organization and binding on all parties. Any breach of a contract, including restricted access, can be a subject of lawsuit by the donor on the repository if not followed. Conversely, if a donor violates a deed of gift by, for example, misrepresenting his or her ownership of the materials or failing to deliver promised materials, the repository can bring suit.

It is also important to clarify policies regarding any subsequent additions to the collection and any subsequent disposal or distribution of materials in the gift. In the sample deeds of gift included at the end of this chapter, there are examples of how a repository can address partial gifts or subsequent gifts with differing levels of formality. The key point is to ensure that the general terms and conditions of the current deed of gift govern future gifts from the same donor. The more complex deeds of gift often include an addendum, which includes the existing terms and conditions and a separate inventory of materials and can, if negotiated with the donor, include any separate restrictions not already articulated in the original deed of gift. Ideally, subsequent gifts should be easy for both the donor and the repository. In addition, if a new donor is donating to an existing collection, such as an heir, the gift would require a new deed.

Another topic of discussion with the donor is the disposition of materials that the repository decides is not appropriate for permanent retention. In each deed of gift, the authorization of the archives program to dispose of materials is explicitly included in the document. This is an important clause for a repository, particularly for collections that sit in the backlog for quite some time or in conditions where extensive appraisal is not available. This clause gives archivists the ability to remove redundant or irrelevant material during processing. The details of the deed of gift dictate how the electronic materials are removed from the collection. Many donors, however, interpret the clause differently. For some donors, the fact that repositories dispose of materials can come as a great surprise, either because they assume that archives keep everything or because they believe that the entire contents of their donation is of great historical value. This clause also fans the common fear of donors that at some point the archives program will sell their collection either due to tough financial realities or because it no longer has research value. Thus, it is important to allay such incorrect assumptions and clarify how archivists process collections and dispose of extant materials.

Some archives programs have a practice of deaccessioning and returning any unneeded material discovered during processing or allow for such a stipulation from the donor. In these cases, it is important to fully document and fully discuss with the donor what is being returned or offered to another archives program. For legal purposes, it does not matter whether the final disposition is disposal or return; as with any clause in a deed of gift, there must be complete agreement on any deviation from standard language, and it must be articulated for anyone who will subsequently work with the collection. There are also potential tax implications for donors, particularly those that have a professional appraisal completed, if a significant portion or the entirety of a collection is not going to be used by the institution for a use related to its primary mission. While this is unusual, it can affect the size of the deduction a donor can claim on his or her income taxes. If large portions of the appraised materials are not included in the donated collection, archivists should advise donors to discuss the implications with their tax advisors.

The concept of donating the "sole copy" of materials has different implications for digital materials. Historically, repositories would have a policy on whether or not they would accept collections that were comprised solely of photocopies. Acceptance would often depend on the research value the copies would provide to the archives program's researcher base. In some situations, there was positive value because the originals were difficult to access or an aggregation of resources better supported research in that subject area. With digital materials, however, this is more problematic as the ability to create a duplicate collection is almost effortless. As a result, repositories must develop methods to evaluate and verify that they are receiving a unique collection. An archives program negotiating with a donor for digital materials may want to include in the deed of gift a clause that if the donor retains a copy of the digital materials, they will not share, give, or otherwise transfer that material to another individual, organization, or entity via transfer or posting on the web. While it may not be the case for all gifts of digital materials, clarifying the issues regarding copies is increasingly more important in deeds or sale agreements.

The issues of ownership and transferring ownership of digital materials are similar for accepting institutional or official records. Many archivists work as institutional archivists with a mandate to preserve the official records of the institution and document its history. When collecting records from the organization itself, a deed of gift is not necessary, but it is still important to ensure that the repository has clearly delegated, written authority from the institution to act as its archives. Institutional archives should have a documentation policy and workflow for records transfers, whether that appears as an accession record, trail of correspondence, or accession/transfer forms. This is particularly important since digital tools have decentralized records storage and creation, which spread it across the organization, leaving the responsibility for collecting archival materials diffused. For example, in the University of California System, official policy dictates that faculty own both the physical materials and copyright for the materials that they create as a part of their teaching and research activities. However, for those faculty members who also have an administrative role, those materials created while in their administrative role are official records and owned by the regents of the University of California.[8]

In most organizations, everything that an employee creates is owned by the organization in a work-for-hire relationship. An institutional archives program thus needs documentation regarding which entities are legally a part of the institution and therefore governed by the delegation of archival authority. Archivists who document universities or colleges are familiar with the fact that records from a sorority or fraternity are not owned by the university and thus should be governed by a deed of gift. At many colleges and universities, student groups are considered a part of the school and thus governed by its records retention schedule, but at other institutions, they are considered independent organizations, and any donation requires a deed of gift.

Best practices for collection management recommend that every gift above a threshold value set by the organization should have a deed of gift. The document clearly spells out the right of the donor to make the gift and the promises of the repository in accepting it. After ownership, the key legal discussion around most deeds of gift is the assignment of copyright.

COPYRIGHT

For most donations, digital or analog, transferring ownership is a fairly straightforward undertaking and normally not fraught with legal pitfalls. Copyright transfer can be much more complicated. Frequently, archivists discover that many of their collections have no deed of gift or the deeds of gift used for many years are vague on the transfer of rights and copyright. These situations are not due to any professional malfeasance but to the fact that until the 1976 U.S. Copyright Act (Title 17), federal copyright protection rested only in published materials, which meant that state copyright laws covered the vast collections of unpublished materials.

The archivist's relationship to copyright changed dramatically with the advent of copyright existing at creation from 1978 onward, including all unpublished materials, and with the rise of the internet and growth of digital donations. Today, copyright is implicated in all aspects of archival work, including access, duplication, preservation, and display. It is important to remember that when assessing copyright issues and digital material, the Copyright Act has remained unchanged in some parts for forty years and refers to technology and practices that were already ten to fifteen years old in 1976. Archivists must try to understand the law within a context that was never anticipated.

The primary issue of copyright with donated material is whether copyright can be donated along with the physical or digital materials. The most important step in discussing copyright at the time of donation is assisting the donor in understanding what he or she owns. Some donors are not aware that they own copyright in the materials that they created and what that means. Even those that have exploited copyrights during their lifetime do not recognize the extent of copyrighted materials in their collections. Also, donors do not understand that ownership of the document or digital file does not constitute ownership of copyright.[9] In the case of unpublished materials, such as correspondence, drafts, and photographs, it is the creator or his or her heirs that control the copyright of those materials.[10] Some donors own only a fractional interest in the copyright, and therefore, they need assistance determining how much they can donate or control. In cases in which materials are already in the public domain for various reasons, donors may not be aware that they do not hold copyright for those materials and therefore cannot control their use. This can come as a surprise to some donors, so it is important to discuss with them the nature of the materials that they are donating and what they own in regard to copyright.

For donors, the primary copyright decision in a donation is whether to donate the copyright to the archives program. Those donors who by the nature of their work have exploited their copyrights prior to donation and expect to otherwise continue to exploit their copyrights or to provide something for their heirs are keen to retain their rights. In these cases, it is crucial for archivists to include in the deed of gift a license for discretionary uses by the repository, irrespective of the grant of copyright, and to explain this to the donor. Discussions with these donors need to focus on the mission of the archives and how the nonexclusive license in the deed of gift is crucial for the repository to perform its work and fulfill its mission.

The sample deed of gift forms at the end of this chapter contain one of these nonexclusive licenses. One individually articulates all of the licensed activity; the other contains a general clause that includes non-limiting examples of common activities like exhibition, display, and research access. Each sample also explicitly notes that the fair use exception of the Copyright Act may also be invoked for a specific use, and therefore, both researchers and archivists are at liberty to make a fair use determination regarding a use of the materials in the gift.[11] The sample deeds also include a catchall statement referring to "statutory copyright exceptions," which include section 108, the library and archives exception, which supports preservation copying, interlibrary loan, and some duplication activities for personal research of particular formats of materials. This section is important for preservation and research services and is used in conjunction with the fair use clause, section 107. It is important for archivists to discuss with donors the access policies and duplication policies of the archives prior to donation so it is clear to all what types of use can be made of the collection, even if donors do not include copyright as part of their donation.

There may be some instances in which a donor does not wish to close materials but wishes to restrict the duplication of materials for research purposes. This is most commonly found in collections in which the donor exploits the copyrights in a collection that contains unpublished materials. In this situation, the archives program must clearly document and abide by such restrictions to avoid violating the deed, risking suit, or ruining donor relations. For example, a donor sued the Smithsonian Institution for breach of contract. The donor, a photographer, added two clauses to the deed of gift—one clause retained copyright, which conflicted with the deed of gift's regular stipulation that transferred copyright, and another clause permitted the Smithsonian the right to use and make materials available for scholarly purposes but specifically denied any commercial use without the donor's permission.[12] Subsequently, the Smithsonian licensed some of the photographs for use in a documentary, as was its usual practice based on its standard deed of gift. The donor sued the Smithsonian for violating the provisions in the deed of gift. The case was later settled out of court. The copyright assignment clause in the deed of gift is an opportunity for archivists to educate donors, discover their wishes regarding the use of their collection, and determine how or if they want to remain involved with the archives program. Archivists must be fluent in the policies of their repository and the copyright needs of their institution while respecting the copyrights owned by their donors.

A new wrinkle in donations today are gifts of materials reserving copyright but with a written expectation that copyright will be transferred to the archives program at a later date, normally after the death of the donor. The key to this arrangement is to document the future transaction in both the donor's will and the deed of gift. Proper documentation of the agreement ensures that all subsequent stakeholders are aware of the donor's wishes and requirements to transfer copyright. A challenge with a separate donation of copyright occurs if the donor would like to have the gift of copyright appraised. This evaluation is a new area for most appraisers, and there is currently very little experience or basis for appraising only the copyright for a set of materials, unless there is a recent market for the works. Ideally, copyright is transferred along with the materials; however, when it is not, donors and subsequent copyright owners must be contacted for each permission request. If this scenario is part of the donor's wishes, then archivists must educate donors on the expectations and responsibilities for managing permissions during their lifetimes and for providing contact information for copyright heirs.

In both deed examples at the end of this chapter, there is a clause that requires donors to provide any information that they have about the copyrights that they own or have transferred. Few donors will be able to provide this information because they have not exploited their copyrights and, in many cases, they do not even know that they own copyrights. However, for those donors who are writers, photographers, artists, and others who base their livelihood on copyright royalties, they likely have documentation about any registered copyrights and particularly any licensed or transferred copyrights with another person or entity, such as a publisher. In some cases, the rights revert from the publisher to the individual after a period of time, such as when a work is out of print if that is a part of the original publishing contract. Documentation of any reversions, where available, should be obtained as well.

It is also important for archivists to ask donors about whether Creative Commons licenses have been used to make materials available. This practice is popular as individuals publish more materials online, often photographs or articles, using various versions of Creative Commons licenses. Creative

Commons licenses were developed to assist creators in clearly articulating the rights and conditions for sharing and use of their materials.[13] While securing copyright documentation from donors is rare, the role of this type of license affects how to structure the deed of gift. This type of documentation allows archivists to discuss with donors any possible previous transfer or licensing of copyrights. Further, it underscores the requirement of writing to secure the legal transfer of copyright.

In specific areas, the Copyright Act (Title 17) addresses digital materials. The Digital Millennium Copyright Act (DMCA), which is incorporated as chapter 12 and sections in chapter 15, only applies to digital materials. As digital donations become more common, this portion of the copyright law will gain importance in the archival profession. For donations, the most important clauses are those that criminalize decryption tools and breaking encryption.[14] The crux of the problem is that if a donation includes an encrypted hard drive and the password is not given to the repository, it is impossible to legally access and preserve the material that the archives program legally owns. Under section 1201, it would be illegal for any archives program from the largest to the smallest to decrypt the hard drive or purchase tools that could access the protected information. In fact, DMCA makes circumventing copy protections or creating and trading in tools that would circumvent copy protections illegal. Even more troubling for archivists is that many software companies are defaulting to copy protection/encryption of documents as a matter of course in creating and saving materials based on the demands of creators for security and privacy of information. For the most part, archivists are navigating the same copyright environment whether they are negotiating a donation of analog or digital materials. However, the specific portions of copyright law that relate to digital materials are particularly antithetical to the work of archivists as currently defined and applied.

The best practices for archivists negotiating copyright for digital donations mirrors the practice for analog materials. First and foremost, archivists must use a deed of gift that specifically and clearly addresses the ownership and transfer of copyright. Also, archivists must understand and be able to explain copyright issues for archival repositories to various types of donors and how those decisions affect the preservation, duplication, and various uses of the donated material. While it is not the end of the world or the end of the donation if copyright is not transferred, helping donors to understand the implications for them to retain copyright is important, including understanding the permissions process and the role and responsibilities that they retain.

It is also important to help the donors understand the extent of their rights over the materials they are donating. As copyright caveats to archivists, take care to explain to donors that the deed of gift that the repository uses specifically addresses copyright exceptions like fair use and, for the sake of the repository's mission, that the repository carves out a nonexclusive license in any gift for preservation reformatting, providing access and displaying the materials, and possibly digitizing materials. Archivists should rethink any gift that would unduly proscribe the ability to fulfill the mission of their repositories to preserve and make available the materials for use.

OTHER INTELLECTUAL PROPERTY

Copyright is by far the most common type of intellectual property found in digital donations, but it is not the only one. Archivists who collect institutional or organizational records or focus on the papers of scientists, designers, and other inventors should be alert to the possibility of trademarks or patents in a donation. Trademark is the use of a symbol, illustration, name, or phrase that is associated with an individual, group, service, or product for the purposes of commerce. Common examples of trademarks are film titles; catch phrases; characters like Snap, Crackle, and Pop; and iconic lettering like the script "K" in Kellogg's. The key components of trademark are that they are unique, not easily confused with another mark, and used in commerce. In order to be enforceable, trademarks must be registered with the United States Patent and Trademark Office (USPTO). The trademark is in force for as long as the mark is used in commerce. Trademarks are unenforceable if they are confusingly similar to another mark used for a similar product or service or if they have become a generic term for a product or service. [15]

Few archives programs have to manage trademarks as a part of digital donations. However, if the donation is coming from a business, group, or individual, it is important to discuss with the donor if there are any registered trademarks in the collection. As with copyright, any transfer of a trademark must be done in writing, and ideally the transfer should also be recorded with the USPTO. [16] If the mark is still in active use, it would be unusual for the donor to transfer the rights to the mark to the archives program. As with copyright, the researcher is ultimately responsible for clearing both copyrights and/or trademarks in a work prior to any use, particularly if commercial. Likewise, the trademark owners are responsible for enforcing the trademarks they hold.

While it is exceedingly rare for archives programs to hold the rights to trademarks, it is not unusual for institutional archives to hold trademarked materials such as images, drawings, and other devices in their collections. These items are then requested by researchers for duplication and use. In many cases, individual items possess both copyright and a trademark. At UCLA, visual depictions of the most iconic building on campus, Royce Hall, are trademarked, and a photograph of the building is also copyrighted. Larger organizations frequently have a trademarks and licensing office, which handles permissions for commercial uses of material owned by the institution. [17] It is important for archivists to understand their institution's licensing policies and whom to contact if a researcher requests a commercial use of material. If the materials depict other trademarks, it is good public service for archivists to remind researchers to clear trademarks if they are intending on making a commercial use. While this does not directly affect the donation process, archivists must consider these potential legal questions and institutional protocols.

Another common area of intellectual property law is patents. Patents are used to protect inventions, objects, or processes and can be obtained for useful objects or designs. Unlike copyrights and trademarks, the period of protection for a patent is relatively: short, twenty years for utility patents and fourteen years for design patents from the date of filing. The power of a patent is to exclude others from making, using, selling, or importing the patented item. [18] Similar to copyrights and trademarks, patents can be transferred but only in writing. As a result of the short duration of patents, it is unusual for archival repositories to receive documentation of active patents and even more unusual for those rights and obligations to be transferred to the archives program.

As archivists bring more contemporary materials into an archives program, it becomes more likely that collections contain records related to an active patent or potential patent. Even though the management of the actual patent would be centered elsewhere in the organization, the documentation supports a significant purpose. Another possible involvement with a patent for an archives program would be managing documentation of the original research, design, and expression of the patentable object, process, or design. In these cases, the issue is secrecy, so most donors will ask for the materials to be closed until after the patent application process is completed. This request adds no additional responsibility on archivists or the repository to manage the patent material beyond what is articulated in the deed of gift regarding access. If a potential donor is active in invention and development, it is always prudent for archivists to discuss whether the donation includes any materials that should be closed from general research access because of possible patent activity.

PRIVACY

Contract and intellectual property laws are not the only legal areas that archivists must be familiar with when negotiating digital donations; increasingly there are concerns about personal privacy and digital materials. In many cases, the discussion of privacy is the same for analog and digital materials. Privacy law is state based instead of a federal law like the Copyright Act, and therefore, it can vary from state to state. Most state laws cover the same four areas of privacy law as first articulated in an 1890 law review article by Samuel D. Warren and Louis D. Brandeis and later widely promulgated in the *Second Restatement of Torts*. The four areas are

1. Publicity—placing a person in a false light
2. Publication of private facts—true information about the private life a person that would be highly offensive to a reasonable person and not of legitimate public concern
3. Appropriation of name or likeness for profit
4. Intrusion upon seclusion or solitude[19]

An additional legal action related to the privacy law's publication of private facts is defamation, which can also be used when personal information is disclosed about an individual. The difference is that for a court to find defamation there must be false statements made about an individual and publication need only be to one person.[20] For legal challenges related to privacy or defamation, the risk for an archives program is generally low. The first obligation of maintaining privacy is with the individual who first violated privacy by taking action to intrude upon it or release the private information. The primary way that archivists and repositories may be liable is by assisting in the publication of private information, such as making it available online. In general, the law recognizes online publication as publication, but the law does not recognize access to content in a reading room for researchers as a form of publication.

Even with publication, court cases related to defamation are difficult to win, and risks are normally small. The real challenge for archivists is to avoid ethical violations or injure the repository's reputation when releasing digital content. Thus, privacy issues must be discussed before a donation is made, and both the donor and the archives program must share long-term responsibility for balancing privacy and access to the content.

In many cases, donors know the most about the contents of their collections and the materials that may be subject to legal privacy. It is their responsibility to help identify these items before donating the collection to an archives program. In regard to third-party privacy, for the most part, it is an ethical responsibility rather than a legal responsibility for the repository. The archives program's main legal responsibility for third-party privacy is to follow any restrictions on behalf of a third party noted in a deed of gift. Violation of those terms may result in legal action against the repository. However, this is a rare occurrence because the third party must both be aware of the restrictions and rely upon them. Conversely, if an archives program gets too overzealous in its desire to root out privacy concerns in digital collections it can establish a higher than normal standard of identifying and eliminating material about third parties, which then becomes a new legal standard.[21] For archivists, the most important guidance on privacy is to be able to recognize when there is a legal or ethical obligation to keep materials private.[22]

The possibility of collections containing confidential materials is another thread of discussion for donors and archivists. Confidential materials are most common in donations from organizations and institutions. Well-known categories of confidential materials include educational records covered by the Family Educational Rights and Privacy Act of 1974 (FERPA), the federal statute that governs disclosure and access. The Health Insurance Portability and Accountability Act of 1996 (HIPAA) is a federal statute covering the storage, transfer, and use of medical information.[23] Institutions with educational and medical records have specific obligations to manage and protect these materials according to federal law. In some cases, archivists encounter donors who have these types of confidential records. Before accepting these materials, archivists must determine whether the donor has the right to transfer the materials to the repository if it is not the home institution for these records. Many donors are unaware of these laws and how they affect access and use of the material.

For the papers of individuals, a common form of confidential material is covered by attorney-client privilege. Records that document the confidential communications between an attorney and his or her client in order to facilitate the provision of legal services are covered, and only the client can waive this confidentiality.[24] This particular form of privilege does not expire, and thus repositories that own such protected materials are in a conundrum when one party owns the records but the right to provide access is owned by another party. This is an important conversation to have with donors who are attorneys and want to offer their legal files to an archives program.

While there may be only a limited concern of legal violation of privacy due to the actions of archivists or their institutions, the larger issue of privacy affects relationships with donors. If there are materials that are not mentioned by the donor that the repository believes are confidential, then archivists have an ethical obligation to raise the issue and resolve it. All deeds of gift should mention that issues of privacy are the responsibility of the donor. Including such clauses in the deed of gift clarifies the donor's responsibilities regarding private materials and any responsibilities they have toward third parties.

As with most legal issues, the same obligations and questions apply to analog and digital materials. However, there are particular privacy issues for donated digital materials. For the most part, standard deeds of gift cover both digital and analog materials. When receiving a digital donation, however, a few special clauses may be necessary to clarify issues of privacy and responsibilities. The first of these is a clause related to the treatment of deleted files and system files that can be found in the course of imaging a hard disk or other storage materials. Ideally it is important that the archives program has a general policy about either retaining or destroying such files. The same goes for the policy of retaining any imaged hardware or removable storage devices as a part of the collection. Those policies and procedures should be articulated within the deed of gift so that the treatment of materials is clear to donors with digital materials. Any exceptions to these policies should be noted in the deed of gift and documented in the collection's accession file.

The same advice holds true for the management of any personally identifiable information (PII) or other confidential information that might be gleaned from digital materials. While most repositories will not have systematic issues with PII, this type of information is more common in the records of organizations, companies, and institutions. In addition, collections of personal papers may contain information such as social security numbers and credit card numbers. There are many tools available for identifying PII as a part of the born-digital processing workflow. Archivists must document the use of these PII tools as part of the repository's procedures for appraising and processing digital donations and verify that those tools are in line with deed of gift agreements.

In regard to best practices for archivists when dealing with privacy issues in donations, first and foremost it is important to discuss all of the implications with the donor and have he or she alert the repository to as much of the underlying privacy issues in the donation as possible. If that is not an option because the donor was not the creator or primary keeper of the records, archivists must discuss what issues they might believe are there and then proceed with greater awareness as to the possible concerns in the collection. Often the background of the creator will point to some obvious areas of concern, such as the person worked in law, medicine, or education. As with any potential donation, it is important to discuss with the donor the repository's policies and procedures regarding the treatment of private, confidential, or sensitive materials uncovered while processing the collection. For the most part, the actions of the archives program will normally be to address ethical issues rather than legal issues when managing privacy concerns.

STRATEGIES FOR DONORS

An understanding of and the ability to navigate the legal issues in archival collections is a mainstay of professional archival practice. It will only become more important with time as the tools for creating digital materials evolve and the potential uses expand while the laws themselves struggle to keep pace. Luckily, today's archivists rely on a growing literature and educational opportunities related to legal issues and digital content. This information informs archival practice and allows archivists to be well positioned to discuss legal issues with their donors and to uphold the promises made in their donor agreements.

While on the one hand copyright and privacy laws do not seem to keep up with modern technologies, there are regular changes to the law through legislation and litigation. Particular to collecting digital materials and a largely unexplored area are the effects of third-party storage and cloud hosting on ownership and access to donated content. This common storage option raises issues of donating materials that are not hosted on the donor's computers or networks. This area is still largely untested from a legal standpoint but will be in the coming years because archivists and donors are still largely tied to their platforms. Regular changes in privacy law regarding the retention of personal information may also affect archival collections. Thankfully, most digital donations will not give rise to thorny legal issues. All donor relationships are based on trust. Archivists have the professional responsibility to help donors navigate any legal questions associated with their donation while at the same time supporting the mission of their institution.

Deed of Gift #1: Transferring Copyright to the Archival Repository

To the Regents of the University of California:

I (we), [Insert donor's name here] of [Insert donor's address here] (hereafter referred to as "DONOR") am (are) the sole and absolute legal owner(s) with full right and authority to enter the Deed of Gift and grant the rights granted herein for the materials fully described in Exhibit A attached hereto and incorporated herein. All such materials are hereinafter referred to as "the Materials."

1. DONOR desires to transfer the Materials as a gift to The REGENTS of the University of California for the benefit of the Los Angeles Campus ("THE REGENTS"), for inclusion and unrestricted access and use in the collection of the UCLA Library.

2. DONOR hereby irrevocably assigns, transfers, and gives all of his (her, their) right, title and interest, including the sole and exclusive copyright in all tangible materials (including without limitation written, audio, video, multi media material or material in any other tangible form now known or hereafter invented), to the Materials to THE REGENTS. To the extent that copyright may be shared with others, DONOR hereby assigns to THE REGENTS all his (her, their) right, title and interest in the copyrights and waives and releases all such rights, whether partial or complete.

3. After execution of this Deed of Gift by DONOR and acceptance by THE REGENTS, title to the Materials shall pass to THE REGENTS upon acknowledgement of receipt of the Materials by the UCLA Library.

4. No term or provision of this instrument shall be interpreted to limit or restrict the fair use rights of THE REGENTS or the UCLA Library or users of the Materials as provided by U.S. Copyright Law, Title 17, U.S.C. ("Fair Use Rights").

5. To the extent that copyright may be shared with others and notwithstanding the Fair Use Rights, DONOR grants THE REGENTS a nonexclusive, royalty free, perpetual license:

   a. To make copies of the Materials for purposes of preservation and creation of a usable archival copy and to permit others to make copies of the Materials consistent with the Fair Use Rights.
   b. To display and reproduce the Materials in exhibitions, catalogs, University publications or advertisements both on and off campus.
   c. To digitize the Materials or use any technological substitute the UCLA Library deems appropriate to preserve and provide access to the Materials.
   d. To provide unrestricted access and use, including Internet or other wireless or digital access to the Materials.

6. DONOR shall indemnify, defend and hold THE REGENTS harmless from any losses, claims, damages, awards, penalties or injuries incurred, including reasonable attorney's fees, which arise from any claim by any third party of an alleged infringement of copyright or any other property right arising out of the access and use of the Materials but only in proportion to and to the extent such liability, loss, expense, attorneys' fees, or claims for injury or damages are caused by or result from the acts or omissions of DONOR.

7. DONOR shall provide THE REGENTS with all information and documentation regarding the provenance of the Materials, including any information relating to intellectual property rights.

8. The Materials will be organized by the UCLA Library and a bibliographic record and/or finding aid will be created to describe the content and arrangement.

9. Donor agrees not to sell, donate, or deposit the Materials, including digital files or copies, at any other institution.

10. Donor grants UCLA the right to store acquired digital content in its entirety for preservation purposes.

11. Donor grants UCLA the right to access all data from digital media included in the Materials, including deleted files, log files, and systems files, and content protected by passwords or encryption. Donor understands and agrees that UCLA may utilize methods to bypass or unlock passwords and/or encryption protections in order to gain access to the data for preservation and scholarly purposes. Any restrictions on access to the Materials requested by the Donor will apply to any such recovered information.

12. The Materials will be physically stabilized and preserved by the UCLA Library including, as appropriate, placing the Materials in non-damaging containers and storing in facilities that provide appropriate temperature and humidity control and security.

13. The Materials will be available to researchers after they have been arranged and described for use.

14. THE REGENTS are authorized to dispose of any duplicate or other material not relevant to the collection which it determines to have no permanent value or historical interest.

15. In the event that DONOR may hereafter donate additional materials to THE REGENTS such gifts shall be set forth in an Addendum to this Deed of Gift and will be governed by the terms and conditions stated above. The Addendum shall include a description of the additional materials so donated and any conditions necessary and pertinent to those specific, newly-donated materials and shall be signed by the DONOR and THE REGENTS.

Signed:(donor) _____

Name:_____

this [type day here] day of [type month here], 20[complete year here].

FOR DEPARTMENTAL USE ONLY

Signature of UCLA Library: Date: _____

_____

Title:_____

Accepted for THE REGENTS of the University of California:

_____

Date: _____

Office of Gift Policy Administration:

_____

Deed of Gift #2: Donor Retains Copyright of Material in Donated Collection

To the Regents of the University of California:

   I (we), [insert donor's name here] of [insert donor's address here] (hereafter referred to as "DONOR") am (are) the sole and absolute legal owner(s) with full right and authority to enter the Deed of Gift and grant the rights granted herein for the materials fully described in Exhibit A attached hereto and incorporated herein. All such materials are hereinafter referred to as "the Materials."

   1. DONOR desires to transfer the Materials as a gift to The RE-GENTS of the University of California for the benefit of the Los Angeles Campus ("THE REGENTS"), for inclusion and unrestricted access and use in the collection of the UCLA Library.

   2. DONOR hereby irrevocably assigns, transfers, and gives all of his (her, their) right, title and interest, exclusive of copyrights, to the Materials to THE REGENTS.

   3. After execution of this Deed of Gift by DONOR and acceptance by THE REGENTS, title to the Materials shall pass to THE REGENTS upon acknowledgement of receipt of the Materials by the UCLA Library.

   4. DONOR retains all rights of copyright in the Materials. However, no term or provision of this instrument shall be interpreted to limit or restrict the fair use rights of THE REGENTS or the UCLA Library or users of the Materials as provided by U.S. Copyright Law, Title 17, U.S.C. ("Fair Use Rights").

5. Notwithstanding, and in addition to, Fair Use Rights, DONOR grants THE REGENTS a nonexclusive, royalty free, perpetual license:

a. To make copies of the Materials for purposes of preservation and creation of a usable archival copy and to permit others to make copies of the Materials consistent with the Fair Use Rights.

b. To display and reproduce the Materials in exhibitions, catalogs, University publications or advertisements both on and off campus.

c. To digitize the Materials or use any technological substitute the UCLA Library deems appropriate to preserve and provide access to the Materials.

d. To provide unrestricted access, including Internet or other wireless or digital access, to the Materials.

e. To use the Materials for educational, research and other noncommercial purposes.

f. To make the full text or full version of the Work available to the public, in digital form, pursuant the Creative Commons Attribution, Non-commercial, No Derivatives license. This means that the Work may be copied and distributed for any non-commercial purpose, provided that DONOR is given credit for the original work, and the Work is not modified, edited, or abridged in any way. See http://creativecommons.org/licenses/by-nc-nd/3.0/

6. DONOR shall indemnify, defend and hold THE REGENTS harmless from any losses, claims, damages, awards, penalties or injuries incurred, including reasonable attorney's fees, which arise from any claim by any third party of an alleged infringement of copyright or any other property right arising out of the access and use of the Materials but only in proportion to and to the extent such liability, loss, expense, attorneys' fees, or claims for injury or damages are caused by or result from the acts or omissions of DONOR.

7. DONOR shall provide THE REGENTS with all information and documentation regarding the provenance of the Materials, including any information relating to intellectual property rights.

8. The Materials will be organized by the UCLA Library and a bibliographic record and/or finding aid will be created to describe the content and arrangement.

9. Donor agrees not to sell, donate, or deposit the Materials, including digital files or copies, at any other institution.

10. Donor grants UCLA the right to store acquired digital content in its entirety for preservation purposes.

11. Donor grants UCLA the right to access all data from digital media included in the Materials, including deleted files, log files, and systems files, and content protected by passwords or encryption. Donor understands and agrees that UCLA may utilize methods to bypass or unlock passwords and/or encryption protections in order to gain access to the data for preservation and scholarly purposes. Any restrictions on access to the Materials requested by the Donor will apply to any such recovered information.

12. The Materials will be physically stabilized and preserved by the UCLA Library including, as appropriate, placing the Materials in non-damaging containers and storing in facilities that provide appropriate temperature and humidity control and security.

13. The Materials will be available to researchers after they have been arranged and described for use.

14. THE REGENTS are authorized to dispose of any duplicate or other material not relevant to the collection which it determines to have no permanent value or historical interest.

15. In the event that DONOR may hereafter donate additional materials to THE REGENTS such gifts shall be set forth in an Addendum to this Deed of Gift and will be governed by the terms and conditions stated above. The Addendum shall include a description of the additional materials so donated and any conditions necessary and pertinent to those specific, newly-donated materials and shall be signed by the DONOR and THE REGENTS.

Signed:(donor) _____

Name:_____

this [insert day here] day of [insert month here], 20[complete year here].

FOR DEPARTMENTAL USE ONLY

Signature of UCLA Library: Date: _____

Title:_____

Accepted for THE REGENTS of the University of California:
Date: _____

Office of Gift Policy Administration

Title:_____

NOTES

1. This chapter is for informational use only and does not constitute nor should be construed as legal opinion or advice. Every effort has been made to ensure that the information presented is accurate, but the law is subject to change after publication. Cultural institutions should obtain the advice of a lawyer in relation to any specific questions regarding their policies and practices.

2. Peter B. Hirtle, Emily Hudson, and Andrew T. Kenyon, *Copyright and Cultural Institutions: Guidelines for Digitization for U.S. Libraries, Archives, and Museums* (Ithaca, NY: Cornell University Library, 2009); Menzi L. Behrnd-Klodt, *Navigating Legal Issues in Archives* (Chicago: Society of American Archivists, 2008).

3. Menzi L. Behrnd-Klodt and Christopher J. Prom, eds., *Rights in the Digital Era* (Chicago: Society of American Archivists, 2015).

4. Association of Research Libraries, "Model Deed of Gift" and "Model Deed of Gift including Mixed IP Rights" *Research Library Issues* 279 (June 2012): 5–6, 7–9, https://doi.org/10.29242/rli.279.

5. Society of American Archivists, *Guidelines for Reappraisal and Deaccessioning*, July 12, 2011, http://www2.archivists.org/sites/all/files/GuidelinesForReappraisalAndDeaccessioningDRAFT.pdf.

6. For an example of a detailed legal negotiation checklist, see Menzi L. Behrnd-Klodt, *Navigating Legal Issues in Archives*, 46.

7. Society of American Archivists, "SAA Core Values Statement and Code of Ethics," May 2011, http://archivists.org/statements/saa-core-values-statement-and-code-of-ethics.

8. University of California, *BFB-RMP-1: University Records Management Program*, 2015, 3, http://policy.ucop.edu/doc/7020453/BFB-RMP-1.

9. Ownership of Copyright at Distinct from Ownership of Material Object, 17 U.S.C. §202 (2010).

10. Copyright Ownership and Transfer, 17 U.S.C. §201(a) (2001).

11. Fair use is the statutory articulation that courts have determined that some uses should be considered fair under the Copyright Act, whether or not they are permitted by the copyright

owner. Fairness is determined by a court considering the four factors articulated in the statute. Limitations on Exclusive Rights: Fair Use, 17 U.S.C. §107 (1992).

12. For an analysis of the case, see Peter B. Hirtle, "Copyright Infringement on the Docket," *Archival Outlook* (May/June 2012): 10, 26.

13. Creative Commons, https://creativecommons.org.

14. Circumvention of Copyright Protection Systems, 17 U.S.C. §1201 (2011).

15. Behrnd-Klodt, *Navigating Legal Issues in Archives*, 266–67.

16. Ibid.

17. If the image is of an individual rather than a building, device, or object, instead of trademark, publicity law may be involved and may need to be cleared for any commercial use.

18. Behrnd-Klodt, *Navigating Legal Issues in Archives*, 269–70.

19. Samuel D. Warren and Louis D. Brandeis, "The Right to Privacy," *Harvard Law Review* 4 (December 15, 1890): 193–220; "Invasion of Privacy," *Restatement (Second) of Torts* §§652A-652I (St. Paul: American Law Institute Publishers, 1977), 3:376–403.

20. Behrnd-Klodt, *Navigating Legal Issues in Archives*, 113.

21. Ibid., 111–13.

22. Society of American Archivists, "SAA Core Values."

23. Family Educational and Privacy Rights, 20 U.S.C. §1232g (2011); Family Educational Rights and Privacy, 34 C.F.R. Part 99 (1988); Health Coverage Availability and Affordability Act of 1996, Pub. L. No. 104–199, 110 Stat. 1936 (1996).

24. Behrnd-Klodt, *Navigating Legal Issues in Archives*, 126–30.

II

Collections and Environments

Chapter Six

Performing Arts Collections

Vincent J. Novara

The lives, careers, and needs of performing arts donors are every bit as complex as the digital content they create. Despite the best intentions of archivists to document and record performance, it remains laced with ephemerality due to limitations of human memory, the degradation of carriers of recorded performance, and the considerable resources required to combat both. Yet, it is this ephemeral quality that imbues performance with such meaning and excitement: the knowledge that what you are witnessing is in some way unique, a moment of creativity that is fleeting even when recorded for posterity.[1] And the notation systems used to communicate how to perform a work are, in the end, instructions that result in these unique moments. Each performance is a singular event.[2] Moreover, each performance is consistently characterized by three elements: a performer or performers, an audience to witness the performance, and the subsequent relationship between the audience and those performing.[3] Recreating all the components of a performance or even capturing them for future generations is currently beyond human capabilities.

Concurrently, a host of other issues complicate performing arts donations to archives, especially those featuring digital material. Contemporary performing and creative artists work with a variety of proprietary applications and formats, many of which are no longer supported or require licenses. The data carriers of their work are produced to either share their creativity, as sketches in the creative process, or as documents of events. It is common that the media they create are massive in size, and a mere representative portion of their careers can easily approach a petabyte in storage. The rights management issues complicate donations in terms of access, academic reuse, licensing, and restrictions required by labor agreements. And, finally, most artists commonly have intersections between their professional work and their personal lives—the machines on which they create are also the machines in which their personal digital lives unfold; their relationships with collaborators and colleagues transcend professional limitations.[4] These factors taken together render each donation of born-digital content and digitized analog content a complicated endeavor.

Yet, these donations have so much to offer the world of the performing arts—for researchers and practitioners alike. Consider reconstructing a past performance. Without some form of performance documentation, artists can only rely on notation, which in some instances is insufficient. That was certainly the case for the award-winning actor Edward Gero when he was asked in 2008 to remount his 1998 performance as Richard Nixon for Round House Theatre's production of *Nixon's Nixon*. Gero stated that viewing a video of his performance kept in the archives was "an indispensable aid" and that he was able to "see first-hand timing and other detailed choices." The digitized video proved an especially useful asset as the recording was made toward the end of the 1998 production's run, and as Gero explained, "Those matured acting choices are not captured in a stage manager's record of rehearsal. . . . A production and performance grows."[5] Such outcomes warrant the complexity and challenges experienced with each digital donation.

This chapter reviews these considerations as they apply to performing arts archival collections. The significance of engaged donor relationships, strategic acquisition, and collaborative appraisal will receive considerable attention throughout. The chapter will also examine select individual artists, ensembles or companies, and performing arts organizations. There are many formats common to the performing arts. The discussions will focus on the audio, video, and photography that document work, the various means of notating and communicating creative intentions, and the numerous forms of records created by artists and organizations.

For much of this chapter, collections and donors from Special Collections in Performing Arts (SCPA) at the University of Maryland will serve as examples to illustrate issues, trends, and future directions. SCPA's collections and donors create and submit digital materials that are representative in building archival collections in the performing arts. Furthermore, SCPA strives to be a true performing arts repository, with equal attention given to dance, music, and theatre and to performative mediums that incorporate those three disciplines, such as puppetry. The collections include all manner of manuscript and media, commercially made or home produced, intended for distribution or for individual use, and from the youngest novice to celebrated professionals. The collected formats reflect that diversity.

EXISTING LITERATURE

In the performing arts, the available literature on digital donations is limited. Case studies on digitization projects and attendant metadata are abundant, but even those articles do not address acquisitions, donor stewardship, and managing expectations. Thus, it is interesting to note that a highly useful contemporary study on the topic of digital donations in the performing arts comes from the field of literature. In the *American Archivist* article "Saving-Over, Over-Saving, and the Future Mess of Writer's Digital Archives: A Survey Report on the Personal Digital Archiving Practices of Emerging Writers," Devin Becker and Collier Nogues report findings from their survey of one hundred writers (especially poets) on personal practices of creating archives. The article suggests the role that archivists can have, at the very least, on advising these actions, with an eye toward creating stable and representative born-digital donations of creative works. Becker and Nogues also address the challenge of the blurring line between the personal and the professional with creative artists. They propose an effective and simple four-step strategy: (1) assemble relevant files into a "Master-Archives" folder on the hard drive of the primary computer used by the writer, (2) utilize an intuitive cloud-storage service to store a copy of the Master-Archives, (3) replace the cloud-storage copy every four months with content from the hard drive, and (4) every year create a "Master-Archives [year]" folder to store the prior year's work on both the primary hard drive and an external hard drive housed in a separate location. The final two steps in this process are iterative and constitute a reasonably easy approach for any artist to manage his or her digital archives on a computer.[6]

The Performing Arts Resources series of the Theatre Library Association (TLA) offers many options to support working with performing arts donors of digital collections. Most of the twenty-seven essays in TLA's recent volume *Body, Mind, Artifact: Reimagining Collections*, copublished with the International Association of Libraries and Museums of the Performing Arts (SIBMAS), is essential reading for understanding the current trends and issues in digital performing arts collections. Predictably, the volume emphasizes theater with dance second, but the wide swath of issues it presents will be useful to any performing arts archivist. The section on digital humanities and the performing arts includes four papers outlining the experiences of digital humanists working with performing arts collections. Two of the papers describe their funding model. As a field of study, the digital humanities are still relatively new, which means that the relationship between these scholars and the archives is developing. For archivists there is great potential to secure support from donors to host residencies for digital humanities scholars. The section on exhibition papers addresses the origins of the collections and how they were donated to performing arts repositories, including some digital content, while still exploring the challenges of collecting on performance in the first place. [7]

Kenneth Schlesinger's edited book *Performance Documentation and Preservation in an Online Environment* is an effective primer for basic concepts and the history of performing arts digital collections, regardless of the vintage. This is especially the case with Cheryl Faver's brief essay, "Archiving and Digital Performance," which outlines key concepts and considerations for building such collections that are still relevant today. Catherine Owen's opinion paper "What Happens When the Money Runs Out?" reviews the financial burden of digitizing performing arts collections and instituting financially viable digital preservation solutions, even for the near term. Finally, Howard Besser's essay "Longevity of Electronic Art" illustrates several points regarding collecting and preserving digital creative output that are still applicable today. [8]

John Calhoun's edited book *Documenting: Scenic Design* reviews the history and challenges of managing digital collections. Wendell K. Harrington's chapter "Preserving Projection" reviews the history of this form of scenic design from lantern slides in the 1800s through today's digital projections. He also discusses the transience of projections, which does not diminish their value to study design or performance. Harrington includes a six-step preservation strategy for digital projection: acquire all documentation, especially "creative correspondence"; archive media files (images, videos, animations, etc.) in an original order with the hopes that the designer has organized the files in folders corresponding to cues and scenes; acquire the script with cues and placement notes or what some stage managers refer to as "prompt books"; preserve the computer programs used for organizing the cues; acquire any documentation of the cues of themselves as seen on stage if possible; and, if possible, include reviews or other commentary if available for context. He encourages archivists to adapt these guidelines to solve many of the collecting challenges for digital content.[9]

Jama S. Coartney and Susan L. Wiesner's article, "Performance as Digital Text: Capturing Signals and Secret Messages in a Media Rich-Experience," describes approaches to collecting digital material. The authors outline a model for incorporating born-digital techniques, such as motion capture, in documenting dance works and movement analysis. They suggest close collaboration between performing artists, digital humanists, and engineers to document performance. The authors discuss the ephemeral nature of witnessing performance and explain that choreographers commonly create unique systems of communicating their works (including, at times, notation), which limits archivists' ability to rely on predictable or repetitive solutions for handling these digital assets or even documenting the process in the first place. The result of such work points to future directions for scholarship in the performing arts and encourages repositories to determine strategies for preservation, while ensuring discovery and access.[10]

Matt Gorzalski's essay, "Archivists and Thespians: A Case Study and Reflections on Context and Authenticity in a Digitization Project," reviews the experiences of a collaborative digital project at Southern Illinois University, Carbondale. As university archivist, Gorzalski collaborated with the institution's theater faculty on a project that revealed differing perspectives on issues of context and authenticity. He argues that such perspectives vary from field to field, especially within the performing arts. A compelling facet of this study was that the digitization project was focused on the scenographic designs of one of the institution's faculty members, which blurred the lines between the donor, creator, project participant, and faculty member.[11]

In "Saving All the Freaks on the Life Raft," Caroline Daniels, Heather Fox, Sarah-Jane Poindexter, and Elizabeth Reilly describe how they documented the underground music community of Louisville, Kentucky. Their Louisville Underground Music Archive (LUMA) project, based at the University of Louisville Archives and Special Collections, included analog materials, digital files, and a variety of audiovisual formats. Much of their article discusses the challenges of working with performing arts donors or often families of recently (and tragically early) deceased musicians. The authors suggest strategies for working with donors who inherently distrust institutions or prefer a post-custodial solution.[12]

Other works related to performing arts collections focus more on the technical challenges. Josh Ranger's AVPreserve blog post from 2014, "For

God's Sake, Stop Digitizing Paper," suggests that archivists must prioritize the conversion of audio and video formats over paper-based materials. Ranger boldly opines: "We should agree to stop digitizing paper and other stable formats for a set period because, in a way, it is bad for preservation." The post offers an impassioned argument about the degradation of media carriers and the race to obsolescence of playback equipment vital for conversion projects. Ranger explains that "when dealing with audiovisual materials, preservation creates access."[13] The Cost of Inaction Calculator, a free online tool available through AVPreserve, underscores Ranger's call to action.[14] The costs of digital conversion, of course, are always a factor for archives programs, but that tangible need can appeal to many supporters who want to make a financial donation.

Another common thread of discussion centers on the question of what constitutes a performance or if performance is truly documentable. Gunhild Borggreen and Rune Gade's 2013 edited volume *Performing Archives/ Archives of Performance* explores this existential quandary. This work focuses on the ephemerality of performance, archives of performance, and the creation of archives as a performative act. More philosophical than practical, the essays deliver a range of perspectives on digital and analog collections. As an example of the range of options in the volume, the opening essay "Archiving Legacies: Who Cares for Performance Remains" by Heike Roms makes the case for collecting a wide range of performing arts materials, while the closing essay "Un/archive" by Marco Pustianaz questions the need to collect broadly and favors more targeted approaches.[15] Such divergent opinions about what and how much to collect prepare archivists for the reticence and reluctance of the artists they will encounter.

Two case studies from experiences of SCPA archivists at the University of Maryland focus on the challenges of digital collections. In their book chapter "Staging an Embedded Appraisal: The Studio Theatre Archives at the University of Maryland," Leahkim A. Gannett, Vincent J. Novara, Kelly Smith, and Mary Crauderueff discuss the use of digital photography to document the company's set models. The authors discuss establishing a records retention schedule with company managers as a method to plan for future accruals of official electronic records. The chapter also describes how archivists worked alongside the company's visionary founder, Joy Zinoman, who was in the process of detaching herself from the company and school she had founded.[16] A second case study, "Is This Enough? Digitizing Liz Lerman Dance Exchange Media," by Bria Parker, Robin C. Pike, and Vincent J.

Novara, reviews a video digitization pilot project. The authors describe the implementation of digitization workflows, including metadata strategies, file storage, and concurrent donor stewardship. This project was part of the original donation agreement between Lerman and SCPA. As an example of the ongoing relationship between archivists and donors, this project involved consultation with the donor and other experts to select videos from the collection for digitization. [17]

The existing literature on performing arts collections illustrates the challenges of managing these complex materials. For archivists, the significant amount of audiovisual material in these collections represents both significant technical issues to overcome and a commitment to resources to provide ongoing access. For donors, the proposition to donate their lifetime of work to an archives program is sometimes intimidating and confusing. It is the responsibility of archivists to develop reasonable expectations with donors. Involving the donor in project planning and execution and enhancing the presentation of the collection as a research tool takes time, but the resulting collections help document artistic productions and performances that would otherwise be lost to their own ephemerality.

TECHNICAL COMPONENTS AND CONCEPTS

Building strong collections of performing arts material requires patience, especially when the bulk of the content is digital. Archivists who work with donors to provide ongoing access to performing arts material have four central issues to consider. First, documenting the performing arts involves a variety of formats—some standard, some novel, some proprietary, many obsolete, and all marching to obsolescence. Second, there are many intersections between what is the donor's work and life. As previously stated, the machines on which they create are also the machines in which their personal digital lives unfold. Third, all performing arts archivists cope with mammoth file sizes for the content, which creates challenges in archival appraisal, processing for access, and long-term storage and preservation. Finally, performing arts materials require careful management of intellectual property rights. The next two sections explore several representative collections from SCPA with the focus on these main issues.

Analog Donations and Digitization

SCPA's collections contain a range of formats representative of the perform-ing arts, both analog and digital. In recent years, SCPA acquired media-rich collections with an expectation by both the donor and the repository that some form of access digital surrogate would be created. Fulfilling these promises has been difficult. Archivists used stopgap solutions to provide access when demand was certain. For many collections, archivists decided to postpone creating digital access until more ideal solutions that adhered to contemporary standards regarding digitization and metadata were available.

Two of the more common means for documenting dance are through some form of written notation—either a system like Labanotation or unique personal notation systems—or through a moving image format.[18] The records of the Liz Lerman Dance Exchange featured both unique personal notation and over 1,400 video items in four formats (VHS, U-matic, Beta, and Hi8). When SCPA began negotiations with Liz Lerman and company leaders about the acquisition of the collection, the shared expectation was a commitment to convert the video from the older formats to digital files. The donation depended on this assurance.

Building on the partnership with the donor, SCPA secured funding from the Dance Heritage Coalition to support a paid intern whose sole project was describing the videos to improve access and to assist with future digitization. The intern worked with a metadata librarian to create information about items selected for the pilot project. The project team worked with the donor to select items for digitization. The videos selected include rehearsal footage, notable performances, and interviews with Lerman. By involving the donor, they ensured that the items digitized were of the greatest consequence for the company's history or possibly of the greatest use for future research projects by Lerman. During the process, project leaders discovered that licensed mu-sic was used in some of the performances. As the company usually did not have releases for the accompanying music, nor from the dancers featured in the works, the project team decided to restrict viewing of the digitized con-tent to on-campus computers maintained by the University Libraries. Project leaders selected one hundred VHS cassettes for conversion.

Alas, technological challenges delayed the work, and it took a decade before the conversion began. Part of the delay was waiting for the establish-ment of a fully operational Digital Conversion and Media Reformatting (DCMR) unit for the University Libraries. This unit contributes to coordinat-ing a wide range of digital projects for the libraries. For this project, the

DCMR worked with an external vendor to complete the reformatting. Because the collection had previously been stored in less than ideal environmental conditions, project leaders expected degradation of the tapes and significant preservation challenges. Luckily, just one VHS tape in the initial selection of one hundred could not be converted. The experiences of the pilot project established a clear workflow for such conversion projects, including the remaining videos from the collection.

Following the pilot, a working group of SCPA archivists and DCMR librarians submitted a Humanities Collections and Reference Resources grant proposal to the National Endowment for the Humanities. The objective of the grant was to digitize the remainder of the video holdings in the collection, preserve the digital content, and provide online access. As part of the proposal, project leaders worked with the donor and members of the company to enhance the metadata for these items. They provided crucial additional contextual information, corrected spellings of names, and identified known dates and places.[19] This type of partnership with the donating institution was beneficial for all involved and for the users of a better-described collection.[20]

Building on this pilot project, SCPA is involved in a similar analog-to-digital conversion project for the open reel tapes of the broadcaster Robert Sherman. His collection featured over 3,500 open reel tapes of four different programs of radio broadcasts of interviews and live performances from his career of over 50 years. The bulk of the recordings are divided into shows on classical music and shows on folk music. Because of the size of the collection, SCPA leaders used a phased approach to conversion, with help from the donor to select topical sets of material.

SCPA recently completed a conversion project of 166 open reels of recordings created by the University of Maryland's Madrigal Singers, an ensemble that existed from 1962 to 1974. With support from donated funds, the collection was digitized, made available through the University Libraries' digital collections portal, and promoted through an online exhibit "The Recorded History of the UMD Madrigals."[21] Following the exhibit's launch, surviving members of the group provided SCPA with contextual information for many of the minimally described recordings. As one result, several of the ensemble's members became donors to SCPA, with new materials or financial support. An understanding of SCPA's work informs their altruism, and the project inspires and engages these donors.

A similar instance of donor involvement was the digitization of the Studio Theatre set model collection. The company's founder and long-time artistic director, Joy Zinoman, took an active role in the selection of models for digitization and which models to preserve physically. Zinoman knew the history of these productions better than anyone at the company, and that knowledge led to discussions about how much of the collection, forty-seven set models that occupied more than 440 cubic feet, should be donated and digitized. Zinoman used the models (with pushpins) to plot the staging for each work for those she directed, an activity of great creativity for a company's productions. Her strong connection to the materials coupled with the emotions of moving into a new phase of her life by leaving the company required archivists to exercise patience and empathy during the donation process.[22]

The James J. Taylor Collection of the Washington Area Performing Arts Video Archive (WAPAVA) represents another important analog-to-digital project for SCPA. Taylor established this organization in 1991 with the goal of creating and preserving a video collection of stage performances in the DC area. During his career in theater as a stage manager, Taylor learned videography through directing programs at a public-access cable channel and later secured permission from the Actors Equity Association (the actors union) to document stage performances in Washington. However, the group limited how the recordings can be disseminated, and at the time of this writing, they do not permit online streaming. The 379 recordings, all in VHS format, represent Taylor's recordings of area theater and dance performances from 1993 through 2004. In December 2004, he donated the collection to SCPA. Taylor died the following year.

Each production in the collection included at least one master and one access copy. The collection was colocated at the DC Public Library and the University of Maryland. The DC Public Library received the access tapes, and SCPA took the masters. Upon receipt of the masters, SCPA converted the VHS tapes to DVDs using a commercial-grade machine. While that method created easier access to the content, the resulting copy was not high enough quality for ingest. To complete that work, archivists would need to send each of the more than six hundred VHS tapes out to a vendor for digitization and then be able to store nearly six hundred hours of digital video.

Starting in 2005, WAPAVA's board of directors began adding new content to the collection. They employed four freelance videographers to record performances directly to digital, saving the files on digital video tape, SD cards, or hard drives. An advisory board of theater professionals, critics, academics, and theater lovers selected the new content. Their criteria for selection included historical and educational value, with special consideration for premieres, unique events, community interest, and specific performers, directors, and designers. The collection includes over 815 productions representing a cross-section of Washington-area theaters from small to large and academic to professional.

Born-Digital Donations

In the past five years, digital collections have become just as common as donations of analog material. Born-digital acquisition creates hosts of new challenges when working with donors and managing materials. One of the first digital donations to SCPA occurred in 2010. Brad Hathaway, an independent DC-area theater critic, contacted SCPA about donating his Potomac Stages collection. Launched as a website in 2001 by Hathaway, the Potomac Stages project included nearly 2,200 reviews of professional and community theater productions in the DC and surrounding area. The site included published criticism and descriptive and historical information about over two hundred venues in the region. Hathaway wrote most of the content.

After the terms of the donation were finalized, archivists harvested the content and structure of the website by using the Archive-It software. The University of Maryland uses this tool each year to collect the content of all websites associated with the institution. The Potomac Stages website consisted of 852 interlinked and distinct URLs, amounting to 18.8 megabytes in size. Archivists created a finding aid for the collection with description at the theater-level linking out to the corresponding page in the site for that theater and the reviews published for its work. The donor kept in close contact with archivists, providing advice on how the materials were described and how the site functioned in the new digital platform. For many performing arts donors, a donation signals the conclusion of a major chapter of a person's life, artistic career, or a project of personal passion. Archivists must be mindful of these emotions and honestly represent what their programs offer in terms of preservation and access.

A more recent born-digital donation to SCPA came from the University of Maryland's School of Theatre, Dance, and Performance Studies (TDPS). Because TDPS was part of the University of Maryland, the collection was treated as a transfer to SCPA. Prior to the transfer, archivists met with the production manager from TDPS to explain how SCPA would preserve, describe, and use the material for future scholarship. The production manager requested more time with the material to impose some order on the files, improve the consistency of the file names, appraise the material for relevance, and ensure that everything intended for transfer was included.

This resulting donation consisted of thirteen terabytes of preappraised records on a single external hard drive. The files pertain to TDPS's collaboration with the National Academy of Chinese Theatre Arts on William Shakespeare's *A Midsummer Night's Dream*, produced during the 2011/2012 academic year. The production began in Beijing at the National Academy and then later at the University of Maryland. The collection includes a complete video recording of the performance in Beijing, along with releases signed by the student performers. That clearance made it possible for SCPA to provide access to the recording on in-house workstations. The digital collection also includes planning documents, digital photographs, production files, student and faculty blogs, promotional materials, scripts, schedules, recordings of rehearsals and performances, interviews with participants, and video footage of sightseeing excursions. The material documents the entire story of the production and the experience for the students and faculty. Thus, the collection is rich in information about how the performance was designed, directed, and intended for execution.

The personal and professional papers of contemporary composers, especially those still living and working, present archivists with complex challenges. For example, the Lawrence K. Moss papers at SCPA are a collection in a state of constant change and enhancement. Moss's composing career spans from 1950 to the present. He currently composes in the music score program Sibelius, a proprietary software. As part of his process, Moss prints out drafts of the scores, marks them with revisions, makes the changes to the electronic file, and then creates a new file instead of overwriting earlier versions. Instead of donating the new material at regular intervals, Moss submits new digital files and analog materials to the archives separately, often not in close succession. The variations are important to researchers, but to fully understand his process, they need access to the digital and analog material. Further, archivists attempting to arrange and describe the collection must consider the sequence of the files and which version of the software was being used to create specific files.[23] Fortunately, Moss wrote the date of each revision on the print versions.

In addition to these digital and paper manuscripts, Moss also donated recordings, concert programs, photographs, correspondence, press clippings, and teaching materials. For a collection of a modern, living composer, the contents were quite representative, but his compositional method coupled with his donating practices required careful accessioning and stewardship. That said, the "master-archives" system proposed by Becker and Nogues was a viable solution in this case, especially if combined with a formalized schedule of physical donations.[24]

In recent years, SCPA experienced consistent submission of born-digital content through transfers of official documents to the archives of performing arts organizations. Initially, SCPA archivists requested that these organizations withhold such submissions until the University of Maryland implemented a more viable electronic records program. That approach quickly changed as archivists determined that collections would be lost due to equipment malfunction, confusion, or inadvertent deletion. Following that reversal of policy, the American Society for Theatre Research (ASTR) submits born-digital records as email attachments or through services like Dropbox on a regular basis. Despite institutional limitations, archivists describe these new accruals of electronic materials in existing finding aids.[25]

NEW DIRECTIONS

In the coming decade, several factors will change the way that archivists approach performing arts collections and other digital archives. All archives programs must anticipate a future that is constantly implementing new strategies to describe, preserve, and serve emerging formats and technologies. The scale of digital preservation will become a monolithic challenge, especially with performing arts collections because of their large file sizes. The types of formats and files as part of digital donations will also vary. When anticipating future formats used by donors, performing arts archivists will have to approach this work with the same boldness and daring of the artists themselves. Consequently, archivists must adapt existing techniques for digital acquisition and descriptive standards to accommodate emerging multimedia formats.

The use of holograms, especially in popular music genres, is just one example of how performance will change in the next few years. Made quite popular with the band Gorillaz starting in 2005 and then with Japanese virtual/humanoid performer Hatsune Miku in 2010, the use of holograms is also common in performances for the South Korean popular music known colloquially as K-pop. As this technology becomes more affordable and easier to create, more performers will use this method, and thus the resulting files will become part of their digital donations. Few archivists have experience with collecting and managing holograms, but this technology offers numerous challenges for archivists to overcome. Furthermore, it is unclear who would have the right to donate the hologram: the artist who used it or the artist who created it? This is to say nothing of contemplating what is real or what is truly possible by real people versus holographic depictions.[26]

Collecting and providing access to research data is an emerging field for most academic archivists, and that includes the performing arts. Thanks to the rise of the digital humanities, this area of research connects archivists, research data librarians, information technology staff, and stakeholders. One area of the performing arts producing considerable research data is the use of motion capture to document, analyze, and communicate about dance. As described earlier, motion capture has more applications than merely realizing special effects in blockbuster movies.[27] However, motion capture is also incorporated into real-time performative settings, as seen with select works of Australian dance company Chunky Move. Founded in 1995 by Gideon Obarzanek, the company works with all manner of new media and regularly works with technological artists in pursuits of new works.[28] The company's work "Glow" from 2007 is representative of where cutting-edge performing artists can take technology and even data. German software artist Frieder Weiss, who collaborated with the company's prior artistic director Gideon Obarzanek, describes the work in a YouTube post as "projections react to the dancer's moving body, graphically illuminating and extending it."[29]

In viewing this type of cutting-edge work, the data projections are equal in consequence to the solo dancer when witnessing the performance. How collaborations will be represented in performing arts collections is something archivists will face sooner than later, especially as they seek to document what Heike Roms refers to as the "body of work."[30] And this is just one of many companies that are devising new ways to incorporate such technology into collaboration and performance.

Another emerging multimedia technology in the performing arts is projection design. This is the art of designing projected images onto surfaces as part of performances, event installation, exhibiting, or advertising. This art has been common in the performing arts since the 1920s, yet the use of digital design technology and the increased use in contemporary theater and dance works make this an area worth consideration.[31] Moreover, as projection design is now almost exclusively a digital art form, keeping up with advances in this field will require close study and vigilance.

As an example of this technology in action, two multimedia design students at the University of Maryland designed projections for the fortieth anniversary gala for Dance Exchange. For that event, the students used digitized images from the collection to create an immersive visual experience for attendees. For preproduction, the designers relied primarily on After Effects for animation, Premiere for video editing, and Illustrator and other Adobe products to create content. When not creating unique content, they pulled stock footage from open online sources. In production, they used different software applications, depending on the circumstance, which made the project even more unique. At the end of the project, the students worked with archivists to document their processes and make the files publicly accessible.[32]

A final challenge for archivists is to rethink gift agreements for digital materials, especially in the case of performing arts collections. These agreements currently work in partnerships with or append existing deeds of gift with donors. Most often these agreements address the most common concerns for a digital donation, such as storage, access, private or sensitive information, and document recovery concerns. But these agreements ignore many other common issues with digital materials, which will only become more common. The 2012 report by the AIMS Work Group highlights many of these challenges, which include: determining rights for duplicating files; disposing of original hardware and media; using "new capture methodologies from a media type not previously encountered; negotiating permission to capture or extract data from a proprietary web service; assessing the feasibility of taking material dependent on software or other programs that require significant commitment to deliver or render; and understanding the licensing and intellectual property rights implications of capturing or copying software as well as data."[33]

Deeds of gift for digital materials must address intellectual property rights and the management of those rights. Further, many agreements between performing artists and archives programs will outline a postcustodial or shared ownership model. Often donors view the archives as a repository for copies of some of their work to be represented and available. Such digital-only donations are reminiscent of the once common practice of donating photocopies of original documents to archives for access purposes. Digital-only donations occur when donors wish to donate a digital copy of their work and maintain the so-called original copy (either physical or digital) in their own personal collections. These donations require clarification on copyright ownership and the ability of the hosting institution to make the donation freely available.

For example, while building collections related to punk music culture, SCPA archivists reported several instances in which donors preferred to maintain originals and donate digital surrogates instead. This is partly due to these individuals, as cultural subversives, having an inherent distrust for large institutions, especially those attached to government agencies like a state university.[34] Additionally, many donors wish to monetize (through sale) or reuse the content (through publishing or reissuing) to continue to earn income from the content. As many performing artists progress through middle age, they often begin to appreciate the value in establishing some form of enduring record of their creativity or participation in their artistic communities.

The payoff of all this work is that archivists are building exciting new collections that document a much fuller sample of society. With punk collections as an example, donors who created the music and shaped the culture are working with archivists at institutions like SCPA, the DC Public Library's Punk Archive, New York University's Riot Grrrl Collection, and the University of Louisville's Underground Music Archive.[35] Collections like this are emerging all over the United States, and digital submissions, even as surrogates, are proving an effective compromise to serve the needs of the donor, the archives program, and eager researchers.

Successful cultivation of donors is built on communication, compromise, and sometimes adapting traditional archival practice to satisfy mutual needs. A clear collection development policy, which includes details on digital materials, allows archivists to share with donors what is possible and not possible. In addition, demonstrating subject expertise will gain the confidence and trust of donors.[36] Familiarity with new technology is a requirement for working in an archival environment and for making connections with the creators of digital content. As archivists continue to digitize analog holdings, that will also move donor relationships into a different phase, especially when donors take an interest in financially supporting the work. No matter the format, one factor that will never cease is the ephemerality of performance. Indeed, performing arts donors will remain every bit as complex as the digital content they create and the digital archives left to the care of archivists.

NOTES

1. This notion of ephemerality is addressed throughout the "Ontologies" section of Gunhild Borggreen and Rune Gade, eds., *Performing Archives/Archives of Performance* (Copenhagen: Museum Tusculanum Press, 2013).

2. Jama S. Coartney and Susan L. Wiesner, "Performance as Digital Text: Capturing Signals and Secret Messages in a Media-Rich Experience," *Literary and Linguistic Computing* 24 (June 2009): 153–60.

3. Melanie Fritsch and Stefan Strötgen, "Relatively Live: How to Identify Live Music Performances," *Music and the Moving Image* 5 (Spring 2012): 47–66.

4. Matthew G. Kirschenbaum discusses this situation as it applies to author Salman Rushdie. Matthew G. Kirschenbaum, "Electronic Literature as Cultural Heritage (Confessions of an Incunk)," *Matthew G. Kirschenbaum* (blog), April 2013, https://mkirschenbaum.wordpress.com/2013/04/06/electronic-literature-as-cultural-heritage-confessions-of-incunk/.

5. This testimonial letter was part of a grant application package and is found in the curator's file for the organization. Edward Gero to the Board of Directors of the Washington Area Performing Arts Video Archive (WAPAVA), October 2013.

6. Devin Becker and Collier Nogues, "Saving-Over, Over-Saving, and the Future Mess of Writers' Digital Archives: A Survey Report on the Personal Digital Archiving Practices of Emerging Writers," *American Archivist* 75 (Fall/Winter 2012): 482–513.

7. Tiffany Nixon and Nicole Leclercq, eds., *Body, Mind, Artifact: Reimagining Collections*, Performing Arts Resources 32 (New York: Theatre Library Association, 2016).

8. Kenneth Schlesinger, ed., *Performance Documentation and Preservation in an Online Environment*, Performing Arts Resources 24 (New York: Theatre Library Association, 2004).

9. Wendell K. Harrington, "Preserving Projection," in *Documenting: Scenic Design*, by John Calhoun, Performing Arts Resources 29 (New York: Theatre Library Association, 2012), 26–27.

10. Coartney and Wiesner, "Performance as Digital Text," 153–60.

11. Matthew J. Gorzalski, "Archivists and Thespians: A Case Study and Reflections on Context and Authenticity in a Digitization Project," *American Archivist* 79 (January 2016): 161–85.

12. Caroline Daniels, Heather Fox, Sarah-Jane Poindexter, and Elizabeth Reilly, "Saving All the Freaks on the Life Raft: Blending Documentation Strategy with Community Engagement to Build a Local Music Archives," *American Archivist* 78 (Spring/Summer 2015): 238–61.

13. Joshua Ranger, "For God's Sake, Stop Digitizing Paper," *AVPreserve* (blog), August 2014, https://www.weareavp.com/for-gods-sake-stop-digitizing-paper-2/.

14. "Cost of Inaction Calculator," https://coi.avpreserve.com/.

15. Heike Roms, "Archiving Legacies: Who Cares for Performance Remains?" and Marco Pustianaz, "Un/archive," in *Performing Archives/Archives of Performance*, eds. Borggreen and Gade.

16. Leahkim A. Gannett, Vincent J. Novara, Kelly Smith, and Mary Crauderueff, "Staging an Embedded Appraisal: The Studio Theatre Archives at the University of Maryland," in *Innovative Practices in Archives and Special Collections: Appraisal and Acquisition*, ed. Kate Theimer (Lanham, MD: Rowman & Littlefield, 2015), 105–18.

17. Bria Parker, Robin C. Pike, and Vincent J. Novara, "'Is This Enough?' Digitizing Liz Lerman Dance Exchange Archives Media," *Provenance: Journal of the Society of Georgia Archivists* 34 (2016): 86–96, http://digitalcommons.kennesaw.edu/provenance/vol34/iss1/11.

18. Coartney and Wiesner, "Performance as Digital Text," 155.

19. Robin C. Pike and Vincent J. Novara, "Preserving and Presenting the Past, Present, and Future of Dance History: Digitizing the Liz Lerman Dance Exchange Archives," July 2016, Humanities Collections and Reference Resources grant application, National Endowment for the Humanities, in author's possession.

20. For more information on the pilot project and the collection, see Parker, Pike, and Novara, "Is This Enough?"

21. "Recorded History of the UMD Madrigals," University Maryland Libraries, http://www.lib.umd.edu/madrigalsingers.

22. "Studio Theatre Archives," Special Collections in Performing Arts, University of Maryland Libraries Finding Aids, http://hdl.handle.net/1903.1/19638.

23. At the time of this writing, Moss is working in version 6 of the Sibelius application, but the latest version of the application is 8.5. Lawrence K. Moss, email to author, December 6, 2016.

24. Becker and Nogues, "Saving-Over, Over-Saving."

25. "Transfer of Official Records," Special Collections in Performing Arts, Michelle Smith Performing Arts Library, University of Maryland Libraries, https://www.lib.umd.edu/binaries/content/assets/public/scpa/transfer-of-official-records-form.pdf.

26. Melanie Fritsch and Stefan Strötgen contemplate the meaning of mediatized performative events and consider the "liveness" of a Gorillaz concert. Melanie Fritsch and Stefan Strötgen, "Relatively Live: How to Identify Live Music Performances," *Music and the Moving Image* 5 (Spring 2012): 47–66.

27. Coartney and Wiesner, "Performance as Digital Text," 156.

28. "Chunky Move," Arts Centre Melbourne, Australian Performing Arts Collection, https://collections.artscentremelbourne.com.au/.

29. Frieder Weiss, "Chunky Move—Glow," September 2013, YouTube, https://youtu.be/C4He543_a80.

30. Roms, "Archiving Legacies," 36.

31. Harrington, "Preserving Projection," 20.

32. Alexandra Kelly Colburn, email to author, December 20, 2016. Ms. Colburn answered questions on behalf of herself and her creative partner Mark Costello. Both are professional designers and graduate students at the School of Theatre, Dance, and Performance Studies at the University of Maryland. The questions were these: Are there particular applications that you work with? If so, for the projections you created (or for other projects), what are the file sizes like? Do you have any archiving/preservation plan in place for your work? Or, how is your work stored and/or backed-up? Is it possible for your work to be studied on a smaller scale, like a laptop screen, desktop screen, etc.? Has your work ever been used as part of a performance? If so, how? (Or, is there an online gallery for me to view, please point me to that.)

33. AIMS Work Group, *AIMS Born-Digital Collections: An Inter-institutional Model for Stewardship*," (University of Virginia Libraries, January 2012), 5, https://dcs.library.virginia.edu/files/2013/02/AIMS_final_text.pdf.

34. Vincent J. Novara, "Collecting Punk: The DC Punk and Indie Fanzine Collection," (PowerPoint presentation, Mid-Atlantic Regional Archives Conference, Roanoke, VA, October 2015), http://hdl.handle.net/1903/18920.

35. "DC Punk Archive: Documenting D.C. Music in Washingtoniana / Special Collections," DC Public Library, https://www.dclibrary.org/punk; "The Riot Grrrl Collection at the Fales Library: Collection Overview," NYU Libraries, https://guides.nyu.edu/riot-grrrl; "Louisville

Underground Music Archive," University of Louisville Libraries, https://library.louisville.edu/archives/luma.

36. Author's conversation with Elizabeth A. Novara, curator for historical manuscripts at the University of Maryland, January 2017.

Chapter Seven

Oral History Collections

Douglas A. Boyd

Oral history and archives programs have always been perceived as intertwined, but in practice, the relationship has been independent and often disconnected. Traditionally, interviewers and archivists have only interacted long after an oral history project was completed, often many years following the active interviewing phase of the project. For decades, committed interviewers conducted oral history projects with a focus on their intended immediate outcomes, such as a journal article, a documentary, an exhibit, a community history, or a book. While some oral history collection initiatives were initiated for "archival" purposes, this usually indicated that a project or interview was being conducted with no specific outcomes envisioned beyond the act of preserving stories for the future. However, even these projects, especially during the interviewing phases, typically operated independently from archives programs. Today, oral history is one of the more popular methodologies utilized by academic, public, and community scholars and by librarians and archivists. Because so many oral history projects will become part of archival collections, it is imperative that archivists play a leading and early role in these projects.

New initiatives to document the history of a person, a place, an institution, a movement, a historical event, or a community are embracing oral history as a method. On the surface, oral history can appear as a simple, friendly, effective, and relatively uncomplicated process needing only a recording device, a list of names and questions, and some time. However, interviewers realize very quickly that good oral history is not simply a recorded questionnaire. Interviewing is a complicated engagement rather than a passive process of simple "listening," and professional-quality recording requires intense focus and attention to detail. Beyond the interviewing phase, archivists who have had experience working with oral history in archives understand that oral history consumes vast amounts of time and resources. The behind-the-scenes work of archival description, comprehensive permissions gathering, working with the complexities of digital audio and video formats, the digitization of older formats, storage and digital preservation, transcription, or providing effective access to interviews are just some of the challenges for archives posed by oral history projects. At the same time, the recollections and memories of those interviewed provide researchers with unique and potentially transformative historical perspectives.

The web-based resource Oral History in the Digital Age provides interviewers, archivists, and practitioners with access to resources on designing and implementing an oral history project and how the resulting interviews can be properly preserved and made more accessible.[1] One of the overarching goals of the project was to acknowledge the convergence of roles and the growing interdependence between those who conduct the interviews, those who preserve the interviews, and those who provide access to those interviews through a variety of modes and to thoughtfully consider possible outcomes for projects from the project design phase to the archives. Interviewers must now have core competencies in digital curation of their files prior to archival donation. Likewise, more archivists are deploying oral history as a methodology for building or contextualizing their collections and engaging communities in new and innovative ways.

The first phase of mainstream popularity of oral history as a practice occurred in the mid-1960s with a growing cross-disciplinary impulse to document history and culture "from the bottom up," coinciding with technical innovations that produced the audio cassette as an affordable and portable recording technology. Widespread oral history interviewing resulted. Columbia University launched the first oral history center in the United States in 1948, followed by the University of California, Berkeley, in 1954. Professionalization was marked by the formation of the Oral History Association in 1967. By the early 1970s, there were oral history centers at UCLA, the University of California, Fullerton, the University of Florida, the University of Kentucky, Baylor University, and the University of North Texas. The introduction to *Oral History in the United States*, compiled by Gary Shumway, claims that in 1965 there were 89 total oral history projects, and in 1971, the figure had grown to 230.[2]

The Louie B. Nunn Center for Oral History at the University of Kentucky (Nunn Center) began recording interviews in 1973, and by 2008, the oral history collection included an estimated six thousand interviews. In the ten years that followed, the collection has doubled in size. Today, the Nunn Center maintains thirty to forty concurrent interviewing projects at any given time. The work ranges from small projects with a community group to larger projects involving family farmers or politicians. The topical areas include the Civil Rights Movement, agriculture, the Appalachian region, politics and public policy, thoroughbred horse racing, coal mining, and the bourbon industry. Prior to 2008, the Nunn Center accessioned an average of one hundred fifty to two hundred interviews in a single year. In 2015 and 2016, the Nunn Center accessioned over six hundred oral history interviews each year; in 2017, the Nunn Center accessioned over nine hundred new oral history interviews.

The Nunn Center's massive rate of growth is indicative and representative of general growth in the popularity of oral history practice throughout the United States and the world. Professional-quality digital recorders are inexpensive and easy to use, and now the ubiquitous smart phone has become a viable option for recording a quick interview. Additionally, the multidisciplinary applications of interviewing methodology within the realms of academia and public history have dramatically expanded. Oral history's applications are no longer isolated to professional historians, folklorists, anthropologists, and archivists. Such interviews have become an innovative model for pedagogy and transforming the classroom experience. Oral history has emerged as a powerful documentary tool in the contexts of conflict, transitional justice, and human rights. Over the years, oral historians have played a significant role in framing history and narrative in the context of the digital humanities. In addition to the work conducted by the relatively few dedicated oral history centers currently at the forefront of the practice, oral history projects are being launched by public libraries, museums, community archives, large and small companies, state and local historical societies, schools, churches, and even neighborhood associations.

While growth and popularity have pushed the traditional definitional aspects of oral history at times, definitions of oral history mostly involve interviewers, interviewees or narrators, research, questions, answers, stories, recorders and cameras, and sometimes transcripts and indexes. In his book *Doing Oral History*, Donald A. Ritchie begins his iconic definition like many others: "Oral history collects memories and personal commentaries of historical significance through recorded interviews. An oral history interview generally consists of a well-prepared interviewer questioning an interviewee and recording their exchange in audio or video format."[3] Ritchie continues where many others have stopped short in defining oral history: "Recordings of the interview are transcribed, summarized, or indexed and then placed in a library or archives."[4]

Archives play an important role in ensuring that the stories recorded in an oral history interview will survive through time and become part of the historical record. In the past two decades, the process of conducting and recording oral history interviews has remained consistent, but for archivists, much has changed related to managing legacy and born-digital oral history interviews. Like other formats described in this book, oral histories are frequent digital donations to archives from academic and community scholars, students, teachers, researchers, librarians and archivists, and various types of organizations. The sources of these donations range from professionally trained oral historians to general practitioners and researchers with some knowledge of oral history methodology and best practices to individuals who have little or no training in oral history but have a passionate commitment to their project. This chapter reviews various ways archivists manage incoming digital archives of oral history projects from these different groups. It draws on experiences of collecting oral histories for the Nunn Center.

EARLY PLANNING AND ORAL HISTORY PROJECT DESIGN

Like other types of digital donations, archivists must take an active role in preplanning and early consultation with the creators of the material. Archivists serve as important advisors to records creators of all types but especially with regard to those constructing and implementing oral history projects. Since its beginnings in 1973, the Nunn Center actively engaged outside partners such as academic and community scholars, students, and community groups in the early phases of oral history interviewing projects. While most libraries and archives may not have an oral history center with staff dedicated to oral-history-based collaboration, even a few simple conversations between archivists and oral history project leaders prior to the interview phase can address questions before they become long-term challenges.

Creating an early connection and dialogue between project partners, interviewers, and archivists can significantly shape a project's scope and help define future outcomes and also ensure mutual agreement and shared expectations between the project creators and donors and those who will be charged with curating the interviews into the future. Archivists can advise in determining the optimal equipment that will be used to record the interviews and how that equipment renders completed files. For example, the data storage needs created by a video project affects the storage costs incurred by the archives following the donation. The archives program may need ample time to budget for such a large donation, or they may decide that a format with such a large data file size is beyond their capabilities to curate and preserve.

Archives may have workflows in place that will optimally be articulated in advance of project implementation. For example, the Nunn Center requires project partners to play a part in describing each interview that is conducted. This involves the interviewer completing a simple informational form to describe the interview immediately following the completion of the interview, which is then included with each donation. This small act makes accessioning interviews much more efficient and adds important descriptive metadata directly from the creators. At any scale, archives programs rarely have the staffing and support to review the complete content of each new oral history donation, which means that most new accessions have limited descriptive metadata. Realistically speaking, it may take many years before archivists can accession these backlog donations and create basic interview-level metadata.

In some ways, the most important role archivists can play early in the project design phase is to advise project partners and interviewers on the appropriate permissions that will be necessary to best meet the needs of the interviewee/narrator, the project creator, and the archives program for the interviewing, research, production, publication, and, finally, the archival phase of the project. The project design phase is the optimal time for archivists and project leaders to discuss any ethical or legal considerations. Project partners and archivists may have different expectations with regard to "outcomes" of an oral history project. While the project designer is typically focused on how he or she will "use" the collection, the archivist is focused on how others will "reuse" the collection. If the project designer intends to donate his or her oral history project to an archives program, discussions about research use must take place. A scholar who is designing a project in order to write an ethnographic monograph will have editorial control over how to grapple with any ethical considerations that arise in an interview. However, once those interviews are turned over to the archives and made available for public access, the editorial control is often challenging to maintain. The archivist plays a crucial role in assisting the interviewer with defining informed consent regarding future archival reuse of the interviews. The concept of informed consent is often oversimplified when it is expressed to interviewees/narrators and focuses primarily on the interviewer's immediate project outcomes.

Input from archivists can play a significant role in defining and communicating the implications of future archival access to interviews following the completion of an oral history project. It is surprising to oral historians and general practitioners that archivists may not always be able to accept certain oral history interviews or collections as donations. This is sometimes the case if an interview represents content that may not be part of an archives program's collection scope or the repository cannot accommodate the recording format. More commonly, if the permissions, releases, or deeds of gift do not address the specific needs of that particular archives program, the archives may be unable to accept the oral history collection.

If the project designer, interviewer, or archivist is affiliated with an institution that requires review and preapproval by the local Institutional Review Board (IRB), it is important to incorporate the archives program into this process. For institutions that require IRB approval, it is imperative in the project design phase that IRB considerations are made in a way that integrates the archives. Too often, IRB application and approval are focused only on the interviewing and active research/publication phase of the oral history process, paying no attention to the archival phase. The Nunn Center has received numerous donations that include signed forms specified by the local IRB but lack any language pertaining to archival intentions or copyright.

Early conversations with archivists can help articulate a more comprehensive IRB application for approval and, more importantly, more clearly articulate the project intentions and the archival agreement so that informed consent can be better understood by all parties involved. In the past few years, the inclusion of oral history as research that required IRB review and approval has been fluid. For several years, there have been signals that oral history (and journalism) would no longer require IRB approval, but this movement has been slow and is often interpreted differently between institutions. Whether an institution requires IRB approval for oral history or not, it is important to stress that all participants consult and adhere to the *Principles and Best Practices* published by the Oral History Association.[5]

The essay "Designing an Oral History Project: Initial Questions to Ask Yourself" summarizes the most common questions to consider prior to implementing an oral history project. It focuses on communicating the importance of archival collaboration to project designers and interviewers. The questions ranged from the existential to the practical: "Why are you doing this project?" and "What is your desired outcome" to "What recording equipment will you use?" and "What are the legal and ethical questions you should be considering?" Each of the questions addressed in some way by an active archival partnership.[6]

The preplanning questions may be similar, but archivists leading oral history projects for their institutions have additional challenges. More and more archives are actively planning and conducting oral history interviewing projects of their own. Archivists leading an oral history project should go through the deliberate process of articulating a mission and a vision for the project that address the questions of "Why are you doing this project?" and "What is your desired outcome from this project?" Answers to these basic questions will help maintain focus and purpose throughout the entire process.

While archivists will never be able to connect with all future donors in the project design phase of every oral history project, it is important to build this into the institution's outreach and communications strategy. Future interviewers and project designers who are in the early phases of their process do not necessarily think to turn to an archivist before a project begins. Often, once these individuals are made aware of an archives program's expertise and willingness to partner, they will seek out that partnership and engage with the archives program. The Nunn Center regularly partners with thirty to forty outside individuals and organizations on interviewing initiatives. Approaching collaboration as an active and ongoing partnership has significantly enhanced the overall quality of the interviews and collections that are donated.

RECORDING TECHNOLOGIES

In general, oral histories should be recorded at the highest quality possible, with external microphones for each person participating in the interview. The Nunn Center provides recording equipment for project partners and has over thirty professional recording kits in circulation. Acknowledging that most archives will not have a dozen or more professional recording kits for their partner oral history projects, an archives program that is actively accessioning oral histories should consider loaning a few kits to outside partners. This will ensure that a project will have the capability to capture a high-quality recording.

No matter how expensive or high quality the recording equipment may be, however, the most important technical aspect of recording oral history is not the technology per se but the operator's mastery of the recording equipment. When an archives program provides the recording equipment, the archivist can have a more standardized approach to training and providing technical support on using the recording equipment. If the archives program does not provide recording kits, archivists who are accessioning oral history files should develop some familiarity with general recording techniques to advise future project partners. This will help elevate the general recording quality of the interviews that will eventually be donated to the archives program.

For decades, oral history was recorded with the goal of being "good enough" for transcription. Best practice is to capture the highest quality recording possible. Most project partners require significant training and time on the recorder before a recording kit is deployed in an actual interview setting. In addition to understanding the basic operation of an audio or video recorder, project partners should be encouraged to take the recording kit home to practice and learn how the audio recorder "listens." The Nunn Center does not currently loan video equipment; however, staff incorporate video recording into the training when necessary.

In the planning phase of oral history projects, leaders must decide if they will conduct audio or video interviews or even a mixture of the formats. The purposes of each project will drive this decision. Each option has advantages and disadvantages. Video recording collects more information about the interviewee, which may have greater potential for use. This option, however, comes with more responsibilities and costs. Interviews conducted on video will require far more resources, such as lights, a camera, and a videographer. The preservation of high-definition video data files (anywhere from thirty to one hundred GB per hour depending on format) or 4K video (which can be over three hundred GB per hour depending on format) will require significant budgetary, technical, and workflow considerations in advance of a project. The logistics of executing video projects are more complicated in terms of scheduling, selecting a location, lighting, framing, storage and preservation, and other variables not present with audio interviews. However, despite the challenges and complications of video, it can be a transformative medium for many oral history projects, especially with regard to future access and use of the collection. In 2017, the Nunn Center installed a video studio for capturing interviews. While this provided a very cost-effective way to capture video, storage costs for the digital files have increased significantly.

Audio-recorded oral histories may seem more "old fashioned" when compared to video, but there are some major advantages to this format. The primary advantage of audio is comfort of the interviewee. Video recording of interviews does involve a camera and lights that must be carefully adjusted and often the addition of a third person (the videographer) in the interview. Further, interviewees become far more comfortable and less self-conscious during an audio interview. Audio projects will be far less expensive than video interviews. The logistics are much simpler for audio interviews; the setup time is minutes rather than hours, and data file sizes for professionally recorded audio will be two GB per hour. A well-recorded audio project may in fact be much more valuable to researchers than a poorly recorded video project. Projects that include both audio and video recordings are becoming more common to highlight certain interviews and subjects with the most effective recording technology. At the same time, researchers are drawn to the details captured in video interviews. The Nunn Center's video recordings are consistently among the most accessed interviews.

Digital audio recordings should be recorded as 24-bit/96-kHz uncompressed WAV files. For video recording, the recommendation becomes more complex due to the variations in cameras and the formats created by the cameras. The challenges of creating and preserving video formats are many and beyond the scope of this chapter. For practitioners, the most important considerations for video interviews are to think through workflows, select formats that are sustainable and interoperable, and pick approaches that the archives program can afford to maintain. As a consideration, a digital video-based preservation package for a single digital video oral history interview now commonly exceeds 200 GB. This file size puts a great deal of pressure on the digital preservation efforts of any archival institution. Considering institutional capabilities with regard to preserving video oral history projects is crucial when working with potential donors or embarking on oral history projects.[7]

TRANSFERRING DIGITAL ORAL HISTORIES

Born-digital material, such as digitally recorded oral history interviews, can be challenging for donors to transfer to archives. The process was much

Douglas A. Boyd

simpler when oral historians and archivists used analog audio cassette tapes. When working with cassettes, the interviewer added information to the label of the cassette and then delivered the collection to the archives. The digital process can be a lot more precarious. The article "The Digital Mortgage: Digital Preservation of Oral History" describes the process and the challenges of digital oral history recordings:

> From the moment an interviewer presses the record button on an audio or video recorder, the interviewer becomes the curator or caretaker of a precious and fragile unique item. Ideally, at the moment of creation, the digital file has begun its journey from the interview context to a stable archival repository ready to ingest the digital file into a sophisticated digital preservation system.[8]

In the oral history context, a set of digital audio or video files can be transferred multiple times prior to the files' donation to the archives. Normally created on flash media such as an SDHC card, the typical project partner may wish to access the recording following the interview. As a common result, the data file then gets transferred from the original flash card to the hard drive on a personal computer. Since the typical project partner may be conducting multiple interviews, they may then erase the flash card in order to free up space on the card to conduct the next interview. When the project partner is ready to make the transfer of data to the archives, the series of audio or video files are often copied to a portable hard drive that is then given to an archivist. At that point, the archivist transfers the files from this portable hard drive, ingesting it into his or her preservation environment. In this model, the file undergoes a minimum of three transfers prior to accessioning.

There are several moments in the transfer process when the digital files are at risk. If the transfer from the original flash card to the personal hard drive fails, the original would have been erased when the project partner cleared off space on the card for the next interview. As a result, the interview is lost before it has been donated to the archives. Irretrievable loss often happens in the form of user error; however, unexplained data corruption is always a risk factor as well.

It is crucial that archivists educate and train project partners to be curators of their digital files prior to donation. This includes close work with project partners to develop workflows that lower the risk to the born-digital interviews and to limit the redundancy of files. The Nunn Center has taken a very "analog" approach to data transfer, which is designed to lower the risk of loss. Since flash media is relatively inexpensive, the Nunn Center provides project partners with enough flash media to record a single interview on each card. Archivists provide project partners with labeled envelopes. Once the interview is complete, the interviewers place the flash card and accompanying paperwork in the envelope. On the outside of the envelope is a preprinted label on which the names of the interviewee and interviewer, the project title, and the interview date are added immediately following the interview. Sometimes donors will drop off interview envelopes one at a time, and sometimes they will drop them off in bulk. It is paramount that archivists engage with the partners in simplified conversations regarding digital curation, data fixity, and redundancy and then forge a plan for data transfer that is comfortable for everyone.

While the envelope system is simple and effective for transfer, it is far from efficient. Seeking a more efficient and remote data transfer solution that would be simple to use and conform to digital preservation standards, I developed Exactly, a tool that creates a user-friendly application for a donor to transfer a digital oral history file to an archives program. Exactly utilizes the BagIt protocol, a digital preservation standard developed by the Library of Congress, to ensure that the fixity and data file integrity are intact upon receipt of the donation. This application utilizes BagIt in a way that does not require users to have advance technical and archival skills. Exactly features simple input lines, preset transfer protocols, and a large "transfer" button. It works via FTP and SFTP transfer protocols, but it also integrates with common tools such as Dropbox and Google Drive. Exactly also includes metadata templates for donors to complete and submit descriptive metadata with the preservation package. The Nunn Center uses this tool as a digital donation system to collect the files and metadata from a growing number of oral history practitioners and project partners. [9]

TRANSCRIPTION

Until recently, transcripts were the only way to optimize the discovery experience when accessing oral history. Transcription, however, also created expensive and burdensome expectations on the archives program. The Nunn Center determined that the most efficient model was to outsource transcription to professional transcription services and utilize students for the quality control and audit phase of the process. At the time of this writing, the going rate in the United States for manually created oral history interview transcripts is between $120 and $140 per interview hour. This estimation is for the completion of the first draft of a transcript. Best practice is to then conduct an audit of the draft transcript: listen to the audio, make detailed corrections to improve the textual alignment of the interview text with the audio, and correct spellings. Even with the help of students, this review makes the process even more expensive. For example, it would have cost the Nunn Center approximately $250,000 to manually transcribe and perform the final audit or authentication for the oral history collections that arrived in 2017 alone. Students are often not an option in the workflow, which means this burden is on archivists or volunteers. Archivists do not have the time to create the transcripts themselves, and it is rare to find a volunteer who is qualified and willing to transcribe interviews in an ongoing way.

The interview transcript was once viewed as the primary access point for oral history interviews in archives, but the high cost of manually generated transcripts has made large-scale transcription a challenge for most programs. The expectation is that a transcript is a verbatim textualization of what was spoken in the recording. While the verbatim aspect of a transcript is a definitional component of what the transcript is expected to be, the interpretation of "verbatim" adds a profound level of subjectivity to the practice. For example, the mere placement (or misplacement) of a comma in a transcribed sentence can completely change meaning. Further, transcriptions completed decades ago were designed to be read and not as an accompaniment to the audio. As a result, early transcribers made the transcripts more "readable," which often deviated in minor and major ways from what was actually spoken in the recorded interview. These practices also created a dilemma when correcting (in text) a known falsehood or "misremembrance" that was spoken. For example, an interviewee stated that he or she graduated from college in 1961, when in fact it was in 1962. The resulting transcript may indicate only the correct date of 1962, even though that was not what the interviewee stated. While these corrections were often handled as editorial insertions in a transcript, heavily edited transcripts can raise complex questions of primacy, authority, and authenticity with regard to the primary source. Several resources concerning best practices for transcribing oral history include the transcribing *Style Guide* published by Baylor University Institute for Oral History and the *Oral History Transcription Style Guide* published by Columbia University Center for Oral History Research.[10]

There have been tremendous advancements with regard to the use of automatic speech recognition (ASR) for use with oral history, but oral history poses many fundamental challenges when applying this technology.[11] Depending on recording quality, accents, and language, ASR can successfully produce a draft version of an interview transcript. Even when most successful, however, a transcript, if verbatim, requires significant cleanup. The expectation of verbatim transcription is a costly goal. While ASR-generated text is far from perfect, it can be very useful for potentially automating the creation of item-level metadata and providing some opportunities for enhancing discovery for users. It can be used by an archives program to efficiently produce a useful draft transcript and automatically create keywords and subjects with more complete descriptive metadata at the time of accession.

METADATA AND DESCRIPTION

There is a massive amount of complex information being communicated throughout an oral history interview, which is compounded exponentially when the interview is part of a larger oral history project or collection. Comprehensive descriptive metadata is the obvious solution to the challenges posed by information overload at both the interview and collection levels. Descriptive metadata at the collection level frames the general concepts that are represented in an archival grouping of oral history interviews. For example, the Nunn Center's "From Combat to Kentucky Oral History Project" provides access to forty-two interviews. Much like a scope and content note for an archival collection, the project webpage introduces the corpus of the interviews through collection-level descriptive metadata and subject headings.[12] An inventory of interviews conducted as part of this project follows the collection description. The inventory contains interview-level descriptive metadata elements, such as interviewee name, interviewer name, interview date, and any noted restrictions. Through browsing, online researchers may click individual records in order to access interview-level metadata. Many of the interviews contain keywords, subject terms, and a description of the content. This sort of interview-level metadata increases the likelihood of effective discovery and engagement with the collection. The challenge for all archives programs is being able to create quality descriptive metadata from thousands of hours of untextualized recordings; thus most oral history collections only have collection-level metadata records.

Current approaches to describing oral history backlogs and incoming digital archives of interviews are, in some ways, similar to how archivists have implemented the More Product, Less Process (MPLP) method for processing backlog archival collections.[13] The notion that archivists would describe, in detail, every single photograph or piece of paper donated to the archives program is unrealistic. Similarly, archivists would not have the time to listen to every minute of recorded audio or video in an oral history collection in order to effectively make the collection discoverable. However, vague collection-level metadata is of little use to the researcher in search of specific information embedded within collections. Since effective discovery experiences working with oral history require detailed metadata describing the specific contents of each interview, it is necessary to explore more efficient ways of creating this descriptive metadata at the item level in order for oral history content to be more discoverable and useful to researchers.

As noted earlier, archivists should advise interviewers and project designers to record some basic information immediately following the interview. Prior to the interview, the interviewer should gather as much information about the interviewee/narrator and the expected topics as possible. This not only makes the questions and conversation much more useful, it creates valuable descriptive metadata for future contextualization and discovery. The Nunn Center developed a protocol for interviewers- and project managers to create some baseline information for each interview. This method encourages the interviewer to immediately reflect on each interview by recording information about the people involved (names, addresses, email addresses, and telephone numbers) and list five to ten keywords that describe important topics or subjects, major themes, and geographic locations discussed in the interview. The protocol suggests that the interviewer write a few sentences to describe and summarize the content and major themes expressed in the interview. The resulting list of keywords, names of people and places mentioned in the interview, and a synopsis of the interview represents important descriptive metadata.

As another path to collecting descriptive information, the Nunn Center's interview information form has become a standard part of documenting each donation of oral histories in advance of accessioning. The form creates a baseline of descriptive metadata prior to the point of accession, which is then used to create a basic accession record for each interview. This simple adjustment to the typical workflow has been transformative for discovery and efficiency.

DISCOVERY AND ACCESS

One of the reasons individuals create oral history projects is to include individual stories as part of the historical record. However, the most cumbersome archival challenges posed by oral history collections relate to access. Archivists provide long-term access to recorded sound and video interviews, but without some form of textual representation, such as transcripts or metadata, researchers cannot efficiently search, discover, navigate, and effectively access the content. In a 2006 essay, oral historian Mike Frisch writes,

> Everyone recognizes that the core audio-video dimension of oral history is notoriously underutilized. The nicely cataloged but rarely consulted shelves of audio and video cassettes in even the best media and oral history libraries are closer than most people realize to that shoebox of unviewed home-video camcorder cassettes in so many families—precious documentation that is inaccessible and generally unlistened to and unwatched.[14]

There are many forgotten oral history projects sitting in boxes or on shelves for decades with no known use by researchers. At the heart of oral history's discovery and access challenges is when the audio or video recordings are completely untextualized. Historically, oral history practitioners perceived an oral history interview recording without a transcript as unfinished and incomplete. Without a transcript, many researchers are unable to take the time or are disinterested in listening to a lengthy oral history recording. Visually or textually scanning transcripts is far more efficient than trying to listen to dozens of hours of interviews. Textualization of the recording transforms the discovery experience for the researcher. The untextualized audio or video recording is, almost always, a disappointing and challenging second choice for the researcher requesting access to an interview. Unfortunately, most oral history collections in archives do not have transcripts, so the untextualized audio and video go unused and undiscovered.

In the past decade, the Nunn Center refocused its efforts to efficiently process incoming collections and to create new approaches to enhancing access to its extensive oral history collection. In 2009, I designed and implemented OHMS (the Oral History Metadata Synchronizer), a web-based application designed to enhance access to online oral histories. OHMS connects the users from a textual search of an interview transcript or index to the corresponding moment in the online audio or video recording. The goal was to more efficiently connect users to the interview itself, rather than limit use to a textual representation.

Indexing in OHMS allows archivists to create segment or story-level metadata, which includes a title, partial transcript, synopsis, keywords, subjects, GPS coordinates, and hyperlinks to external resources, such as a photograph that represents the content being discussed in the segment. The resulting index generates natural language terms that map to meaningful topics for searching and discovery. Those search results then connect to specific moments in the actual interview. The OHMS indexing process does not replace existing transcripts or make transcription work obsolete, but it is a powerful and inexpensive option (approximately one-tenth of the cost of transcription) to provide enhanced access to oral history interviews.[15]

In 2012, the Nunn Center received a grant from the Institute for Museum and Library Services (IMLS) to assist in making the extant version of OHMS a free and open-source system for use by small and large archives programs. Publicly released in 2014, OHMS is now being utilized to enhance access to online oral history collections by institutions all over the world. At the Nunn Center, OHMS has transformed users' experiences and altered workflows. Enhanced access is now the expectation, and at the time of writing, the Nunn Center's online interface averages ten thousand to twelve thousand uses of oral history interviews each month.

As more archives implement OHMS, leaders of oral history projects expect that their donations will be quickly indexed and made available online. The Nunn Center creates an average of nearly one thousand indices each year but does not have the capacity to index all incoming interviews. The use of OHMS has also changed how the donors or creators of the material organize their digital content. For example, in 2017, the Nunn Center received an oral history collection of sixty-four interviews documenting experiences during Hurricane Sandy. This collection was created in 2013 by students at Kean University under the leadership of Dr. Abigail Perkiss. What made this donation unique was the fact that the digital oral history interviews in this collection were accompanied by OHMS indexes created by students in an introductory digital humanities course at Stockton University in 2014. The students, in this case the creators, used OHMS to index the interviews prior to donation.[16]

Today, there are numerous simple and free options for presenting oral history online. Increasingly, platforms such as WordPress, Drupal, and Omeka, when combined with the OHMS user experience, provide incredibly powerful frameworks for presenting oral history project websites and digital exhibits. In 2018, the Nunn Center will release a suite of plug-ins for integrating OHMS with Omeka. The combination of these two systems provides a user-friendly and free platform for creating project exhibits and websites that become a powerful opportunity to digitally connect archives, the community, and donors.

ETHICS, RIGHTS, AND PERMISSIONS

Archivists leading or partnering with oral history projects must consider the various legal and ethical issues that may arise during the interviewing, archival, and publication phases of a project. Even the most mundane oral history project can involve significant privacy risks. There was a tremendous safety when analog tapes and transcripts were waiting for researchers in archival boxes on the shelves of archival repositories. Because few people utilized oral history sources and "publication" mostly meant an interview would be quoted in a print publication that would have low academic distribution, the risk was relatively low.

Today, online access to oral history's audio and video recordings and searchable transcripts or indexes is the expectation of researchers and a stated outcome for project leaders. Audio recorders contain Wi-Fi chips, which make it possible for interviewers to upload a file to SoundCloud moments after completing the interview. After files are reviewed and added to online collections, it only takes a day or two for Google to crawl the content of new interviews. Further, free tools such as OHMS provide granular access to individual moments in audio and video interviews. What is recorded and released to the public now is much more accessible and discoverable than just a decade ago. While greater access and discovery experiences to oral history collections have long been the goal of archivists, this means that one of the most personal primary sources in archival collections is now accessible and shareable with anyone who has an internet connection. It is crucial that archivists and project partners work together to better understand and assess potential risk, secure the proper paperwork, and, most important, better define informed consent in this new era of digital access.

If informed consent is the most important goal, the interview deed of gift is the most important piece of documentation collected during oral history projects. Archivists, trained practitioners, and other interviewers must understand the significance of the deed of gift. For all types of oral history projects, the best practice is to have the interviewee or narrator sign a deed of gift following the interview. Of course, the interviewer conducting the session should discuss this document with the interviewee prior to the actual recording. Signing a deed of gift after the interview is completed should be a simple step in the process and not a surprise to the interviewee.[17] The Oral History Association's "Principles for Oral History and Best Practices for Oral History" clarifies rights and ownership issues for oral history projects. The document explains:

> Interviewees hold the copyright to their interviews until and unless they transfer those rights to an individual or institution. This is done by the interviewee signing a release form or in exceptional circumstances recording an oral statement to the same effect. Interviewers must insure that narrators understand the extent of their rights to the interview and the request that those rights be yielded to a repository or other party, as well as their right to put restrictions on the use of the material. All use and dissemination of the interview content must follow any restrictions the narrator places upon it.[18]

The Nunn Center regularly provides the option for interviewees or interviewers to restrict interviews or collections at the point of donation to the archives program. The deed of gift used by the Nunn Center includes restrictions for the interviewees to limit access for a number of years or during their lifetimes. These two options both have finite end points. The Nunn Center also allows a third category for customized restrictions, such as limiting access until a book is published. The challenge is to combine this customary form of restriction with an additional, finite end point, such as a specific date for removal of the restriction since, using this example, not all books are published.

A "sealed" or restricted interview is an agreement between the interviewee, project partner, and the archives program to prohibit or manage permissions regarding public access to interviews. For decades, the "unanswered question" was whether an archival restriction could stand up to legal requests, such as an open records request or a subpoena. In 2011, a legal case involving Boston College and an oral history project documenting detailed life stories and activities of former members of the Irish Republican Army became the definitive precedent. This case was complex, but the outcome for archives was clear. Archival restrictions will not hold up in the face of a legal subpoena.[19]

Search engines such as Google and archival discovery tools such as OHMS have changed the process and capabilities of access for oral history collections. While the intention of these technologies is to promote access and research, archivists must work with donors and project partners to minimize any potential privacy risks to interviewees or narrators. A good oral history interview focusing on life history could discuss a person's parents, a person's education, and a person's childhood friends. With those three facts, in addition to an email address, someone could potentially reset an interviewee's bank password or have access to other deeply personal information.

The concept of informed consent must be dynamic and changing. Pre-internet consent meant something altogether different from consent today. It is the responsibility of project designers, interviewers, and archivists to convey a realistic sense for what archival access to oral history means. The act of oral history interviewing creates a trust relationship between interviewer and interviewee. If the archival institution is not part of the interviewing project from the beginning, then it is the responsibility of archivists to understand what type of promises were made and the original level of consent given. Without a clear sense of the parameters of the agreement between the interviewer and the interviewee, then archivists can only rely on the terms of the deed of gift when creating access to the resulting collection. At the same time, the archives program assumes potential risks for the content that they are, in effect, publishing to an unrestricted public platform. The act of providing access to a massive amount of personal information puts individuals and archives programs at potential risk.

The article "Informed Accessioning: Questions to Ask after the Interview" describes a reflective assessment process created for the Nunn Center to "consider and document the presence of sensitive, problematic, or deeply personal details" prior to providing access to the interviews.[20] For the Nunn Center, this reflection and assessment occurs at two points in the life cycle of an oral history interview. The first assessment occurs immediately following the interview and is conducted by the interviewer. The second assessment occurs when archivists work directly with the interviews to either transcribe or, when using OHMS, to index an interview. At both of these points, the assessor (interviewer/archivist) is most acutely aware of what is being said in this interview at the detailed level. The reflective assessment involves the interviewer or the archivist working with the material to ask himself or herself the following questions and include his or her answers with the interview documentation:

1. Does the interview contain personal information, such as a physical address, healthcare information, a phone number, a social security number, or anything else that potentially poses a privacy risk?
2. Does this interview contain confidential or sensitive information about anyone, such as discussions of personal tragedies, medical conditions, sexual abuse, or violence?
3. Does this interview contain criminal allegations against another party?
4. Does this interview contain potentially slanderous or libelous language pertaining to another living person?
5. Does this interview reveal institutional, trade, or corporate secrets?
6. Does this interview use culturally insensitive language?[21]

Affirmative answers to any of these questions do not result in archivists editing, restricting, or censoring the content. Instead, this information creates a sense of informed accessioning that empowers an archival institution with knowledge of the contents of a donated oral history interview. With this knowledge, archivists can make better decisions with regard to future access. For both born-digital and legacy collections, this reflective assessment is crucial to determining if sensitive content exists and what risks might be associated by providing online access to the interview.

PERSPECTIVES

Oral history interviewing today is experiencing an explosive phase of growth inside and outside of the academy. There is a major increase in the general awareness of oral history as a practice in the public consciousness. The relationship between archivists and oral history practitioners is emerging as more of a continuous and collaborative partnership rather than a transactional relationship. The closer work between archivists and oral history donors results in making donations of digital archives more accessible and available to researchers much faster than ever before.

Although archivists do not need to be experts in all aspects of the oral history process in order to effectively engage with creators of oral history collections, archivists who work with oral historians or oral history collections would benefit from actively seeking a core frame of reference with regard to the phases of the oral history process. Training sessions, workshops, professional literature outside of the archival domain, ally organizations such as the Oral History Association, and available online resources such as "Oral History in the Digital Age" are effective ways for archivists to seek out professional development opportunities, remain current on best practices for preserving and providing access to oral history, and also better understand the project design and interviewing phases of oral history projects.

Oral history is most useful when discovery is optimized. Optimal discovery environments have, in the past, required exhaustive resources, resources that simply have not been affordable for most archives. This is changing. Archives now have powerful and inexpensive tools to efficiently process, preserve, and provide innovative access to oral history materials. Through active and sustained collaboration and engagement, individuals, communities, and archives can work together to overcome the challenges and limitations of the past. Enhanced access to incoming and past digital donations of oral history materials may, in fact, change the historical record in truly profound and potentially transformational ways.

NOTES

1. Oral History in the Digital Age, http://ohda.matrix.msu.edu.

2. Gary L. Shumway, *Oral History in the United States: A Directory* (New York: Oral History Association, 1971).

3. Donald A. Ritchie, *Doing Oral History: A Practical Guide*, 2nd ed. (New York: Oxford University Press, 2003), 19.

4. Ibid.

5. Oral History Association, *Principles and Best Practices for Oral History*, 2009, http://www.oralhistory.org/about/principles-and-practices/.

6. Douglas A. Boyd, "Designing an Oral History Project: Initial Questions to Ask Yourself," Oral History in the Digital Age, 2012, http://ohda.matrix.msu.edu/2012/06/designing-an-oral-history-project/.

7. Douglas A. Boyd, "Case Study: Is Perfect the Enemy of Good Enough? Digital Video Preservation in the Age of Declining Budgets," Oral History in the Digital Age, 2012, http://ohda.matrix.msu.edu/2012/06/is-perfect-the-enemy-of-good-enough/.

8. Douglas A. Boyd, "The Digital Mortgage: Digital Preservation of Oral History," Oral History in the Digital Age, 2012, http://ohda.matrix.msu.edu/2012/06/the-digital-mortgage/.

9. Bertram Lyons, "Exactly: New Tool for Digital File Acquisitions," *AVP* (blog), January 13, 2016, https://www.weareavp.com/exactly-a-new-tool-for-digital-file-acquisitions/.

10. Baylor University Institute for Oral History, *Style Guide: A Quick Reference for Editing Oral History*, 2015, https://www.baylor.edu/oralhistory/index.php?id=931752; Columbia University Center for Oral History Research, *Oral History Transcription Style Guide*, 2018, http://www.ccohr.incite.columbia.edu/services-resources/.

11. Doug Oard, "Can Automatic Speech Recognition Replace Manual Transcription?" Oral History in the Digital Age, 2012, http://ohda.matrix.msu.edu/2012/06/automatic-speech-recognition/.

12. "American Veterans: From Combat to Kentucky, Student Veterans Oral History Project," Louie B. Nunn Center for Oral History, University of Kentucky Libraries, https://kentuckyoralhistory.org/catalog/xt734t6f4g1b.

13. Mark Greene and Dennis Meissner, "More Product, Less Process: Revamping Traditional Archival Processing," *American Archivist* 68 (Fall/Winter 2005): 208–63.

14. Michael Frisch, "Oral History and the Digital Revolution: Toward a Post-documentary Sensibility," in *The Oral History Reader*, eds. Robert B. Perks and Alistair Thomson, 2nd ed. (London: Routledge, 2006), 102.

15. Douglas A. Boyd, "OHMS: Enhancing Access to Oral History for Free," *Oral History Review* 40 (January 2013): 95–106.

16. Dan Royles, "Teaching Digital Humanities with Oral History: The Staring out to Sea Oral History Project and OHMS in the DH Classroom," *Oral History Review* 43 (September 2016): 408–20.

17. John A. Neuenschwander, *A Guide to Oral History and the Law*, 2nd ed. (Oxford: Oxford University Press, 2014).

18. Oral History Association, *Principles and Best Practices*, 2009.

19. John A. Neuenschwander, "Major Legal Challenges Facing Oral History in the Digital Age," Oral History in the Digital Age, 2014, http://ohda.matrix.msu.edu/2012/06/major-legal-challenges/; Society of American Archivists Oral History Section, "Archives, Oral History and the Belfast Case: A Re-focused Discussion," 2013, https://www2.archivists.org/groups/oral-history-section/the-belfast-case-information-for-saa-members.

20. Douglas A. Boyd, "Informed Accessioning: Questions to Ask after the Interview," Oral History in the Digital Age, 2015, http://ohda.matrix.msu.edu/2015/03/informed-accessioning-questions-to-ask-after-the-interview/.

21. Ibid.

Chapter Eight

Architectural and Design Collections

Aliza Leventhal

As the corpus of this book demonstrates, digital records are complex and require expertise and resources that archivists and archives have had to quickly (as quick as archivists can) adapt to the demands of the hybrid (digital and analog) collections being donated. Digital design records are no exception and have created additional anxiety for archivists of these subject-specific collections due the variance in the software producing these records and their limited relationship with the broader digital preservation world on this niche discipline. As a result, best practices for the preservation and access of digital design collections are still in their infancy.

The digital drafting and modeling tools that can be classified as computer-aided design (CAD) and building information modeling (BIM) software are what come to mind most often when thinking about the landscape of digital design records. While this is not inaccurate, it is an oversimplified assessment. The entire architecture and design business, like most businesses, has gone almost entirely digital—accounting to project management to contract deliverables. Additionally, the blanket CAD and BIM categories poorly represent the numerous file types that make up the "alphabet soup" of records produced throughout the career of a designer.

In 2012, the Architectural Records Roundtable, now the Design Records Section, of the Society of American Archivists (SAA) established the CAD/BIM Taskforce. Since that time, this group has worked to establish best practices for the accessioning, processing, describing, preserving, and providing access to digital design records. The work of this taskforce has been framed by both discussions within the Design Records Section's membership

Table 8.1.   Files and formats in architectural and design records

.DWG	.DXF	.DGN	.RVT	.RTE	.WRM
.SHP	.BMP	.MB	.STEP	.STL	.3DM
.PPT	.XLSX	.DOCX	.PDF	.SKP	.BZM
.AI	.PSD	.INDD	.JPG	.TIF	.GIF
.PY3	.DYF	.MP4	.MPEG4	.F4V	.VRMAT

and the work that has been done so far by the greater archival community around tools and workflows to document and store files and data.[1] The taskforce first compiled a bibliography of significant research efforts on the preservation of complex digital design and design-related (e.g., GIS data) records and then surveyed the existing holdings of archives collecting architecture and design records.[2] Following the 2016 SAA annual meeting, the taskforce developed reference resources to introduce archivists to the various design software that will be needed to access digital files in architectural collections. During the 2017–2018 academic year, the taskforce explored the frequently asked questions of archivists working with digital design records and how to better utilize the donor agreement to ensure the necessary information and resources are included with the donation.

Digital design records pose new challenges that require archivists to be proactive and technologically savvy. Hardware and software obsolescence are well understood issues in the archival field, which are further compounded by the expensive, proprietary, and quickly changing versions of design software. Additional intervention by archivists throughout the cycle of records creation is crucial to the success of collecting digital design materials. Although archivists are decades behind in starting these conversations with architects and other design records creators, it is not too late to catch up and get ahead of the foreseeable digital challenges. Archivists need to reach out and engage with current record creators and potential donors early on to raise their awareness of the challenges and value that their records hold. These very conversations have been happening more publicly at meetings such as the Designing the Future Landscape: Digital Architectural, Design, and Engineering Assets Summit," hosted by the Library of Congress, the Architect of the Capitol, and the National Gallery of Art; and the Building for Tomorrow Forum, funded by the Institute of Museum and Library Services (IMLS). These recent events attracted a broad spectrum of stakeholders from practitioners and academics to technologists and archivists.[3] By taking preemptive measures to understand the context about the workflow and materials in the anticipated collections, archivists can confront many of the additional technological challenges and better understand the environment where those records were created.

This chapter analyzes the who, what, and how of digital design records. The "who" covers a brief history of architectural archives advocacy, the issues that leaders have addressed in developing donor relations, and some of the changes to that dynamic with consideration for new digital records challenges. The "what" provides an overview of the most prevalent design software and compares the digital files to their analog predecessors that have been superbly covered in Waverly Lowell and Tawny Ryan Nelb's *Architectural Records: Managing Design and Construction Records.*[4] Recognizing that the future holds untold and possibly greater challenges than we can anticipate at present, the "how" offers recommendations for archivists to approach their digital design records and better prepare their institutions to collect these digital archives.

WHO

Collecting Institutions

Design records have been a constant challenge for archivists to collect. Design records are collected by institutions around the world, all with unique collection policies that determine which designers and firms they collect records from and what types of records they collect. Design archives are located within academic institutions, museums, cultural institutions, and government agencies. The type of collecting institution, its collecting policy, and its resource and staff capacities, all affect what types of records an institution can or chooses to collect. From the oldest collections in the United States established by Columbia University's Avery Library and the Library of Congress's Prints and Photographs Division to the relatively young collections of the University of California, Berkeley's Environmental Design Archives (founded in 1953) and the Canadian Centre for Architecture in Montreal (founded in 1979), collecting design records has been a strategic and focused effort.[5] Digital design records have a significant cost associated with them to have the necessary infrastructure and staff expertise to properly process, preserve, and provide access; as a result, many institutions have been cautious in bringing digital design records into their holdings.

The proactive conversations and happenings around digital design records today are built upon the early efforts focused on analog records, which began in 1973 with establishment of the Cooperative Preservation of Architectural Records (COPAR). The group focused on the preservation of architectural materials and coordinated the formation of local and state groups called "committees of COPARs." Throughout the late 1970s and into the early 1980s, COPARs promoted regional advocacy and educational programs focused on architectural records. The groups worked directly with collecting institutions, practicing architects, and architecture firms to support the preservation of architectural records within offices and advise on the donation of design records to archives.[6]

The collecting policies of institutions specifically focused on design records have diverse motivations that include: their current students, faculty, or alumni; a geographic region; women or specific demographic of designers; or a specific design style or period of designers. Every building is the result of design and construction records, which results in design records appearing in collections at institutions beyond those with defined collecting policies. This ubiquity is why understanding the information the records hold and what the best practices are for preserving, describing, and providing access is crucial and should be of interest beyond the niche community.

Architectural and design archivists have continued to employ the proactive approaches used by the COPARs, especially as the use of computers became standard within the design professions. This has even led, in some cases, to institutions creating decades-long relationships and ongoing deed of gift agreements with active architects and designers. This donor model allows for a more thoughtful and gradual accessioning of materials rather than the more rushed or less contextualized donations that can come from the retirement of an individual, the closing of a practice, or the posthumous donation. This type of early intervention by archivists with records creators helps contain some of the additional frustration or confusion expected while accessing and interpreting the digital materials.

Some of the early digital design collections, such as those featured in the Canadian Centre for Architecture's three-part exhibition *Archaeology of the Digital*, demonstrate the experimental nature of early technology adopters within the architecture and design world.[7] While some of the experiments have become normalized features of current CAD, BIM, and similar software, much of that early work was difficult to replicate, interpret, and access. Further, the practices of current designers and their approach to technology have changed dramatically. These early projects exemplify the importance of contextual conversations with the creators. Such conversations set a precedent for designers to push the technology at their disposal, not only to create more challenging geometric designs and structures but also to manipulate the technology beyond its intended function. The latter resulted in the import and export of files and data across software to facilitate more interdisciplinary work.

These first experiments and collaborations illustrate a central point: the designer's approach to digital design is just as much an artistic expression as his or her analog-based drawings and sketches are. In the digital realm, they appear more constrained and rote due to the tools and features each program provides and thus are not as readily appreciated for their artistic quality. It is important to articulate the nuance of each designer's use of software to realize his or her artistic and design expression.

Donors

The majority of design records collected are related either to a specific designer, design firm, or firms in related fields, such as real estate or development, that have a portfolio of properties. Occasionally, an entire collection is based on a specific project, place, or building. As briefly mentioned earlier in this chapter, design records are typically donated at the end of a career, the closing of a firm, or posthumously. These traditionally timed donations were more easily accepted and processed when the records were paper based, but with the rise of digital records, this significant lag time between creation and donation causes substantial challenges for preserving and providing access to the files.

Recognizing this issue, institutions and donors have become more proactive and are developing new donor agreements and donation schedules. Yale University's Architectural Archives collaborates directly with designers and their firms. Yale archivists and company archivists make collective decisions about what analog and digital content from closed projects should be transferred to Yale or kept by the firm. Through this relationship, similar to the donations made for the *Archaeology of the Digital* exhibit, the institution and designers have an open line of communication. Because of the frequent exchange, archivists are able to learn more about the designer's intent, techniques, workflows, and tools; this facilitates better description and access mitigation by the institutional archivist, which benefits researchers.

There are significant benefits to earlier intervention of archivists with their potential future donors, but there are also concerns about overextending the archivist's influence over the selection of materials donated. Appraisal and accessioning guidelines must be flexible, just as archivists must be aware of new types of records produced by their donor community. Archivists are committed to facilitating access to original records rather than being curators of historical documentation. Experience has shown that what records a donor finds valuable may differ from the collecting interests of the archives. Close communication and sharing collection development strategies of the program are effective ways to clarify what archivists can and cannot do to help their donors.[8]

The appraisal grid provided in Lowell and Nelb's *Architectural Records: Managing Design and Construction Records* serves as starting point for potential donors to determine which types of records have enduring value.[9] By creating a more symbiotic relationship, or framework for those relationships to develop, archivists can help designers identify research value in their project records beyond their immediate utilitarian purpose. This approach results in the added benefit of collecting more comprehensive and contextualized project records.

Researchers

Design records have a traditional researcher community of architectural historians. With the development of digital design records, the potential research pool broadens as the records themselves include a wider range of topics, including software, programming, and the actual designs. As new techniques and tools are developed, so are new academic disciplines, such as software studies and the more established digital humanities. As demonstrated by panelists at the 2017 Designing the Future Summit, hybrid technologists and architectural historians were the first researcher groups to use these collections. They understood the capabilities and purpose of the software used and also the nuanced designs created with that software. Early forays into this research have included documenting the user community's response of version upgrades of a specific software (e.g., Rhinoceros 3D), applying digital forensics to expose the digital palimpsest and evolution of a design, and establishing a language of design, such as building off of the concept of shape grammar first introduced in the 1980s.[10]

This type of research, much like digital design collections in archives, is still relatively new, and without more examples of how the records *can* be used, it is difficult for the archival community to confidently establish standards for how researchers might access and use content. At the 2017 Designing the Future Summit, this discussion came up several times, revealing that practitioners, archivists, technologists, and scholars were all looking to each other to determine what was both the realistic and ideal level of access to provide users of digital design records. Because digital records can be easily duplicated and because the file directory of these records can be significant to scholars, it would be advisable and useful to this community to have unfettered access to both the files and the digital environment (suites of software and any unique hardware they were created in). It would be incredibly expensive and difficult to provide this level of support. The disruptive nature of digital design software on the design profession has had a ripple effect on archival and scholastic professions interested in these records, requiring additional skills from the former and opening up new lines of inquiry for the latter.

WHAT

As predicted by Genevieve Greenwald-Katz in 1976, the speedy adoption of software within the design world would need to provide a way for architects to do things they cannot do, do well, or are not interested in doing.[11] The expense of computers and the limitations of early versions of software from the 1960s through the early 1990s meant that these technologies were only used by a small group of avant-garde designers cum technologists. The experimental records of that group of early adopters demonstrated some of the most difficult challenges that digital design records pose for archivists.[12] Similarly, the software produced by architects and designers, such as Frank Gehry's Gehry Technologies, Beverly Willis's CARLA, and Sasaki's Smart-Plan, exemplified the creativity and technical capabilities of designers impatient for tools to support the work they envisioned. With such variation of file types and software used, archivists are concerned about deciphering the nuances and intention of files, identifying authorship and provenance of the collaborative work within a single file, and understanding how the software functioned at the time the record was produced (vs. current versions of that software).[13]

Since it was first released in December 1982, Autodesk's AutoCAD software has held a monopoly on the market. This early software offered architects many of the capabilities identified by Greenwald-Katz to improve the designer's daily workflow. More recently, Autodesk's Revit software allows architects to create and quickly adjust 3D models. AutoCAD and later Revit in the 2010s represent disruptive technologies of their respective times for the field of architecture. Disruptive innovation or technology was widely introduced in the mid-1990s and refers to the products that create new markets and competitive advantages. AutoCAD introduced simplified utilization of parametric geometry and thus removed limitations of time and difficult calculations so designers could more quickly test complex constructions. Similarly, Revit removed additional barriers that CAD had not addressed, including the incorporation of product-specific components, simplified batch changes to categories of components, and additional layers of data about the site and the functionality of the building.

As a result, files created using AutoCAD and Revit are the most commonly found design-specific formats in the collections of architecture and design firms and architectural archives. This near monopoly was confirmed in the responses to two surveys conducted by the SAA's Design Records Section's CAD/BIM Taskforce in 2015 and 2016. The below figures demonstrate overlap in the software used by active firms (figure 8.1) and those in existing collections with institutional archivists (figure 8.2). Figure 8.2 gives archivists an idea of what software they can expect to see in future collections. Architects and designers follow the precedent of the early digital design adopters by challenging the limits of the latest software, promoting the interoperability of data and file types, and encouraging others to develop technological skills such as script writing.

Despite the changing landscape of design documentation, there are some parallels between digital and analog design records. For analog architectural records, archivists identified four general categories of material: project list, files, photographs, and drawings.[14] For digital materials, software allows architects to create three broad types of content: plans and models, rendering, and project data. These categories reflect the changing language and outputs of modern designers and thus are not exact replacements for the analog categories. The three groupings attempt to provide some context for understanding how the software in the modern designer's arsenal are used and help the researcher decipher the purpose of the files associated with a project.[15]

Plans and Models

Software programs focused on creating plans and models have replaced traditional design drawings that will be part of the contractual deliverables.

8.1: What software does your firm currently support and/or use?

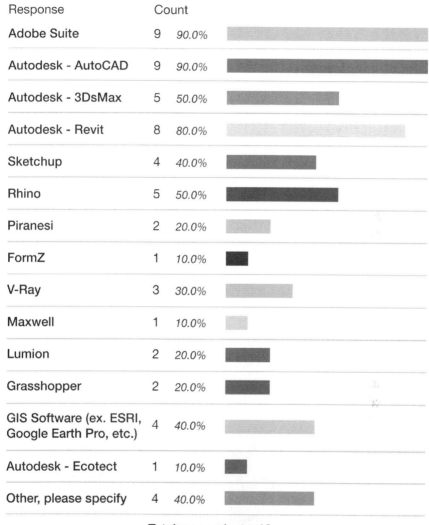

Response	Count	
Adobe Suite	9	90.0%
Autodesk - AutoCAD	9	90.0%
Autodesk - 3DsMax	5	50.0%
Autodesk - Revit	8	80.0%
Sketchup	4	40.0%
Rhino	5	50.0%
Piranesi	2	20.0%
FormZ	1	10.0%
V-Ray	3	30.0%
Maxwell	1	10.0%
Lumion	2	20.0%
Grasshopper	2	20.0%
GIS Software (ex. ESRI, Google Earth Pro, etc.)	4	40.0%
Autodesk - Ecotect	1	10.0%
Other, please specify	4	40.0%

Total respondents: 10

Figure 8.1. What software does your firm currently support and/or use?

These are also the most ubiquitous software programs throughout the architecture, engineering, and construction (AEC) industries. Autodesk's Auto-

8.2: What file formats do you have in your holdings?

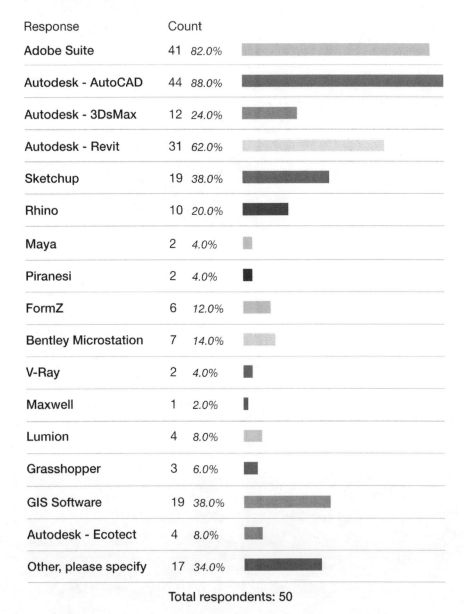

Response	Count	
Adobe Suite	41 *82.0%*	
Autodesk - AutoCAD	44 *88.0%*	
Autodesk - 3DsMax	12 *24.0%*	
Autodesk - Revit	31 *62.0%*	
Sketchup	19 *38.0%*	
Rhino	10 *20.0%*	
Maya	2 *4.0%*	
Piranesi	2 *4.0%*	
FormZ	6 *12.0%*	
Bentley Microstation	7 *14.0%*	
V-Ray	2 *4.0%*	
Maxwell	1 *2.0%*	
Lumion	4 *8.0%*	
Grasshopper	3 *6.0%*	
GIS Software	19 *38.0%*	
Autodesk - Ecotect	4 *8.0%*	
Other, please specify	17 *34.0%*	

Total respondents: 50

Figure 8.2. What file formats do you have in your holdings?

Table 8.2. Categories of digital materials for architectural and design records

Plans and Models	Rendering	Project Data
AutoCAD	V-Ray	Esri ArcGIS
MicroStation	Lumion	Google Earth Pro
ARCHICAD	Maxwell Render	Ecotect
CATIA	3dsMax	Honey Bee*
Revit	Maya	Dragonfly*
SketchUp	form•Z	Elk*
Rhino	Piranesi	Butterfly*
Grasshopper	Adobe Creative Suite	Ladybug*
Dynamo*		
Civil3D*		

CAD and Revit products are the most popular software packages among designers for producing the contractual deliverable documents; however, there are similarly functioning CAD programs such as Bentley Systems' MicroStation, ARCHICAD, and CATIA. The transition from CAD to BIM, a market almost entirely dominated by Revit, represents a shift from a strong 2D drawing tool that replicates the sketching process with its layers functionality to a robust 3D tool that builds all views of a structure simultaneously and captures significant metadata about the model. Each software has its own strengths and supports the work of architecture, landscape architecture, civil engineering, and other built-work design fields.

A brief history of a few Autodesk products demonstrates the rapid development of business-crucial software for architects and designers. Since the introduction of AutoCAD in 1982, the company has released thirty-one different versions of the popular software.[16] In comparison, Autodesk first released Revit in 2000, and in less than twenty years, it has gone through thirty different version releases. The constant version updates have created issues for practicing architects, who are not able to easily open files created in the newer versions of the software using older software and may lose data when they open files created in older software versions when they open them in newer versions. The complications of forward and backward compatibility are not unique to these products, but this challenge is particularly difficult for archivists and researchers who want to navigate and confirm the integrity of the files.

CAD software, especially the widely adopted AutoCAD, redefined the field of architecture. Similar to the ways that Microsoft Word changed word processing and writing habits, CAD software provided a familiar environment with the ability to make shortcuts for tedious and time-consuming tasks while still allowing users to make multiple variations quickly, work in layers, and create precise lines. Revit, and other BIM software products, made it possible for architects and designers to create 2D and 3D design simultaneously. Revit produces impressive 3D renderings, which are automatically generated as 2D components drawn into the model. The ability for the Revit and AutoCAD files to export into Drawing Interchange Format (DXF) allows for smoother interoperability of the files. CAD and BIM programs allow users to work on files created in earlier versions of the software, but minor degradation of files occurs during the conversion process.

SketchUp, Rhino, and Grasshopper are also common modeling software programs, but they create less granular outputs than AutoCAD or Revit. Rhinoceros 3D, colloquially referred to as Rhino (figure 8.3), was first released in 1994 as a dynamic tool that renders mathematical representations of 3D geometry.[17] The representations are simultaneously flexible and accurate, which allows the created files to maintain integrity when opened in other software and to support future actions, including final fabrication.[18] Sketch-Up (figure 8.4), a tool used by architects, civil and mechanical engineers, planners, and urban designers, was first released as a Google product in 2000. It has become a staple tool for quick design massing using triangulated geometry. Grasshopper (figures 8.3 and 8.5) is a visual programming language first released in 2007. Originally, it was built as a plug-in to Rhino that builds generative algorithms to create patterns and other detail features that would otherwise be incredibly labor intensive. These programs embed limited details into their models, which makes the files "light" and easily manipulated. For designers, such modeling programs make it much faster to make changes and create multiple versions than the more clunky, but data-rich, Revit environment.

Rendering

Architectural renderings or illustrations are no longer limited to 2D images. Software can now create animation, photorealistic elements, and 3D representations. Digital renderings are increasingly photorealistic and interactive, entering into the experiential technology realms of augmented reality and virtual reality. They are digitally produced by taking a file through a combi-

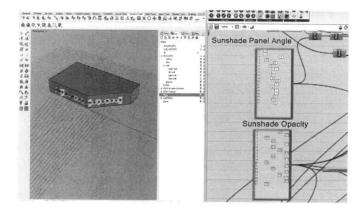

Figure 8.3. Using Rhino and Grasshopper to adjust files

nation of software. As an example of the process, the user creates the initial file using AutoCAD or Revit and then imports that file to Photoshop, Illustrator, or InDesign (all part of the Adobe Creative Suite) to add artistic features. The Adobe Creative Suite is an integral piece of the rendering process because it allows for further editing. Because these Adobe products are so widely used outside of the AEC industries, there are fewer preservation or access challenges for archivists.

Designers and architects use other software programs that support animation features and integration or plug-in capabilities, which is an important contextual part of a file's development and evolution. The most popular software packages with these capabilities include Piranesi, V-Ray, form•Z, Maxwell Render, Maya, 3ds Max, and Lumion. Piranesi is the oldest of this group of software, with its first release in 1981.[19] Although Piranesi began with CAD products, it expanded to include GIS (geographic information system) data and most popularly to 3D paint rendering and 3D viewer systems. First released in the early 1990s, 3ds Max and form•Z provide platforms for 3D and animated renderings.[20]

Lumion and Maya appeared on the market in 1998. Both software products focused on high-end visualization technology, with Lumion being very customizable and user friendly. Because of its dynamic visual effects and virtual production tools, Maya appeals to companies focused in video production, video game development, and 3D printing. V-Ray built its user base by providing plug-ins for existing rendering, and later modeling, software. It was first released in 2002 as a plug-in for 3ds Max to provide illumination

Figure 8.4.   SketchUp

and other accentuating features in rendering software. Maxwell Render is a stand-alone rendering tool for film and animation with the capacity to plug-in to 3D and CAD programs. Through such plug-ins, architects and designers can merge the functionalities of various programs to produce the most visually stimulating and engaging representations of their plans and built work.

While these software programs demonstrate the breadth of tools and features available to designers, rendering often relies upon the digitization of hand-drawn or existing analog records that can be edited and enhanced. Digitizing design records is a similar practice to that of any other record type. Although architects and designers often scan their preliminary sketches to incorporate them into presentations or to use them as base drawings within their design software programs, they are typically unaware of digitization best practices. Digitization requires access to large format scanners or cameras that can create high-resolution files. The files must be of high enough quality to capture all details and subtleties of the analog drawings, such as annotations and other added notes. These digitized versions of original renderings represent an important challenge for archivists, especially if the files have been modified.

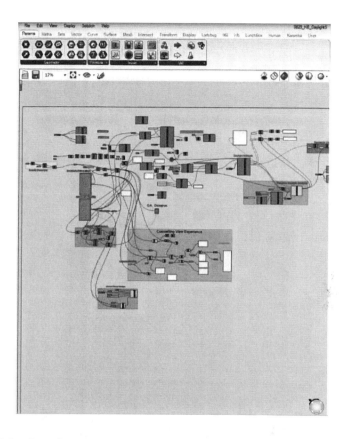

Figure 8.5. Grasshopper

Project Data

Each project contains additional associative and crucial data. This information is not managed by the previously mentioned software and is separate from the plans or models. The most crucial data is typically GIS and topographic related, while contextual information about decision-making processes and specifications about projects are captured in word processing documents and direct correspondence with the clients. The GIS files often require cleaning, editing, or analysis by the project team before they can be imported into AutoCAD, Revit, or any of the rendering software for layering of design and building massing. Esri's ArcGIS, first released in 1999, offers extensive data sets with built-in analytical and integrative features that allow designers to build maps and make data-driven design decisions. Similarly,

Google Earth Pro—a virtual globe, maps, and geographical information program—offers a wide range of geographic data and visualizations that can be
utilized for rendering and site positioning.

In addition to using geographic information data, the AEC industry has
embraced environmental and sustainable design tools. Environmental analysis tools, such as Ecotect, are often designed as Revit plug-ins (or with plug-
in functionality) to augment the BIM environment. Ecotect was acquired by
Autodesk in 2008, which recently announced the discontinuation of this program, as most of its features have been integrated into the Revit environment.
Other software in this category include the "zoo" of software oriented toward
sustainability and energy use, such as Ladybug, Honeybee, Dragonfly, Elk,
and Butterfly.[21]

These software programs, and their varying levels of interoperable file
types, have created an entirely new landscape of architecture and design
records. While final contract deliverables are still printed with wet stamps
and signatures, this practice is becoming less frequent as companies and
clients now use BIM as a contract deliverable and electronic signatures.[22]
This new electronic deliverable poses significant promise and challenges for
the design and facility management professions. From the record standpoint,
the digital deliverable contains the details contractually agreed upon, the
client's expectation of how architects will incorporate that into their BIM
file, and how that will be represented in the model a client receives at the end
of a project. There are established levels of detail (LOD) that can be specified
in the contract (figure 8.6), but the architect will still create and include
notes, schedules, specifications, and other documentation throughout the design phases, including construction documents and construction administration files. Architects place high value on these materials, particularly because
having that information exist outside of the BIM allows the digital model to
stay lighter and easier to work within. As a result, archivists and researchers
may encounter models with intentionally unfinished areas or missing details,
which are included with other documentation connected to the project.

The various files created by current software packages are becoming a
significant part of archival collections from designers, architects, and firms.
As the digital deluge will only accelerate in the coming decades, archivists
must stay abreast of the technological changes and innovations in the design
field. The next "cutting edge" technology and design tools will span the
spectrum of physical and digital with fabrication (3D printing and computer
numeric cutting) and include virtual, augmented, and mixed realities. These

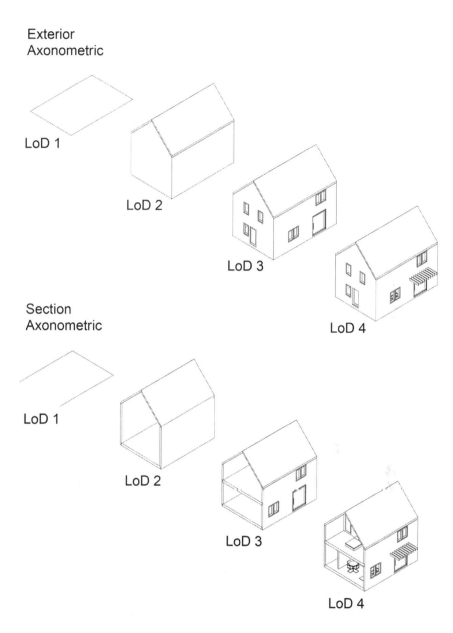

Exterior
Axonometric

LoD 1

LoD 2

LoD 3

LoD 4

Section
Axonometric

LoD 1

LoD 2

LoD 3

LoD 4

Figure 8.6.   Levels of details for renderings

exciting platforms allow designers to engage with their clients, and they also
provide a new perspective for designers to experience their initial and developed designs. The design field is full of experimentation. Professionals are

creating digital spaces where designers and technologists come together to push the limits of their skills and imaginations, much like the early days of design software that was "broken" and adjusted by the individual designer. The capacity for 3D printing, laser cutting, and a larger-scale fabrication within firms reaffirms the ephemeral nature of the files and by-products of designers' records. These innovations, however, may hinder the ability of archivists to capture the design process in total.

HOW

For archivists, it is especially important to advocate for the utilitarian and intrinsic value of digital design records, which have not yet reached that status of art as the hand-drawn sketches and drawings of previous design generations have achieved. When the donations were analog, the biggest concerns were mostly preservation related, such as mold, the fragility of the paper, off-gassing from reproduced prints, and physical storage. While these are serious concerns and continue to strain budgets and stress archivists, these records survived in awkward storage spaces and imperfect climates for sometimes decades. Digital records do not have the same shelf life as their analog counterparts, and thus much earlier intervention is required. Some of the most pressing concerns for archivists are software licenses, versioning, copyright, access restrictions, the steep learning curve for archivists to familiarize themselves with the functionality and uses of the various software by designers, and the volume of records that must be appraised before (or more likely after) accessioning the collection.

Building on the categories and appraisal grid established by Waverly Lowell and Tawny Ryan Nelb for analog materials, archivists can better manage and crosswalk the digital records to their analog predecessors.[23] Although most architecture and design records are made digitally in the present, this does not mean design firms have become paperless offices, especially since many contract deliverables still require physical signatures and stamped drawings. This analog approach is changing, as clients want their deliverables as digital records and increasingly as dynamic models for facilities management purposes.

This shift in deliverables is a pressing motivator for determining best practices for preserving the complex digital files that make up the visual materials in design records. To fully document the process of digital design, archivists must understand how the creators used technology. This means that archivists should have a working familiarity with basic software packages, like the Microsoft Office Suite and Adobe Creative Suite, and have experience with the more elaborate design software programs specific to the design field. Further, archivists with responsibility of digital design records need subject-matter expertise to understand the context in which the material was created.

The 2007 MIT FACADE (Future-proofing Architectural Computer-Aided Design) project examined the role of digital design files in the life cycle of modern architecture and construction with the intention of developing strategies for long-term preservation of these records. Through both the MIT FACADE project and the follow-up Harvard University FACADE2 project (2011), archivists developed a stronger understanding and intellectual control of the various types of data produced throughout the design and construction process. These two projects resulted in a potential strategy for long-term preservation and the building of an open-source repository, known as the Curator's Workbench. Both of these projects were IMLS funded and provided crucial lessons for the community around the nuances of the ecosystem that produces these records and the scalability of processing large collections that contain digital design files.[24]

The complexity of design software and the niche quality of the built and environmental design fields means that it is highly unlikely that an open-source version of any CAD, BIM, or related software will be developed. This limits the options for archivists to provide access to these proprietary file types. At the time of this writing, there have been two successful methods of providing access to dynamic digital design files, but both require access to the proprietary software. The first has been done at the Canadian Centre for Architecture, which has obtained copies of software directly from the vendors or through assistance by practitioners and has been able to use older versions of software to "up-save" the files to be accessed through free readers that are also offered by the software vendors.[25] The second has been through the development of Emulation as a Service at Yale University, where Euan Cochrane and his team have built emulation environments for the original early versions of software to work within their original operating system environment.[26] While the conversation continues to develop, emulation appears to be a viable option for providing accurate representation of the digital design files and the functionality of the software used to design them.

Emulation is a process for accessing original software in a compatible environment with a current platform; it is not a digital preservation practice.

This process requires having copies of the original software and some sort of approved licenses for those software packages from the vendor. Jeff Rothenberg, a senior research scientist at the RAND Corporation, was an early and strong advocate for emulation. He was skeptical about the integrity of the data and functionality of files accessed through other methods, such as migration, and argued that emulation was a better method.[27] Emulation poses its own challenges, namely access to the software packages and necessary licensing. Securing individual licenses to each version of the software can be an expensive endeavor for most archives programs, not to mention the cost of servers and storage of the files and software. A consortial approach may make it possible for multiple archives programs with design records to share the financial burden of storing and providing support for the emulated software.

Digital design records present challenges on technological, legal, and curatorial levels. Technological issues continue to be the most pressing, complicated, and overwhelming for archivists. Better communications between the archival community and software vendors will help clarify needs and perhaps create software products geared toward accessing legacy content. Such conversations would benefit from the presence of records creators, but that requires additional efforts from archivists to educate design professions about the long-term significance of their records. Nonprofit organizations, such as the Software Preservation Network (SPN), are exploring frameworks to create a dialogue between cultural heritage institutions and software vendors. One of SPN's goals is to resolve legal concerns about the access and use of current and legacy software.[28] Further, SPN supports efforts such as a recent grant program through IMLS for archives and libraries to preserve legacy software, which has significant positive implications for digital design records as their collecting institutions begin to develop digital preservation programs.[29]

A number of legal issues surround the management of digital design files. These include access, ownership, the use of software, and reproduction rights. File ownership and copyright for the actual project records are perhaps the most challenging legal issues. Although it is not explicitly the result of the use of digital design records, donations of these materials to archives programs have raised concerns about the copyright of the project records. In many cases, the records are not owned by the donating designers but rather their clients. During discussion with donors, as part of the formal donor agreement process, archivists must seek clear documentation about the contractual agreements for project records. This documentation establishes whether the donor can transfer access rights for the material to the archives program. During early consultations with potential donors, archivists should emphasize that designers should not release exclusive ownership of their project deliverables to the client.

ACTIONS

The legal and technological issues of managing digital design records are many but not insurmountable. Archivists are best prepared to develop standards and best practices for the long-term preservation of these fragile materials. That longer view means focusing on areas often ignored by other stakeholders, which include the potential research value of the material, early interaction with potential donors, developing open access platforms to support various file types, and creating best practices and workflows for ingest and delivery. Sometimes taking risks and trying new approaches are the only ways for archivists to make progress with records created by architects and designers that are sometimes difficult to use and access. The CAD/BIM Taskforce has led the way in making recommendations, such as adding an informational interview to the process of donating a collection. As archivists continue to learn about the digital design landscape and the evolving areas of research and discourse around the built and spatial design professions, archives programs will be better prepared to approach the technical and legal issues and incorporate solutions into existing professional practice. What follows are some simple recommendations to help keep archivists current with the challenges of digital design materials.

Crosswalk the Files

The categories established by Waverly Lowell and Tawny Ryan Nelb for analog materials are a valuable baseline for understanding the digital files. With these groupings in mind, archivists can crosswalk, or draw parallels, between digital and analog files when possible (e.g., floor plans, sections, details, perspectives). It also allows archivists to identify new types of records with no precedent (e.g., animated renderings, energy studies, algorithm-based design commands). Further, the analog framework applies to accessioning, appraising, and describing design collections, which may be analog, digital, or a hybrid collection.

Table 8.3 is a reference table of the record categories and types identified by Lowell and Nelb and some of the most common software used to create those types of documents in current practice. This table crosswalks record types to the corresponding software that is used in current practice to produce that same record type. Based on conversations with practicing architects, planners, and landscape architects, it is clear that projects continue to move through phases, but the records produced at each phase are not as separated. Rather, the software transcends the project phases, and project teams regularly continue to work from the same CAD or BIM model throughout the evolution of the project. As previously described, many of the software programs in current use are intended to be used in tandem with other software to produce richer files. These practices are reflected in the table with multiple record types being matched with the same software and several software programs being matched to a single record type.

Think Broader

Successful management of design records starts long before the deed of gift is signed. Archivists must begin the donor process with a broad view. They should approach the donor and collection comprehensively, considering all parts of the donor's professional environment from his or her technological milieu, to record-keeping practices, and consultant and prime relationships. Each facet of his or her work has implications for archivists attempting to decipher the nuances of the digital design practice of yesterday, today, and tomorrow.

Because collections are rarely of a single project's records from a donor, understanding the workflows of designers or their office is informative beyond recognizing the phases of projects. Further, better understanding these workflows allows the archivists to identify how, why, and which software programs and their unique versions were used throughout each project. Having conversations with donors about their use of collaborative technology, including how they interacted with and shared digital materials with consultants, clarifies issues of provenance, coauthorship, and ownership.

Information about the donor and how he or she created records affects how the archives program can manage the collection. A new collection of design files may result in an archives investing in hardware, software, storage, or preservation services. Creating access points through a stable platform and a multifunction user interface may also be needed for researchers to actually use the collection. Gathering technical and collection information

Table 8.3. Software used in the production of project records

Project Phase	Record Category	Record Type	Software
Preliminary Design Schematic Design Design Development	Design Development	Sketches	Adobe Creative Suite, Scanned hand drawings, Bluebeam
Preliminary Design Schematic Design	Design Development	Schematics	Esri ArcGIS, Google Earth Pro, Ecotect, Adobe Creative Suite, AutoCAD, MicroStation, CATIA, ARCHICAD, SketchUp, Revit, Grasshopper, Rhino, Revit, Bluebeam
Preliminary Design Schematic Design Design Development	Design Development	Presentation Drawings	Adobe Creative Suite, V-Ray, Lumion, Maxwell, 3dsMax, Maya, form•Z, Piranesi, Revit, AutoCAD, CATIA, ARCHICAD, MicroStation
Design Development Construction Administration	Construction Drawings	Final Drawings / Record Set (includes: Site Plans, Flood Plans, Elevations, and Sections)	Revit, AutoCAD, CATIA, ARCHICAD, MicroStation, Rhino, Grasshopper, Dynamo, ESRI ArcGIS, Google Earth Pro, Ecotect, Adobe Creative Suite, Bluebeam
Design Development Construction Administration	Construction Drawings	Bid Sets	Revit, AutoCAD, CATIA, ARCHICAD, MicroStation, Adobe Creative Suite, Bluebeam
Design Development Construction Administration	Construction Drawings	Field Sets	Revit, AutoCAD, CATIA, ARCHICAD, MicroStation, Adobe Creative Suite, Bluebeam
Design Development Construction Administration	Construction Drawings	Electrical Plans	Revit, AutoCAD, CATIA, ARCHICAD, MicroStation, Adobe Creative Suite, Bluebeam
Design Development Construction Administration	Construction Drawings	Mechanical Plans	Revit, AutoCAD, CATIA, ARCHICAD, MicroStation, Adobe Creative Suite, Bluebeam

Design Development Construction Administration	Construction Drawings	Plumbing Plans	Revit, AutoCAD, CATIA, ARCHICAD, MicroStation, Adobe Creative Suite, Bluebeam
Design Development Construction Administration	Construction Drawings	Structural Plans	Revit, AutoCAD, CATIA, ARCHICAD, MicroStation, Adobe Creative Suite, Bluebeam
Construction Administration	Construction Drawings	As-built / Design Build	Revit, AutoCAD, CATIA, ARCHICAD, MicroStation, Adobe Creative Suite, Bluebeam
Design Development Construction Administration	Construction Drawings	Details	Revit, AutoCAD, CATIA, ARCHICAD, MicroStation, Adobe Creative Suite, Bluebeam

contributes to the appraisal and, later, access to the collection. This includes learning about the folder structures for projects, how consistently the structure was used, and if any file naming conventions were adopted. Figure 8.7 illustrates how the fast-paced and deadline-driven environment of design professions does not inherently support consistent project folder structure. The inconsistency of the organization of project records adds further appraisal and processing challenges for archivists. Often archivists spend extra time dissecting the organization of project records and exploring the significance, if any, of the nonstandard folder structures.

A consistent project folder structure does not hinder the creative process of designers, and it makes the work of archivists and researchers much easier. At Sasaki, an international interdisciplinary planning and design firm, designers follow a consistent file structure as depicted in figure 8.8. Their approach enables multiple disciplines to work together and makes the management of projects more efficient. In particular, the standardization of file structures has reduced the time required for new team members to get up to speed on where records are stored throughout the life of each project.

Additionally, archivists must understand the project closeout process for each firm or individual practitioner. Further, the existence of records retention programs at firms and those practices will inform archivists of the comprehensive nature of the collection and of potential data and record loss in any transfer or transaction. In most firms, projects are housed on a "billable drive" as the work progresses. Once the project is completed, the project folder and all the files associated with the project are moved to an "archives

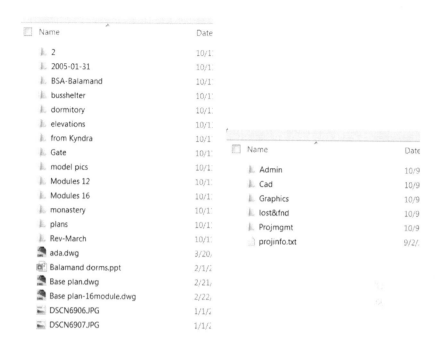

Figure 8.7.   A convoluted folder structure

drive," which is often more affordable storage and less heavily trafficked by project teams. With the rise of cloud-based software (e.g., GreenBIM, Autodesk's A360), the use of cloud storage is ever increasing within the design industry, but due to the nature of the size of these project files, most firms continue to maintain their own servers for their project files. The details of when a project's records were moved from the billable drive to the archives drive can be useful in understanding how or why the xref links of CAD, BIM, and Adobe Suite files have broken. This information may also explain trends in how a collection of project records all experience the same unique issue due to an incomplete migration of the project records. For archivists, this type of information can resolve simple technological challenges, such as reconnecting broken xref links or clarifying the timeline when particular design software and specific versions were used.

Often designers are not thinking about the nuances and idiosyncratic aspects of their work. They must be prompted to share this type of information that will be invaluable for archivists and future researchers to make sense of the hodgepodge of digital records that make up their collections. What fol-

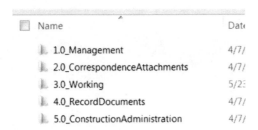

Figure 8.8. A tightly organized folder hierarchy

lows are basic questions to help archivists start conversations with creators and keepers of design records. They are by no means comprehensive, but the answers often lead to deeper details that help archivists prepare for these complex donations of digital archives.

QUESTIONS TO ASK DONORS

1. How are project records organized?
2. What is your office's project folder structure?
3. What are your file naming conventions?

   a. How can you/I identify the deliverables to the client?
   b. What are the documents that best document the decision-making process of your projects?

4. What software do you use in your firm?

   a. How many versions of the software were used to create the materials being donated?
   b. What activities/documents do you use/produce from this software?
   c. Can you provide copies of this software with your donation?

5. What is the average size (GB, TB, PB) of your project folders?

   a. What is the range in size of project folders?

6. What documents can you provide for each project in the following categories?

   a. Contracts
   b. Project staff
   c. Additional services and repeat work for that client

7. Are all of your project deliverables in a packaged format (avoiding disconnecting xrefs that would need to be relinked)?

   a. What formats do you have the packaged deliverables in?
   b. Are deliverables digital or analog?
   c. Either way, do you have a signed/stamped copy for all built projects?

8. Do you hold the copyright to all project files included in the donation?

   a. Can you identify the projects that you do not have copyright?
   b. If you do not have copyright, can you help the archivist contact clients about obtaining approval for the archives to provide access to these materials?

FORWARD THINKING

Considerable work remains before archivists are fully prepared for the long-term management of digital design records. Through research, case study sharing, and broadening the community discussing the issues at hand, archivists have developed actionable solutions and resources. The challenges of digital preservation and access will forever be evolving as the technology producing and the people creating these records will also change. Preparing for digital design materials must be a flexible process to accommodate for constant change. Thankfully, archivists should expect phases of built design work to persist from preliminary and schematic design through design development and construction administration. By understanding these consistent elements and communicating with the people involved in each phase, archivists will be well positioned to respond to new challenges.

The CAD/BIM Taskforce has supported a number of research initiatives related to design records. The group is building resources and raising awareness for understanding these materials and sharing that information with the larger design archives community. Presentations and publications focused on design software and digital design practices demystify this medium, which raises the communal knowledge that will allow a larger group to investigate the more difficult questions. By educating other archivists, this process has raised more questions than it has answered, but it has also identified priorities, strengths, and weakness.

Rather than being held captive by the technology, archivists want researchers to be able to use technology to better understand and perhaps liberate the content of digital design collections in new and exciting ways. By addressing both the legacy and expected design software, archivists are approaching the issue of access comprehensively to develop a lasting strategy that can (hopefully) accommodate the changing technological landscape and emerging research needs as they develop.

NOTES

1. MacKenzie Smith, "Future-Proofing Architectural Computer-Aided Design: MIT's FA-CADE Project," DSpace@MIT, https://dspace.mit.edu/handle/1721.1/46329; David Peyceré, "Gau:di Programme Case Studies on Preserving Electronic Documents," 2006, http://www.icam-web.org/data/media/cms_binary/original/1163002339.pdf; DURAARK: Durable Architectural Knowledge, http://duraark.eu/.

2. Aliza Leventhal and Inés Zalduendo, "Draft Bibliography on Studies Dealing with Legal, Technical, and Curatorial Issues Related to Born Digital Architectural Records," Society of American Archivists, 2013, https://www2.archivists.org/sites/all/files/AR%20Taskforce_Born%20Digital%20StudiesBibliography_AL+IZ_FinalDraft_revised.pdf; CAD/BIM Taskforce, "Survey Results, Digital Design Holdings," Society of American Archivists, 2016, https://www2.archivists.org/sites/all/files/20160508_SurveyResultsDigitalDesignHoldings.pdf.

3. Aliza Leventhal, "Designing the Future Landscape: Digital Architecture, Design, and Engineering Assets," Library of Congress, November 16, 2017, http://loc.gov/preservation/digital/meetings/ade/ade2017.html; "Building for Tomorrow: Collaborative Development of Sustainable Infrastructure for Architectural and Design Documentation," Harvard University, 2018, https://projects.iq.harvard.edu/buildingtomorrow/home.

4. Waverly Lowell and Tawny Ryan Nelb, *Architectural Records: Managing Design and Construction Records* (Chicago: Society of American Archivists, 2006).

5. Society of American Archivists Design Records Section, "Find Built Environment Records," https://www2.archivists.org/groups/design-records-section/find-built-environment-records.

6. Society of American Archivists, "Cooperative Preservation of Architectural Records (2009)," https://www2.archivists.org/sites/all/files/copar-committees-2009.pdf.

7. Matthew Allen, "Archaeology of the Digital," Domus, May 15, 2013, https://www.domusweb.it/en/architecture/2013/05/15/archaeology_of_thedigital.html.

8. These include the clarified collection policy and mission statement of collecting institutions. "Donations to the Environmental Design Archives," UC Berkeley Environmental Design Archives, http://archives.ccd.berkeley.edu/donations.

9. Lowell and Nelb, *Architectural Records*.

10. These three projects were shared by active scholars at the November 2017 Designing the Future Summit hosted by the Library of Congress, Architect of the Capitol, and the National Gallery of Art.

11. Genevieve Greenwald-Katz worked for the New York-based firm Max O. Urbahn Associates and was an organizing member of the AIA's task force that developed its affirmative action plan for women architects. Genevieve Greenwald-Katz, "Computers in Architecture," in *AFIPS Conference Proceedings: 1976 National Computer Conference* (Montvale, NJ: American Federation of Information Processing Societies, 1976), 318, https://www.computer.org/csdl/proceedings/afips/1976/5084/00/50840315.pdf; American Institute of Architects, *Affirmative Action Plan for the Integration of Women in the Architectural Profession* (Washington, DC: American Institute of Architects, 1975).

12. Early adopters included Peter Eisenman, Chuck Hoberman, Shoei Yoh, and Frank Gehry, who were all featured in the CCA's *Archeology of the Digital* exhibit.

13. The 2013 CAD/BIM Taskforce's initial report outlines the fundamental concerns around digital design records. Report available at https://www2.archivists.org/sites/all/files/CAD%20BIM%20Taskforce%20Report%202013.docx.

14. Lowell and Nelb, *Architectural Records*, 101.

15. The author developed these categories based on conversations with design professionals and the descriptions of the software by their developers. There are additional software programs, such as GIS (geographic information system) programs and data sets, that do not fit into these categories but can be compared to the topographic maps previously used by architects and designers for determining the qualities of a site. Some project data is held within the BIM or CAD models and also in word-processing files and in correspondence with the clients.

16. Shaan Hurley, "AutoCAD Release History," *Between the Lines: Autodesk, Technology, Design and More* (blog), http://Autodesk.blogs.com/between_the_lines/autocad-release-history.html.

17. "The History of Rhino," McNeel wiki, September 2015, http://wiki.mcneel.com/rhino/rhinohistory.

18. "What Are NURBS?" Rhinoceros, 2018, https://www.rhino3d.com/nurbs.

19. "About Us," Piranesi, 2018, http://www.piranesi.co.uk/about.html.

20. "Autodesk 3ds Max Software Celebrate Its 20th Anniversary," Autodesk, July 2010, http://investors.autodesk.com/news-releases/news-release-details/autodesk-3ds-max-software-celebrates-its-20th-anniversary; "About AutoDesSys," form•Z, 2018, http://www.formz.com/home/aboutus.html.

21. Ladybug Tools, https://www.ladybug.tools/.

22. Many firms use proprietary software to ensure the legitimacy and legal authenticity of electronic signatures. Archivists who work for these firms need to establish protocols and workflows to ensure all project record elements, including signatures, are appropriately documented.

23. Lowell and Nelb, *Architectural Records*, 84–85.

24. Tom Rosko, "Curating Architectural 3D Models: FACADE; Future-Proofing Architectural Computer-Aided Design," (PowerPoint presentation, Society of American Archivists Meeting, Architectural Records Roundtable, August 12, 2009), https://www2.archivists.org/sites/all/files/saa-facade_2009.pdf; "Curators-Workbench," GitHub, 2018, https://github.com/UNC-Libraries/Curators-Workbench.

25. Jessica Lee Hester, "The Quest for a Universal Translator for Old, Obsolete Computer Files," Atlas Obscura, March 8, 2018, https://www.atlasobscura.com/articles/how-to-open-old-computer-files.

26. Euan Cochrane, "Emulation as a Service (EaaS) at Yale University Library," *The Signal* (blog), August 2014, https://blogs.loc.gov/thesignal/2014/08/emulation-as-a-service-eaas-at-yale-university-library/.

27. Jeff Rothenberg, *Avoiding Technological Quicksand: Finding a Viable Technical Foundation for Digital Preservation* (Washington, DC: Council on Library and Information Resources, 1999), https://www.clir.org/wp-content/uploads/sites/6/2016/09/pub77.pdf; Stewart Granger, "Emulation as a Digital Preservation Strategy" *D-Lib Magazine* 6 (October 2000), http://www.dlib.org/dlib/october00/granger/10granger.html; Leslie Johnston, "Considering Emulation for Digital Preservation," February 2014, *The Signal* (blog), https://blogs.loc.gov/thesignal/2014/02/considering-emulation-for-digital-preservation/.

28. Patricia Aufderheide, Brandon Butler, Krista Cox, and Peter Jaszi, *The Copyright Permissions Culture in Software Preservation and Its Implications for the Cultural Record* (Washington, DC: Association of Research Libraries, 2018), http://www.arl.org/storage/documents/2018.02.09_CopyrightPermissionsCulture.pdf.

29. Software Preservation Network, http://www.softwarepreservationnetwork.org/; "FCoP: Software Preservation in Libraries and Archives," Software Preservation Network, http://www.softwarepreservationnetwork.org/temp-projects/.

Chapter Nine

Congressional Collections

Danielle Emerling

Throughout the second half of the twentieth century, staffing in congressional offices grew to support the expanding responsibilities assigned to members of the US Congress. An increase in staff precipitated growth in records production, and the concept of modern congressional papers collections was born. Since the 1970s, Congress has adopted electronic technologies that affect how members produce, consume, and communicate information. The digital materials created by members of Congress continue to increase in complexity and size. Congressional offices create and manage digital materials that are broad in content and format, from constituent emails and press videos to Facebook pages and legislative memoranda.

When a senator or representative leaves office, due to his or her retirement, death, or loss of an election, the materials created by the congressional office may become the purview of collecting repositories across the country. The digital components of these political collections present new opportunities for scholarship, but the archives programs taking custody of these records must carefully consider how to best appraise, describe, manage, preserve, and provide access to these digital archives. This chapter looks at digital donations of political papers with a specific focus on congressional collections. It reviews the types of digital content contained in political collections and describes the best archival practices to make these materials available for researchers.

THE NATURE OF CONGRESSIONAL COLLECTIONS

The records of Congress document the democratic process, the development of public policy, and the federal body closest to the people. Archivists have long recognized the numerous challenges associated with managing these records. Modern congressional records are large, complex, and contain a variety of formats, including paper, analog audiovisual materials, and digital files. While full of rich resources, researchers often find political collections cumbersome and difficult to use. Identifying materials with enduring value from the vast panoply is complicated by the fact that the records of Congress are not administered uniformly. Congressional records are created by numerous collaborating entities, such as the executive and judicial branches and outside interest groups. Further, the primary materials generated by Congress are separated into official and private records. [1]

The official records of Congress are those created, maintained, or received by committees related to legislative, oversight, and executive business. They remain in the custody of the federal government, and once inactive, they are transferred to the Center for Legislative Archives at the National Archives and Records Administration (NARA). These are differentiated from the personal papers of members of Congress, which include materials created or received by the individual as documentation of his or her political career. They are preserved either as evidence of the organization and functions of the member's office or as information about the individual member, and they include materials created and received by office staff. [2]

Because members of Congress own their personal papers, they decide where to place their collections. If a member chooses to send his or her papers to a repository located in his or her home state, federal funds are available to pay for the transfer of boxes from the Washington, DC, area to the repository. Members contact archives programs at academic institutions, historical societies, and others that collect political papers that are topically, geographically, or politically similar. Other times, they may donate their papers to their alma mater. While most members give little thought to their collections until they are leaving office, some politicians create centers within academic institutions while they are in public office. For example, the University of Louisville's McConnell Center offers civic education and leadership development programs and houses the McConnell-Chao Archives. [3]

As the creator, the politician can stipulate closure periods, something that is usually negotiated with the collecting repository. While no statute dictates what a member must do with his or her papers, in 2008, House Concurrent Resolution 307 passed unanimously and urges that "Members' Congressional papers should be properly maintained" and that members should "take all necessary measures to manage and preserve their papers."[4]

Personal congressional papers most often bear the name of the member of Congress who created them, but congressional papers have more in common with organizational records than those of an individual. Congressional papers document an office—or, more often, offices—and the sometimes hundreds of staff members who worked in those offices over several years. For instance, one senator who served for thirty years employed more than three hundred people throughout that time. In addition to the office in Washington, DC, this member had four smaller home state offices.

Depending on a repository's preparedness, acquiring a modern congressional collection can be "an archivist's dream" or the stuff of nightmares.[5] Acquiring collections can be, as one archivist put it, "high stakes, high profile, and come with even higher donor expectations."[6] Modern congressional papers are behemoths, often measured in the hundreds or thousands of linear feet, that require storage, the attention of knowledgeable archives staff, a healthy budget, and sometimes years of dedicated processing.

Acquiring a collection that contains desirable documentation also depends largely on how a congressional office closes. When a member of Congress leaves his or her elected position, he or she may have only weeks to vacate the office. Closing an office involves multiple tasks, not least of which is boxing records and memorabilia that were not previously transferred to a storage facility. Most staff immediately begin searching for new employment, leaving a small number of people to close the office. Members are often given postelection temporary office space, which one member described as being like "congressional refugees."[7] The politician has the responsibility to choose an archival repository and arrange for the transfer of the papers or find his or her own storage solution.

Closing an office is made worse for those leaving unexpectedly when no transfer plan is in place. For example, the death of the person or loss of election exacerbates the process. A repository receiving such a collection may have little idea what the collection contains or what resources are necessary to support it. Once the collection arrives, the archivist must inventory each box and hard drive to create processing plans and timelines and make appraisal decisions. This is no small task when modern congressional collections are measured in the hundreds and thousands of feet and terabytes of digital records.

Appraising and arranging congressional papers requires an understanding of the dynamic nature of Congress, including its powers, rules, and schedule; the functions of an office; and the individual member's career. Archivists writing about appraisal have urged retaining less of these bulky collections. The Minnesota Historical Society established strict appraisal guidelines to heavily weed materials, many of which were duplicative and tangential.[8] Further, some archivists suggested cooperative approaches regionally and nationally that would consider the duplicated series in collections across the country or in each congressional delegation and keep only the most unique parts of each collection.[9] Effective appraisal and the use of the More Product, Less Process (MPLP) method for processing reduces a congressional collections' size by 25 to 75 percent.[10] Arrangement is based largely on the functions of the office, with common series including legislative materials, constituent services, press relations, personal and political materials, and office management files.

DIGITAL MATERIALS IN CONGRESSIONAL OFFICES

While Congress has been using electronic technologies since the 1970s, the bioterrorist attacks on Congress in 2001 and 2004 "greatly accelerated" the move to digital materials. Requirements to irradiate all incoming mail slowed correspondence with congressional offices and made electronic communications more efficient. Although digital production has increased in congressional offices, consistent management of those records has not. Digital technologies must be approved for use in the Senate or the House of Representatives, but members enjoy a great deal of autonomy in choosing how technologies are adopted and how their records are managed. Offices deploy different electronic systems to manage constituent correspondence and casework, and staff manage records creation and retention in varying ways.[11]

Only a handful of congressional offices employ archivists or systems administrators. Senate offices are required to have systems administrators, but these roles are sometimes delegated to an existing staff member. Offices use numerous formats and storage methods for digital files.[12] Most office staff members save files to both personal locations (e.g., individual server managed spaces or removable media) and a shared office drive managed on a local server.[13] Staff files include a range of format types, such as textual documents, photographs, and audio and video files. Each office has at least one organizational filing structure to follow; however, staff organize files in whichever way they find most useful. Inconsistent management of these office records often means that no single file naming convention exists, duplicate materials are often saved in multiple locations, and the depth and breadth of records varies for each staff member.

Additionally, the member of Congress and each member of staff maintain an individual email account. Members of Congress and their staff members may conduct official business through personal email accounts because their records are not subject to the Freedom of Information Act or the Federal Records Act.[14] Again, their papers are considered to be their personal property, so they have broader discretion than the members of the executive branch in managing their records.

In spring 1994, Massachusetts senator Ted Kennedy became the first member of Congress to create a website, and it helped launch the legislative branch into the new world of the web.[15] At present, every member of Congress maintains a website, and each office is responsible for updating its website. The Library of Congress has collected member websites from the end of the 107th Congress through the 112th Congress. In addition, NARA has harvested congressional websites since the end of the 109th Congress.[16]

Members of Congress have also embraced social media. In 2013, the Congressional Research Service reported that 84 percent of representatives and senators were registered on Twitter, and 90 percent were registered on Facebook.[17] These technologies allow members to share information, voice their positions on issues, lobby for desired political outcomes, and communicate with citizens, activists, and leaders of movements. In less than a decade, social media platforms have created new ways for members of Congress and the public at large to participate in the political process.[18] As of 2015, the Senate Sergeant at Arms Office had approved three vendors, Archive Social, Archive-It, and Hanzo Archives, for archiving websites and social media connected to congressional offices.[19]

Members' posts to social media may be more frequent than updates to the website, and occasionally, the posts are related to a specific event. For example, in June 2016, Democrats took over the Senate floor to advocate for stricter gun control laws following a shooting that left fifty dead at a gay nightclub in Orlando, Florida. Holding the Senate floor began with a Tweet from Connecticut Senator Chris Murphy and lasted for nearly fifteen hours, during which time the hashtag "#filibuster" trended on Twitter.[20] In a case such as this, there is no entity charged with archiving the event on social media. For public tweet text created between 2006 and 2017, the Library of Congress maintains an archive; however, in December 2017, the Library announced that it would no longer archive all public tweet text but would collect tweets on a selective basis.[21]

Constituents communicate with congressional offices in a variety of ways. One of the more unique digital materials created in congressional offices are through the Constituent Services Systems (CSS), also known as Correspondence Management Systems (CMS). Staff use the CSS and CMS primarily to respond to constituent contacts made via mail, phone, email, and fax and to track when a response was made.[22]

Congressional offices began using automated systems (CSS and CMS) to manage constituent correspondence in the late 1970s, and the use and complexity of the systems has only increased since then. For example, in the mid-1990s, the Senate approved the use of proprietary systems created by outside vendors. At the same time, the Senate Archivist worked with the Senate Sergeant at Arms Office to create the "archive format," a set of thirty-two fields, so that data could be exported to an archival repository. In 2016, Senate offices were given the ability to export the "Senate data interchange format," which includes two hundred additional fields. Senator Harry Reid was the first to export data in this new format. Offices may export communication with constituents including correspondence, greetings, casework, and requests for the member to intervene on an individual's behalf. The exported information usually includes a form letter library, correspondence records, indexing data, incoming email text, and additional files attached to the records. Increasingly, these databases may manage more than correspondence and include social media, schedules, and more in a congressional office.[23]

Although not all congressional offices develop records management policies, guidance is available from the Senate Historical Office (SHO) and the Office of Art and Archives (OAA) of the House of Representatives. Early guidelines for managing electronic records in congressional offices recommended titling documents and folders consistently, ensuring the migration of permanently valuable information to print or new systems, and transferring permanent records to an "archival transfer medium," which at the time was CD-ROM. Offices were also instructed to retain system technical specifications and information about file content, structure, and context.

For managing email, guidelines emphasized retaining substantive communications, deleting messages of "transitory value," and using a document management system for filing permanent messages into "archive" folders [24] The guidelines also recommend exporting email, calendars, and other types of folders from Microsoft Outlook/Exchange to Outlook Archive/Personal Storage Table format (PST).[25] In 2012, the Advisory Committee on the Records of Congress reported that many offices complied with these recommendations, and there were an increasing number of members of Congress working with SHO and OAA to prepare their digital collections for donation.[26]

BEST PRACTICES FOR DIGITAL POLITICAL COLLECTIONS

The growth of digital materials in congressional offices (and the way in which they are managed) affects how archives programs will be able to provide access to those political collections. Archives programs with political collections have experienced an increase in digital content. In response, archivists have worked to establish best practices for electronic material to incoming congressional collections. Literature on acquiring, processing, and providing access to digital congressional materials is limited but growing. Members of the Congressional Papers Section (CPS), formerly the Roundtable, of the Society of American Archivists are taking the lead to create, collect, and share methods of dealing with digital content in political papers. The survey information and case studies that follow offer a window into those emerging practices.

Acquisition

When acquiring digital archives from donors, archivists search for information about how the records were created and maintained. In most cases, this investigation yields mixed results—the information is frequently lacking, formats for storage were not necessarily good choices for preservation, and metadata may not be applied or saved uniformly, if at all.[27] This reality is no different for congressional papers. Further, having a deed of gift, or a memorandum of understanding, that specifically addresses the digital files and what the repository will and will not do with the files can help the repository to take appropriate appraisal and preservation actions.[28]

The CPS conducted surveys in 2009, 2014, and 2015 to discover what digital materials are being donated with congressional collections and how they are being managed by collecting repositories. According to these surveys, collecting repositories were receiving a broad range of digital materials, the most common being digital photographs, audiovisual materials, and text documents. Digitized materials and archived email were the next types of formats to be noted. Less commonly, repositories reported receiving CSS databases, websites, social media accounts, and calendars. In 2015, most respondents indicated that social media accounts and websites were not transferred with collections, and for repositories that did receive those materials, some harvested the sites themselves.

While the 2014 survey showed that most institutions were discussing formats and other technical issues with donors, it reported that few institutions were discussing the content of the digital materials or setting expectations with donors about how materials would be managed. The 2015 survey further explored the topic of donations and found respondents were attempting to put policies and procedures into place but struggled with the details. For example, half of the collecting repositories communicated with donors about preferred file formats, which included PDF, JPEG, and TIFF, but none of the respondents reported a 100 percent success rate in receiving those formats.

According to the surveys, most archives programs received digital donations when an office closed, but those who communicated with offices were sometimes able to set up periodic transfers. The periodic transfer option was the preferred method because it helped with planning, allowed more opportunities to converse with donors about what files were, and ensured that formats complied with standards. When offices transferred files, most respondents indicated that files arrived on external hard drives or on another type of removable media. Respondents noted that external hard drives were the preferable method for transfer because the files captured the breadth of the organization, hard drives were convenient, and donors understood how to use the drives. Archivists further reported that they were not always receiving the full scope of digital materials or receiving them in a preferred manner and format.[29]

The survey responses indicated that communication with congressional offices was the key to obtaining digital materials. Communication with donors should occur at least at the beginning of the acquisition process, if not sooner. Respondents mentioned successful communications included highlighting the special needs of electronic records and what the repository would do to care for them. This communication included talking with IT personnel and other staff members with knowledge of electronic records, reassuring staff that the security of electronic records would be taken seriously, and communicating in person or via phone rather than email.[30] Archivists have also developed formal guidelines and checklists to aid repositories in discussions about identifying document and system types, outdated formats, and even digital files stored on portable electronic devices, such as the once ubiquitous Blackberry.[31]

In addition to communication with offices, archivists must communicate up in their organizations. Administrators, government relations officers, development professionals, and anyone who interacts with congressional offices must know that expertise in managing these collections exists within their institution. The "high stakes" nature of these collections means there can be numerous individuals involved with negotiating the donation. Archivists are available to ensure the transfer of records is handled properly, to discuss professional practices, and to explain the ways a collection will be used to enrich teaching and research.

Finally, communication with archivists on Capitol Hill is essential. Archivists in the SHO and the OAA know the appropriate contacts to expedite records transfer and can advise repository archivists and offices when questions arise. There are not always archivists in members' offices, but when there are, collection transfers occur much smoother. Archivists in congressional offices have a better understanding than most other staff members of the full scope of records in an office and how they were managed. These archivists can also help to communicate the repository's needs and wishes to the staff and to the member of Congress.

Two examples from the field underscore the importance of communication and planning. In 2015, Congressman Nick Joe Rahall of West Virginia donated his papers from thirty-eight years (1977–2015) of service in the US House of Representatives to the West Virginia and Regional History Center of the WVU Libraries. Rahall, a longtime member from the southernmost district in the state, lost his 2014 reelection bid in a surprising upset. As mentioned previously, closing an office involves numerous tasks that are complicated when done under significant time pressure. The transfer of the collection was handled primarily by the university's government relations staff without much consultation with the center or the congressional papers archivist.

The collection arrived without any digital records. The archivist was able to contact the former chief of staff and learned that the office's share drive had not been transferred before the office closed. While removable media, such as floppy disks and CDs, was stored in some of the more than two thousand boxes of papers, the share drive, emails, website, and social media accounts were missing. The constituent services data was also not included with the donation. The former chief of staff shared the name of the vendor, and the WVU Libraries purchased the data directly from the vendor, a costly transaction that not all collecting repositories can afford. The data arrived in the mail on a CD and thumb drive.

Contrast this scenario with Senator Jay Rockefeller who represented West Virginia in the US Senate for thirty years (1985–2015). In 2013, he announced his plans to retire from Congress, giving his office ample time to plan. Rockefeller hired an archivist several years before this announcement, and two more archivists closed the office. Additionally, staff visited collecting repositories and compared budget, staffing, and storage facilities. Ultimately, the collection arrived at WVU Libraries in November 2014. The donation included the share drive of the Washington, DC, and state offices; an archived website and archived Facebook, Twitter, and YouTube accounts; and archived staff email accounts on external hard drives and thumb drives. The archives also received several hundred CDs and DVDs with videos, presentations, and audio recordings, all of which provided a complete snapshot of Rockefeller's time in office.

This donation was nearly an ideal scenario for acquiring the digital materials in a congressional collection, but even with archivists on staff, there were challenges. For example, while accessioning electronic records, the congressional papers archivist realized that the CSS data was missing. After contacting the closing archivist and the Senate Historical Office, the archivist learned that the data was still under review by the Senate Sergeant at Arms Office. With the help of the Senate archivist, the archived constituent correspondence data for the entirety of Rockefeller's career was eventually transferred to the repository.

From Accession to Access

Once a collection has been transferred to the repository, archivists should inventory and prepare the digital materials for accessioning immediately. Inventory preparation involves, to the greatest extent possible, counting and describing all digital materials that were transferred, including external hard drives, materials on other removable media dispersed in boxes, and anything transferred via email or cloud storage services, such as Google Drive, Dropbox, or Microsoft OneDrive. The inventory will allow the repository to identify any missing materials; prioritize materials based on importance, danger of loss, and uniqueness; and begin to assess replication across digital and paper materials.[32]

Accessioning workflows for digital materials generally follow the same steps as non-congressional collections. Accessioning includes transferring digital materials from removable media to a clean computer using a write blocker for certain removable media, copying files to safe and trustworthy storage, and performing a virus scan. Documenting accessions and providing additional metadata to reflect the origin, content, and context of the digital materials are important for collection management. Naming and describing accessions to reflect names of staff members, topics, and dates is useful for appraising, arranging, and describing congressional digital materials.[33]

Archivists likely will find a "comprehensive approach" to processing congressional digital materials useful. This approach to hybrid collections involves arranging and describing paper and digital in an integrated way, balancing donor concerns with researcher needs, and processing with access in mind.[34] Processing may be prioritized for collections and series that are not encumbered by closure periods or materials with potential privacy concerns. Finally, an understanding of the office's organization and records management strategy, in addition to being familiar with staff roles and areas of expertise, can help archivists to identify existing organization and context for digital materials.

Best practices for processing digital materials include keeping access in mind, attempting to mirror the arrangement of digital and paper materials, and describing digital materials in online finding aids. Also, archivists should understand that various approaches to access are influenced by available IT support, privacy concerns, and closure periods. The following two examples demonstrate these best practices in action.

In 2009, Senator Edward E. (Ted) Kaufman was appointed to fill the Senate seat left vacant when Delaware's longtime senator Joseph R. Biden Jr., was elected vice president of the United States.[35] After his term ended in November 2010, Kaufman donated his papers to the University of Delaware with no access restrictions. Office files and documents were acquired as Kaufman vacated his offices in Washington, DC, and Wilmington, but the senator's electronic files were not transferred until 2012.

These records were stored on a hard drive and given directly to a library administrator, which unfortunately bypassed standard accession procedures for manuscript and archival collections. The Kaufman electronic records were copied onto a library server without archival procedures to ensure authenticity and integrity of the files. Missing from the electronic collection were staff email accounts and archived social media and website files. Library systems staff were able to "scrape" the site, saving one snapshot before it was taken down permanently by the Senate. The site was made available through the University of Delaware Library's website and marked as an "archived" copy.

Beginning in 2013, archivists worked with systems staff to create a "dark" archive, a secure area of the server only accessible from a stand-alone electronic records workstation, and made a working copy of the files in a separate location. The Digital Record Object Identification (DROID) tool identified file formats and exported a log of files that included sizes, names, and checksums. Using Microsoft Excel's conditional formatting function, archivists identified duplicate files or files with the same checksum. Identifying which files were originals and which were duplicates proved challenging. Because of the method in which the files were transferred from the hard drive, a number of the creation dates had been changed to the date on which the transfer occurred. Additionally, files were sometimes stored in multiple locations. For example, congressional delegation photographs of international trips were stored in a folder labeled as such, but at least two additional staff members retained copies in their files.

In most cases, archivists found it was most efficient to retain the set of duplicate files that were easy to find and identify, particularly those with descriptive file names. The archivists tried to delete folders that contained multiple duplicate files and avoided appraising at the item level. In other words, they would not search through folders for a single duplicate file. While not all duplicate files could be easily disposed, a number of folders were deleted, reducing the total size of the working electronic records copy from ninety to sixty gigabytes. The archivists also performed some initial arrangement as they disposed of files. They deleted empty folders and condensed files contained within multiple folder levels.

Next, archivists scanned the records for personally identifiable information (PII), such as social security numbers. They used Identity Finder, a software suite to which the University of Delaware subscribed. After receiving the report, archivists spot checked and found that most sensitive information was actually a false positive. In a couple of cases, the sensitive information was redacted, and a note was made in the document explaining why redactions took place. Archivists performed minimal arrangement. They moved some extraneous files into appropriate series, batch renamed some files with more descriptive information, and reformatted some files for access. The entire process took several weeks to complete.

For access, the archivists considered a virtual reading room, reading room access on-demand, or a reading room access with a use copy available at all times. For reasons of IT support, the potential for sensitive information, copyright concerns, and time, archivists chose the latter approach. Library IT staff set up a dedicated computer workstation in the special collections reading room. This access point provided a read-only "user" copy of the records, which could not be modified. To maintain control over unwanted copying of the materials, the machine was not connected to the internet, and ports were inaccessible. Researchers could browse directories and files as if they were looking through a directory on their own computer, facilitated through the Firefox web browser. Discovery was facilitated through an EAD finding aid, which allowed the integration of the description of both paper and digital records. Digital records were described as a subseries of each appropriate series, and detailed scope and content notes and also access information were provided for each subseries of digital materials.[36]

A second example of applying best practices to digital collections demonstrated that sometimes it may not be possible to process an entire collection at once and the processing must be piecemeal. In 2014, Senator Jay Rockefeller's papers arrived at WVU Libraries with more than two thousand boxes of papers and a full cadre of digital materials. The collection is closed for twenty years, but materials previously made available to the public, such as press releases, may be opened for research. The archives received the office share drives from Washington, DC, and West Virginia on an external hard drive. The content included seven hundred gigabytes of materials arranged by staff member and office function. The CSS data, more than 2,400 digital photographs from the Senate Photo Studio (SPS) and Legislative Activity Reports, arrived after the papers and the share drive.

The congressional papers archivist copied these materials to a dedicated workstation, using a write blocker and Data Accessioner, and transferred them to a server managed by the WVU Libraries. A second working copy was placed on local storage for processing. Using the box-level inventory prepared by the office archivist, the congressional papers archivist identified several hundred CDs and DVDs stored in record cartons that contained digital information. The archivist continues to accession materials from this media.

Due to the closure period, the archivist prioritized the collection's press materials for processing. This part of the collection was opened for research in May 2016. The archivist identified digital press materials on the office share drive. Photographs, press releases, video and audio interviews with journalists, and news clippings were part of the "press" folder and found in folders maintained by individual staff members. The archivist and a graduate assistant processed the paper and digital press materials simultaneously, which made it possible to appraise for redundant materials and to identify gaps across the paper and digital files. For instance, several boxes of daily clippings and indexes, which were news stories and summaries from approximately 2005 to 2009, provided to the senator each day, were discarded because the same materials were maintained digitally by the office. In another example, digital photographs from the SPS contained very different content from the twelve linear feet of print photographs saved by the office press staff.

The archivist appraised photographs from the SPS at the item level, and redundant photographs were discarded. This work was accomplished using Adobe Bridge to review files and metadata. Photographs dating from 1985 to approximately 2002 were digitized by the SPS, while photographs from 2003 to 2014 were born-digital. The metadata in the born-digital photographs was invaluable when describing these photographs and making them accessible online through the libraries' Samvera digital platform. All photographs were in the JPEG format and were preserved and made accessible in that format.

The digital collection contained textual files, such as clippings indexes and press releases. Many staff members used WordPerfect for word processing. Archivists batch migrated these materials to PDF using an inexpensive application called WPD Converter. The files remained in PDF format for preservation and access purposes.

Using ArchivesSpace, the archivist created a finding aid for the collection, which included a description of the paper and digital materials in the press series.[37] A digital object link connected the finding aid descriptions to the materials available online. The SPS photographs were described at the folder level in the finding aid and linked to more than 1,500 photographs available online. Currently, access is on-demand for those digital materials that have not yet been made available online. When a researcher requests access, some files can be shared through the University's Microsoft One-Drive cloud storage system, which allows for permissions and time limits on files. In-person researchers may use any reference computer in the reading room, though protocols for access have not been established.

Because of the size and complexity of Rockefeller's digital archives, the amount of time needed to process the digital materials, in-house technical support, and the archivist's other responsibilities, the WVU Libraries contracted with the digital preservation company Preservica to more easily manage the congressional born-digital assets. While processing using the Preservica software is just beginning, the expectation is that it will bring together the voluminous digital materials together, identify duplicates across all digital materials, and automate description in ArchivesSpace.

Constituent Services Systems

Archivists recognize the potential for the data exported from CSS, but both the complexity and format of these exported systems have posed challenges for repositories. Data from modern systems arrives as flat ASCII text files with a library of attached records. Institutions have been reluctant to purchase the proprietary systems because of high upfront costs of contracting with vendors and the resources that would be necessary to maintain the proprietary systems in the long term. Further, systems intended for office use are not designed for research. Exported issue mail, both physical and electronic, may be coded with thousands of subject codes unique to each office, have multiple attachments, and contain sensitive personal information.[38]

Some question the research value of constituent correspondence and the ongoing costs to provide access. From the perspective of users, researchers have pointed to the difficult nature of finding and coding letters to quantify information. Conversely, scholars have used constituent correspondence for numerous inquiries related to the public's views on major issues before Congress.[39] Providing researchers with searchable data, rather than paper records, could only make this type of research more efficient and accurate.

Beyond academic scholarship, the data and correspondence exported from various systems have applicability for journalistic and civic projects seeking to better understand public engagement and establish accountability. Since the 2016 presidential election, public interest in how constituents communicate with Congress—and how representatives respond—has increased. For instance, in March 2017, ProPublica, an independent nonprofit newsroom that produces investigative journalism, asked readers to share correspondence from their members of Congress about the Affordable Care Act to fact check the messages received by constituents.[40]

Attempts to process these databases have yielded mixed results. Naomi Nelson writes that automated CSS records are "well suited for aggregate, quantitative research," but she cautions that inconsistent and missing data and duplicate records, in addition to large file sizes, are impediments to realizing the promise of the data sets.[41] Further, database development is outside the scope of most archivists' expertise and requires significant support from IT professionals.

In 2014, a project at Middle Tennessee State University's Albert Gore Research Center successfully created a searchable database of Tennessee congressman Bart Gordon's Intranet Quorum (IQ) data. The database is available to individuals from a wired campus computer on a case-by-case basis. The same year, the Robert C. Byrd Center for Congressional History and Education in Shepherdstown, West Virginia, worked with an IT professional to develop a database to read the CSS data from Senator Byrd's office. However, due to problems with the way data had been exported and security protocols, the project was not completed. In 2015, archivists at the University of Montana imported the data from Montana senator Max Baucus's office into a Microsoft Access database, but import errors made the dataset unusable.[42]

In 2016, WVU Libraries began developing of a system that was able to access and search the CSS data from Senator Jay Rockefeller's office. The tool also has built-in functionality to visualize the data geographically.[43] The system requires further development, but a group of congressional archives are exploring possibilities to utilize the system for providing access to multiple congressional CSS datasets.

LOOKING AHEAD

The call for better communication between repositories and congressional offices is not new but is more pressing with the increasing amounts of digital materials. Digital archives require early intervention, advocacy, and ongoing curation by archivists to successfully preserve and provide access. Staff in congressional offices are overwhelmed as they grapple with managing documentation in various formats, and archivists should see this as an opportunity to provide guidance. Repositories need to work closely with their congressional delegations, advocate for the resources provided by the SHO and

OAA, and encourage offices to hire archivists. Archivists managing congressional papers do the community a service when they share practices and challenges. The Electronic Records Committee of SAA's Congressional Papers Section facilitates sharing as archivists continue to develop best practices.

The addition of digital materials has made congressional papers more complex and unwieldy. Efforts in the past for redefining congressional collections and cooperative approaches to appraisal are perhaps even more applicable, but these recommendations must be updated to ensure they meet the needs of appraising incoming hybrid collections. Congressional archivists must rely on each other and look for partners, such as librarians with expertise in government information, to better appraise these massive collections.

Archivists need to consider what it means to "web archive Congress." Large swaths of government information are published exclusively online, and members of Congress interact with a variety of constituencies via their websites, Facebook, and Twitter accounts. Congressional archivists are looking to other stakeholders, like state archivists, the Government Printing Office, and the Federal Web Archiving Working Group. Online projects like the End of Term Web Archive provide information about the gaps between presidential administrations, which adds new details to the history of political transition and provides a model for congressional archivists to consider.[44]

Finally, born-digital records, digitized materials, and the data that describes them have potential for computational analysis. Available data in congressional collections includes CSS datasets, and archivists are beginning to think more broadly about congressional digital materials as data. The potential for this type of analysis is evident, but these new sources documenting Congress raise new methodological and ethical questions for archivists and scholars. These sources will require more intervention from archivists and librarians to help researchers not only discover them but also provide context for their creation and guidance for new ways of engaging with them.

No longer are congressional papers a typical type of manuscript collection with traditional series, formats, and arrangement patterns. Digital materials add to the complexity and difficulty of managing congressional collections. Examples from the field show that progress can be made in appropriately acquiring, accessioning, processing, and providing access to digital materials in these collections. In the future, better communication with donors, collaborative appraisal projects, and innovation in providing access to data in the archives will aid archivists in managing digital archives.

NOTES

1. Karen Dawley Paul, *The Documentation of Congress: Report of the Congressional Archivists Roundtable Task Force on Congressional Documentation* (Washington, DC: Government Printing Office, 1992), 102–20.

2. Karen Dawley Paul, "Congressional Papers and Committee Records: Private vs. Public Ownership," in *An American Political Archives Reader*, eds. Karen Dawley Paul, Glenn R. Gray, and L. Rebecca Johnson Melvin (Lanham, MD: Scarecrow, 2009), 91–94; Karen Dawley Paul, Robin Reeder, and Richard Hunt, comps., *Advisory Committee on the Records of Congress: Fifth Report*, December 31, 2012, https://www.archives.gov/files/legislative/cla/advisory-committee/fifth-report.pdf.

3. McConnell Center, http://louisville.edu/mcconnellcenter.

4. "Expressing the Sense of Congress That Members' Congressional Papers Should be Properly Maintained and Encouraging Members to Take All Necessary Measures to Manage and Preserve These Papers," H. Con. Res. 307, 110th Congress (2008), https://www.govtrack.us/congress/bills/110/hconres307.

5. Lauren R. Brown, "Present at the Tenth Hour: Appraising and Accessioning the Papers of Marjorie S. Holt," in *An American Political Archives Reader*, eds. Karen Dawley Paul, Glenn R. Gray, and L. Rebecca Johnson Melvin (Lanham, MD: Scarecrow, 2009), 19.

6. Linda A. Whitaker and Michael Lotstein, "Pulling Back the Curtain: Archives and Archivists Revealed," in *Doing Archival Research in Political Science*, eds. Scott A. Frisch, Douglas B. Harris, Sean Q. Kelly, and David C. W. Parker (Amherst, NY: Cambria, 2012), 115.

7. Steve Israel, "The Humiliations of Life after Congress," *New York Times*, December 16, 2016.

8. Mark A. Greene, "Appraisal of Congressional Records at the Minnesota Historical Society," in *An American Political Archives Reader*, eds. Karen Dawley Paul, Glenn R. Gray, and L. Rebecca Johnson Melvin (Lanham, MD: Scarecrow Press, 2009), 181–95.

9. Patricia Aronsson, "Appraising Modern Congressional Collections," in *An American Political Archives Reader*, eds. Karen Dawley Paul, Glenn R. Gray, and L. Rebecca Johnson Melvin (Lanham, MD: Scarecrow Press, 2009), 145–64.

10. Cynthia Pease Miller, *Managing Congressional Collections* (Chicago: Society of American Archivists, 2008), 60–73.

11. Elisabeth Butler and Karen Dawley Paul, "Electronic Record Systems on Capitol Hill: Finding and Obtaining What You Want," in *An American Political Archives Reader*, eds. Karen Dawley Paul, Glenn R. Gray, and L. Rebecca Johnson Melvin (Lanham, MD: Scarecrow Press, 2009), 131–32.

12. "Ask a Systems Administrator Series: Volume Two—Office Experiences," *Electronic Records Committee: A Working Group of the SAA Congressional Papers Section* (blog), April 25, 2016, https://cprerc.wordpress.com/2016/04/25/ask-a-systems-administrator-series-volume-two-office-experiences/.

13. "Ask A Systems Administrator Series: Volume One—Departing Staff Files," *Electronic Records Committee: A Working Group of the SAA Congressional Papers Section* (blog), April 11, 2016, https://cprerc.wordpress.com/2016/04/11/ask-a-systems-administrator-series-volume-one-departing-staff-files/.

14. Erica Werner, "When It Comes to Saving E-mails, Congress Makes Its Own Rules," *Associated Press*, March 15, 2015, https://www.pbs.org/newshour/politics/congress-rules-saving-emails.

15. Chris Casey, "20 Years Ago: Sen. Kennedy Announces First Congressional Website," *Epolitics.com*, June 4, 2014, http://www.epolitics.com/2014/06/04/20-years-ago-sen-kennedy-announces-first-congressional-website/.

16. "United States Congressional Web Archive," Library of Congress, https://www.loc.gov/collections/united-states-congressional-web-archive/about-this-collection; "Congressional and Federal: Government Web Harvests," National Archives, available at, https://webharvest.gov/.

17. Eric Matthew Glassman, Jacob R. Straus, and Colleen J. Shogan, *Social Networking and Constituent Communications: Members' Use of Twitter and Facebook during a Two-Month Period in the 112th Congress*, Congressional Research Service, March 22, 2013, https://www.fas.org/sgp/crs/misc/R43018.pdf.

18. Libby Hemphill and Andrew Roback, "Tweet Acts: How Constituents Lobby Congress via Twitter," Proceedings of the 17th ACM Conference on Computer Supported Cooperative Work and Social Computing, http://share.iit.edu/handle/10560/3195.

19. Adriane Hanson, "Donations of Digital Records from Congressional Offices: Lessons Learned from the 2014 Election Cycle," *Electronic Records Committee: A Working Group of the SAA Congressional Papers Section* (blog), June 2015, https://cprerc.wordpress.com/case-studies/donations-of-digital-records-from-congressional-offices-june-2015/.

20. Eyder Peralta, "Democrats Hold Senate Floor until Early Thursday in a Push for Gun Control," *National Public Radio*, June 15, 2016, http://www.npr.org/sections/thetwo-way/2016/06/15/482182468/live-video-democrats-to-hold-floor-indefinitely-in-push-for-gun-control; Rachel Dicker, "Democrats Are Holding the Senate Floor Indefinitely for Gun Control, and the Internet Is Going Nuts," *US News and World Report*, June 15, 2016, https://www.usnews.com/news/articles/2016-06-15/chris-murphy-launches-senate-filibuster-for-gun-control-and-the-internet-is-going-nuts.

21. Gayle Osterberg, "Update on the Twitter Archive at the Library of Congress," *Library of Congress Blog* (blog), December 26, 2017, https://blogs.loc.gov/loc/2017/12/update-on-the-twitter-archive-at-the-library-of-congress-2/.

22. Butler and Paul, "Electronic Record Systems," 132.

23. Society of American Archivists Congressional Papers Section CSS/CMS Task Force, *Archiving the Constituent Services Data of the U.S. Congress*, November 2017, https://www2.archivists.org/sites/all/files/2017_CSS_CMS_Report.pdf.

24. Karen Dawley Paul, *Records Management Handbook for United States Senators and Their Archival Repositories* (Washington, DC: United States Senate, 2006), 51.

25. Office of Art and Archives, Office of the Clerk, United States House of Representatives, *Records Management Manual*, February 2014, 4.

26. Paul, Reeder, and Hunt, *Advisory Committee*.

27. Susan E. Davis, "Electronic Records Planning in 'Collecting' Repositories," *American Archivist* 71 (Spring/Summer 2008): 169.

28. Hanson, "Donations of Digital Records."

29. "Analysis of 2009 Congressional Papers Roundtable Electronic Records Survey Results," *Electronic Records Committee: A Working Group of the SAA Congressional Papers Section* (blog), 2009, https://cprerc.files.wordpress.com/2015/05/analysis-of-2009-cpr-electronic-records-survey_0.pdf; Danielle Emerling, Adriane Hanson, Laura Litwer, "Where We Are and Where We Need to Go: Surveying the Digital Archiving Practices of the Congressional Papers Roundtable," *Archival Outlook* (January/February 2015): 12, 28–29; Danielle Emerling, "Donation of Digital Records: Preferred File Formats, Social Media, and Schedules," *Electronic Records Committee: A Working Group of the SAA Congressional Papers Section* (blog), February 15, 2016, https://cprerc.wordpress.com/2016/02/15/donation-of-digital-records-preferred-file-formats-social-media-and-schedules/.

30. Laura Litwer, "Donation of Digital Records: Donor Communications," *Electronic Records Committee: A Working Group of the SAA Congressional Papers Section* (blog), March 1, 2016, https://cprerc.wordpress.com/2016/03/01/donation-of-digital-records-donor-communications/.

31. Miller, *Managing Congressional Collections*, 55–56; "Electronic Records Checklist for Congressional Offices," *Electronic Records Committee: A Working Group of the SAA Congressional Papers Section* (blog), https://cprerc.files.wordpress.com/2015/08/electronic-records-checklist-for-congressional-offices_0.pdf.

32. Ricky Erway, *You've Got to Walk before You Can Run: First Steps for Managing Born-Digital Content Received on Physical Media* (Dublin, OH: OCLC Research, 2012), http://www.oclc.org/content/dam/research/publications/library/2012/2012-06.pdf.

33. "Sample Repository Documents," *Electronic Records Committee: A Working Group of the SAA Congressional Papers Section* (blog), https://cprerc.wordpress.com/sample-policy-and-procedures-documents/.

34. Laura Carroll, Erika Farr, Peter Hornsby, and Ben Ranker, "A Comprehensive Approach to Born-Digital Archives," *Archivaria* 71 (Fall 2011): 61–92.

35. A report about the Kaufman records originally appeared as "Establishing Electronic Records Management at the University of Delaware: Accessioning and Appraising the Electronic Records of Senator Edward E. (Ted) Kaufman," *Congressional Papers Roundtable Newsletter*, Fall 2013, 3–6.

36. "Edward E. 'Ted' Kaufman Papers" University of Delaware Special Collections, Finding Aids, http://www.lib.udel.edu/ud/spec/findaids/html/mss0660.html.

37. "Senator John D. (Jay) Rockefeller IV Papers," West Virginia University Libraries, Finding Aids, https://archives.lib.wvu.edu/repositories/2/resources/1.

38. Society of American Archivists, *Archiving the Constituent Services*.

39. Ibid., 14.

40. Terry Parris Jr., "Is Your Member of Congress Telling It Straight on the ACA? Help Us Fact Check Them," *ProPublica*, March 10, 2017, https://www.propublica.org/getinvolved/item/help-us-fact-check-members-of-congress-on-the-affordable-care-act.

41. Naomi Nelson, "Taking a Byte out of the Senate: Reconsidering the Research Use of Correspondence and Casework Files," in *An American Political Archives Reader*, eds. Karen Dawley Paul, Glenn R. Gray, and L. Rebecca Johnson Melvin (Lanham, MD: Scarecrow Press, 2009), 235–52.

42. Society of American Archivists, *Archiving the Constituent Services*, 11–12.

43. "Constituent Correspondence Data Tool Archival Repository," GitHub, https://github.com/wvulibraries/rockefeller-css.

44. End of Term Web Archive: US Federal Web Domain at Presidential Transitions, http://eotarchive.cdlib.org/.

Chapter Ten

Email

Matthew Farrell

Email, the formats, systems, and standards involved in transmitting text and other computer files over the internet, has been a powerful tool touching disparate aspects of contemporary culture for decades. Conversations that used to take place over phone lines or in face-to-face meetings occur asynchronously and may involve many more participants than other forms of communication. While this can lead to a growth in volume of the written record, thereby allowing users of archives another window into the lives, activities, and functions of those people and organizations documented in archival records, there are increased challenges presented as well. Individual approaches to organizing and managing email varies wildly from person to person and organization to organization. The large volume of email messages exchanged in our daily lives only compounds this. There is also the tendency to mix personal and professional messages into an email account, which leads to a potential minefield of sensitive or personal information alongside innocuous correspondence. While such intermingling is nothing new to archives, email is often considered as a whole as opposed to a set of individual messages stored in a system. But email can be considered from both a holistic and atomistic perspective; the lens through which to view a potential email acquisition will likely depend on a number of factors, including its creators and the archival institution.

This chapter gives a brief overview of the history of email communications and introduces important technical standards and concepts involved in the transmission of email messages. It then discusses efforts by archivists over the last fifteen years to address the challenges presented by the prominence of email messages in the lives and work of sources of archival and manuscript material. Two case studies are covered to illustrate different approaches to email acquisition from donors—total account acquisition and selective acquisition after pre-transfer appraisal by curators and records creators. These examples and best practices came from the experiences of archivists working at Duke University's David M. Rubenstein Rare Book and Manuscript Library. The chapter closes with a look ahead to the future of tools that will enhance the use of email by researchers and the management of these digital archives by archivists.

ORIGINS OF EMAIL

In the 1950s, the military in conjunction with IBM developed technology for computers to send data to other computers over telephone lines. They released this technology to the public in 1958. Investment in the nascent networking methods made communication between computers more efficient and a created a more centralized communication approach (i.e., computers communicating with each other through a computer center). More localized projects throughout the 1960s created systems for individual mainframe computers to communicate. University campuses were the locations for these types of networks. The Triangle Universities Computation Center (TUCC) connected computers at North Carolina State University, the University of North Carolina at Chapel Hill (UNC), and Duke University. Similarly, a network connected Princeton University and Carnegie Mellon University. The primary focus of these data-sharing initiatives was database and software sharing, not individual person-to-person communication.[1]

In 1969, the United States Department of Defense Advanced Research Projects Agency (ARPA) funded and built a network to allow computers to communicate across multiple institutions. The network, known as ARPANET, connected computers through the Transfer Control Protocol and Internet Protocol (TCP/IP).[2] In 1971, ARPANET supported an electronic mail function.[3] This feature became so popular that internal ARPANET reports called "its use by researchers for collaborative work the 'largest single impact'" of the network.[4]

Email also became a motivating factor behind the development of networks outside of the ARPANET, including Usenet.[5] This network was developed by college students at UNC and Duke as a system for sharing and distributing electronic newsletters. By distributing their network to other colleges and universities, Usenet became popular with "many schools that had no other access to a national network." Usenet and similar independent networks developed email and email-like methods of sending messages, which were imitated by commercial email services by the mid-1980s, though often using idiosyncratic transmission methods.[6]

The introduction of consumer-focused internet services, such as America Online or CompuServe in the 1980s and 1990s, brought email services to a wider group of less technologically savvy users. Likewise, email client software for both individual and enterprise-level consumers during this time allowed for businesses and home users alike to receive, compose, send, and organize email messages. From a business perspective, the benefits of email systems were numerous, including increased efficiency of communication and the keeping of an automatically generated record of communication, potentially more accurate than phone logs or memoranda. On the other hand, the ease with which email message could be composed and sent presented new challenges. In their book on the history of computers, Martin Campbell-Kelly and William Aspray explain, "Electronic mail was a completely new communications medium . . . and brought with it a range of social issues that fascinated organizational psychologists and social scientists. For example, the speed of communications encouraged knee-jerk rather than considered responses, thus increasing rather than decreasing the number of exchanges."[7]

Sometimes, the increased volume of messages could be handled by the email service or clients, but limits on attachment file size and total inbox size restrictions were common throughout the 1990s. When Google launched its Gmail service in 2004, a new account came with one gigabyte of storage and ten megabytes per attachment—unheard of at the time for a free service. Since that time, the trend for both enterprise email systems and public individual systems was to offer inboxes that are virtually unrestricted in total size or, at least, unrestricted to the end user and abstracted away by systems departments.

The volume of messages produced continues to challenge archives programs. The vast number of messages in email accounts dwarf an individual's capacity to absorb the information contained within, to say nothing of the potential legal (e.g., educational records, health information, human resources information) or ethical (e.g., personal information in a business account) implications of accessing such information. Another challenge is the complexity of the format itself. While email messages are often plain text wrapped in headers that can be accessed in text editors with minimal massaging, modern email clients handle attachments, calendar information, task lists, and other functionality. Email clients handle these sets of information and function differently and generate various formats for offline backup, storage, and potential archival transfer.

COMPONENTS OF AN EMAIL MESSAGE

Email messages are governed by different standards documents ("standards," for the purposes of this chapter, is a general term not to be confused with standards documents produced by the Internet Engineering Task Force and Internet Society). The current standard for the structure of an email message's transfer is the Simple Mail Transfer Protocol (RFC 5321).[8] The standard for the structure of a message's content is the Internet Message Format (RFC 5322). RFC 5322 "specifies a syntax only for text messages."[9] Other RFC documents describe the transmission of attachments via email and together make up part of the Multipurpose Internet Mail Extensions (MIME) series. At its most basic, an email message is made up of a series of header fields followed by a body. RFC 5322 specifies that these should both be in ASCII encoded text, though the MIME documents describe ways in which email may encode HTML and other types of formatted text to be transmitted "either by extending the syntax provided [by RFC 5322] or by structuring such messages to conform to [RFC 5322]."[10] Because RFC 5322 specifies ASCII encoded text, the bodies of many email messages can be viewed in a text editor, even if the header fields and attachments cannot be viewed.

SELECTED EMAIL FORMATS

Personal Storage Table (PST)

The Personal Storage Table (PST) is a format used by Microsoft in a suite of messaging applications, most commonly Outlook. Though officially described as an open format, it is proprietary and controlled by Microsoft. The file is stored on a user's local machine, and copies of the email messages, calendar events, and similar objects are copied from the email account's server to the local folder. Enterprise systems administrators may set limits to what is stored locally and what is only stored on the email server. Outlook users can create PST exports of their entire account or specified folders within their account. Once exported, the PST files and their contents can only be successfully re-rendered in another copy of Outlook. Several software applications can convert PST to more open file formats, both commercial (e.g., Aid4Mail or Emailchemy) and open source (e.g., libpst/readpst). It is important to note that, however, depending on the conversion file format, attachments, calendar events, to-do lists, and other Outlook objects may not be handled in the same manner that PST handles them, potentially leading to loss of these objects in the converted copy. From a preservation standpoint, PST is proprietary and, while in popular use, may not be long lived.

Microsoft Mail Message (MSG)

Microsoft mail message (MSG) files are individual email messages exported from Outlook. Like PST files, MSG files are an open proprietary format maintained by Microsoft. Further, MSG also requires Outlook or conversion programs to render the content in other applications.

MBOX

MBOX refers to a family of formats developed over time. An MBOX file may contain one or more email messages.[11] In fact, when using Emailchemy to convert an email account to MBOX, by default Emailchemy creates one MBOX file for each folder in an email account. MBOX is the export format used by Gmail and can be understood by the open-source Thunderbird email client. Because of the specification to encode text as ASCII, MBOX files can also be parsed in a text editor, though doing so may be less desirable for the user as header information and attachments may render as characters unreadable to the human eye. Compared with PST, the openness and relative simplicity of the MBOX family of formats indicate that it is a more stable option for long-term preservation.

Electronic Mail Format (EML)

Electronic mail format (EML) was developed by Microsoft for both Outlook and the discontinued Outlook Express. Because EML complies with RFC 5322, different email clients can open the format. Unlike MBOX, EML files are generally composed of one email message. Attachments can either be included in the EML file as MIME content (as described by the MIME series of documents) "or written off as a separate file, referenced from a marker in the EML file."[12] Like MBOX, because its compliance with RFC 5322 leads to the use of ASCII text, EML files may also be opened in text editors with accurate rendering.

EMAIL PROJECTS

Managing the Digital University Desktop (MDUD), 2003–2006

In 2003, archivists, records managers, and archival educators together from UNC and Duke University launched the Managing the Digital University Desktop (MDUD) project. The project focused on the proliferation of unorganized records, duplicative copies of those records, and nonrecords created during the shift from paper to electronic record creation. The project team's goals included documenting and analyzing user needs and developing educational modules for staff, faculty, and administrators at institutions of higher education in the creation, organization, and management of electronic records, with emphasis on email records. [13] Not coincidentally, North Carolina has long considered email messages in their public records statute. [14]

In addition to conference presentations, major outcomes of the MDUD project included two in-depth FAQs—one related to electronic records writ large and the other devoted specifically to email. The audience for these FAQs were records creators, rather than archivists and librarians. Though the FAQs were specifically aimed at affiliates of UNC and Duke, the principles were applicable to more general audiences. The FAQs featured an informal style, reminiscent of other filing and records management guidelines for records creators. There was a lack of specifics about what, technically, an email message is compared to other text-based computer files. At the very least, the project enabled records creators to do their own filing and appraisal. These instructions were based on records management principles, which encouraged the responsible retention of appropriate email records and their transfer to the archives.

Collaborative Electronic Records Project (CERP), 2005–2008

Starting in 2005, the Smithsonian Institution Archives collaborated with the Rockefeller Archive Center on a three-year project "to develop the methodology and technology for managing and preserving the born-digital materials in archival collections." [15] From the beginning, the project team narrowed its scope to email. Like the earlier MDUD project, project leaders developed best practices and related guidance, but unlike MDUD, these guidelines were "to assist *depositors* and *archivists* with email management" (emphasis added).[16] Project leaders recognized that both records creators and archivists needed help managing and preparing email records for transfer to archives programs.

One phase of CERP allowed participants to test various tools for transferring, converting, and processing email messages and attachments. The project team made file format recommendations for both messages and attachments and partnered with the Preservation of Electronic Mail Collaboration Initiative (described below) to develop an XML schema for long-term preservation of email. As another outcome, CERP suggested an ingest package architecture for depositing archive information packages (AIPs) into DSpace repositories and released an archival parser application for use. At the time of this writing, the Smithsonian Institution Archives has released a successor to the CERP Parser, called DArcMail, which added a graphical user interface and other features.

Preservation of Electronic Mail Collaboration Initiative, 2007–2009

Email per se, has been managed within and by the email client. There are several benefits to approaching email in such a way. First, it abstracts the conversation around either the "record-ness" or value from the item to a more holistic level. An archivist need not work closely with the donor or record creator to individually appraise email messages; rather, the creator can put as much or as little effort into pre-transfer appraisal as he or she wishes. This may lead to challenges during processing (e.g., through transferring junk, spam, and other nonrecord messages), but it makes the pretransfer appraisal phase less onerous on the donor. Total account preservation also allows archivists to make decisions about other parts of an email account in addition to the content of the messages. A person's calendar events may not be as important as an archival record, but there are scenarios in which having several years of scheduled appointments helps reconstruct an organization's history or a specific period of an individual's life. When working with the records of an institution, business, or other organization, archivists may focus on acquiring the accounts of key personnel or offices. This approach will cut down on the duplication of email messages sent office wide or organization wide.

Total account preservation addresses some of the challenges of collecting email but introduces barriers to processing and making available email to researchers. Collecting all or most of a donor's email account translates to large number of individual email messages. Though file size for individual messages is negligible, many thousands of messages and attendant attachments create a relatively large storage footprint. Further, by collecting the messages in larger quantity, staff may have a more difficult time identifying messages with potentially private or sensitive information. Specific tools are needed to help archivists identify sensitive data patterns and to parse language with a degree of nuance. Before duplication of an account is initiated, archivists expect the owner or manager of the account to remove transitory and otherwise non-permanent records. But as the capstone policy of the National Archives and Records Administration (NARA) makes clear, there are many instances of email collections that contain content with limited archival value.

In 2014, the Duke University Archives used NARA's protocol for a pilot project. Following the retirement of university provost Peter Lange, the university archivist and digital records archivist worked with his technical support staff to acquire email backups created each year of his tenure as provost, 2001–2014. The provost used Lotus Notes for email until approximately 2006 when Duke began using email systems supported by Microsoft. His IT support staff migrated the earlier emails to Outlook's PST format at the time of the switch, so the eventual acquisition comprised fifteen PST files totaling twenty gigabytes. Archivists focused on processing the paper records from his office and delayed the review of the email files. In addition, the email files fit within Duke's policy that administrative records receive a twenty-five-year restriction, with exceptions made for the office of origination and entities who have received permission from the office of origination.

Just after acquisition of the material, the University Archives received two reference requests for information from the Lange Papers. The first was from University Counsel, requesting any information pertaining to ongoing litigation. The other was a researcher who obtained permission from the provost's office to view restricted records pertaining to a research topic of interest. In both cases, the requests came with specific time periods and keywords. To address these requests, archivists created use copies of the PST files in question, opened the copies in an instance of Microsoft Outlook, and then ran Identity Finder (then a standalone product, now part of the Spirion suite) with the search specifically scoped to email and keywords. Although time consuming, this approach allowed archivists to successfully respond to both requests for information from email files. This approach was not generalizable to the rest of the corpus of email in the collection because Identity

Finder searches for data patterns (e.g., social security numbers, bank account numbers, passwords), keywords, or regular expressions. In the original PST files, neither Identity Finder nor the open-source application bulk_extractor could identify messages with possible restricted content as per the Family Educational Rights and Privacy Act (FERPA), the Health Insurance Portability and Accountability Act of 1996 (HIPAA), human resources or personnel records, and Duke-specific restrictions around information related to the board of trustees, donors to the university, and other financial or legal information.

After the pilot project, the ePADD email ingest software from Stanford University had reached a point of stability that could support public use. At present, Duke archivists are using ePADD to work with Lange's email. Their first challenge was to get the PST files into MBOX, the format expected by ePADD. After experimenting with the open-source libpst/readpst command line application, archivists settled upon the commercial Emailchemy and Aid4Mail products to convert the files. Libpst/readpst has been in a beta release for a number of years, and its output was difficult to standardize. After creating MBOX copies of the PST files, archivists imported individual MBOX files into the software. That approach relied on two premises: the email messages from the earliest year will remain under restriction until 2026, and because of potential sensitive information, archivists will need to review messages before releasing the files to researchers. The current goal of the project is to remove non-permanent material and identify files with potential restrictions. Output from ePADD will be stored in MBOX format as archivists explore other potential preservation formats.

Facilitating this work is ePADD's combination of regular expression search, entity identification, full-text indexing of both email content and attachment, and natural language processing (NLP) tools. Regular expression search currently allows users to identify common data patterns, such as social security numbers and credit card numbers. While these two types of information appear rarely in email, there is a particularly high level of sensitivity around this personal information. The entity identification and full-text indexing allow archivists to efficiently search for the names of members of the board of trustees so that archivists can apply appropriate restrictions to messages that involve board business with some level of confidence.

NLP tools create what ePADD calls "lexica," which are groups of related terms. The software will aggregate any email messages or attachments that feature one or more of the terms in a given lexicon. The software comes packaged with several example lexicons, but users can edit or add their own. At Duke, archivists created a handful of lexica related to an academic setting and their campus culture.[17] These Duke-centric terms could then be searched when the records were available for use. For example, these terms will make it possible for researchers to locate messages related to the Duke lacrosse case. With these search tools, archivists can flag the most sensitive permanent records for appropriate restriction, filter out the records that should not be retained, and create notes about content for future archivists who will review the collection at the time the collection is open for research.

Archivists at Duke encountered many challenges with the NLP lexicon tool. In many cases, the initial search across a collection was time consuming and devolved into review at the item level. This was particularly the case for reviewing email from members of the board of trustees who were often copied on messages that were not directly related to board business. Further, processing at a granular level may result in a tendency to restrict more materials. When working with the NLP lexicon tool, archivists must have a tolerance for false positives—messages that are identified because they include one or more terms from a lexicon but are not actually related. Adjusting the terms included in a particular lexicon removed some of these false positives. For example, archivists removed the word "threat" from the lexicon because it appeared so frequently and did not have the connotations usually associated with the word.

There are technical issues in version 5.0 of ePADD that still need improvement. For example, to use ePADD, email must be either imported as MBOX files or directly imported from a live email account. This requires users to find a solution to convert other email format into MBOX. Likewise, ePADD's default configuration has a strict limit on the amount of computer memory it is allowed to use, reducing the size of MBOX file that may be imported. There are workarounds for this, which requires a level of comfort with command line work or basic knowledge of Java virtualization. Luckily, the ePADD project team continues to add new features and develop the software to meet emerging needs. Like other open-source software projects, there is a growing community of users who support the further development of ePADD for use by archivists.

MANAGING EMAIL COLLECTIONS

Opportunities for Pretransfer Appraisal

Archivists also collect email by identifying and targeting a subset of email messages from a user's account. Such a targeted approach is useful when collecting the records of individuals related to one area of their life or professional output. For example, a researcher may be interested in a collection created by a writer, especially his or her correspondence with other writers and publishers. But the researcher would have little interest or reason to review email related to the writer's personal finances. Similarly, the donor would want the archives to preserve his or her professional and literary output but omit or restrict more sensitive material such as financial records or family content. In a perfect world, donors and creators logically organize their email the same way that they keep their analog and even digital materials. Some people use folders to manage their email accounts, which make appraisal and the creation of categories for research use somewhat easier. But, many email users, including archivists, have no logical structure to organize their email. This is mostly due to the sheer volume of incoming and outgoing messages.

When acquiring portions of a donor's email, an archivist must consider how to manage sent messages. The structure and organization of sent messages depends on the email system and client used by the donor. Microsoft Outlook stores all outgoing mail in a generic sent folder—mixing email messages of all kinds together. In Gmail, the software generally tags an entire thread of email messages, rather than only received messages. The macro approach for managing sent email in a donation is for archivists to acquire the entire sent folder, with the expectation that there is material to eliminate or restrict. Another option is for archivists to conduct a number of keyword searches within the sent folder and copy relevant sent messages to another folder for transfer to the archives. Instead of sorting through sent mail folders, archivists may decide that enough of the conversation is documented in the received messages (a reply email usually includes the text of the message to which it responded). Each approach depends on the donor's wishes and the ability of the archivists to fulfill those expectations.

During conversations with donors, archivists may choose to demonstrate the use of a tool like ePADD for accessing email collections. Such a program can be installed on a local computer in order to present donors with concrete examples of how email can be searched and displayed. Archivists at Duke often work with donors to identify names of family members and other search terms for on-site demonstrations and later screening during processing. Even if a donor has organized his or her email prior to transfer, archives staff should run the standard set of analysis tools for other digital acquisitions (e.g., virus and malware scans and sensitive information analysis) to search for sensitive content.

Duke's Rubenstein Library (of which the University Archives is a part) receives annual transfers of selected email from poet and author Stephanie Strickland. Her work appears both in traditional print and experimental electronic formats. The donor's email system is Gmail, which takes a tagging approach to email organization rather than Microsoft Exchange Server's and Outlook's folder/subfolder methods. Each year, Strickland tags messages that she wishes to transfer to Duke with an agreed upon tag (i.e., in the format *Duke_Keeper_yyyy*, where *yyyy* is replaced by the year she tagged a conversation). When archivists receive her yearly transfer of email, they analyze the acquisition with bulk_extractor and a virus scanner before adding summary description to the extant finding aid.[18] This yearly procedure is not More Product, Less Process (MPLP), but it is similar in that it requires only the baseline of nonautomated work on the part of archives staff and a reliance on the appraisal decisions made by the curator and Strickland when the gift agreement was originally negotiated.[19] This arrangement works for everyone involved in managing the Strickland Papers.

Choosing Methods

Though the collections and approaches described above were not mutually exclusive, a comparison highlights some of the decisions to consider when acquiring email. Accepting bulk sets of email on offer often translates to a larger chance of sensitive information to process. At Duke, Lange's staff rigorously sorted his email into relevant and personal folders, but those subjective decisions did not fully separate the personal and professional information. As a result, personal correspondence with colleagues and family mixed with professional business, and sometimes both types of information appeared in the same message. The collection also included forwarded messages and responses that mixed official business with more personal details. In the case of the Strickland collection, her level of review before transferring content to the archives resulted in a lower incidence of messages that require additional restrictions. The pretransfer appraisal approach lends itself more to MPLP processing of archival records. Processing each annual addition and updating the finding aid is a much more efficient process than acquiring the entire email account at one point in time. This approach works well for this collection, which is singularly focused on Strickland's literary output. In manuscripts collections with a wider focus on all aspects of a donor's life, such selection may highlight the subjectivity inherent in appraising archival collections.

The complexity of an email collection may, to an extent, mirror that of the physical records as well. This mirroring allows archivists to plan for processing and secure the necessary software and technology. The focus of the Strickland Papers is her literary and academic output. Personal and family information exists in the collection, but this content was minimized because archivists advised the donor before the transfer. In the case of the Lange Papers, physical records and email messages contained a large amount of restricted content. Prior to Lang's retirement, archivists worked closely with the provost's office to determine how and what to restrict. Because of the mixed nature of personal and business content in the collection, archivists were unable to find a suitable tool to appraise the email records. The temporary solution was to store the acquired PST files in secure dark storage until such time as tools became available with built-in functionality for natural language processing.

LOOKING FORWARD

As current and previous projects indicate, software for working with email messages is still in development, and the landscape of what applications and processes are available is always changing. Tools exist to aid archivists in the identification and classification of email messages with various sensitivities. That said, there is still a fair amount of human intervention required to use these tools effectively. The work currently underway with the Lange Papers is only the first pass at assigning restrictions and gaining intellectual control over the email records.

NLP tools are good at parsing and grouping related information, but the ambiguous nature of language makes review of individual emails a necessary precaution. The BitCurator NLP project, funded by the Andrew W. Mellon Foundation, is developing NLP software for specific use in libraries and archives.[20] The new tools are intended to analyze born-digital materials such as text-based email messages. In addition, archivists have a significant influence on these initiatives. The project's advisory board includes archivists

228   *Matthew Farrell*

who are either currently part of or were previously associated with the epADD project.

Development of sustainable, open formats for preservation purposes will increase the longevity of email collections in archives programs. The products from CERP/EMCAP include a documented XML schema for storing, describing, and providing access to email messages. This format may gain wider adoption and become a preservation format for email. At present, MBOX is open and widely used, but as a format, it features a lot of variation when implemented. At the Rubenstein Library, MBOX is the preferred medium-term preservation format with monitored consideration for migration when another format supersedes it.

Finally, archivists recognize that there is not a one-size-fits-all solution to managing, preserving, analyzing, and providing access to email. In November 2016, the Digital Preservation Coalition and the Mellon Foundation formed a task force of librarians, archivists, and industry leaders to address the shared challenges of long-term preservation of email. Leaders of the task force for email archives declared that "the preservation of email . . . cannot rely on a single, comprehensive solution, but on the coupling and interaction of a variety of solutions covering the entire range of archival activities."[21] The group is focused on analyzing current tools and systems used to preserve email and identifying gaps in current functionality. The task force has released a draft of its report.[22] The report covers in great technical detail the challenges inherent in preserving email, different models for conceiving of email systems, and how email maps to different life-cycle models familiar to archivists and records managers. Such groups aim to better articulate how archivists can manage digital donations of email in the short term and medium term. In recent years, records creators and archival institutions have moved beyond merely printing important messages and filing them as physical records. There is still no single agreed-upon standard for approaching the management of archival email records, but archivists are developing new tools and methods to solve the access and preservation issues for a form of communication that dominates our working and personal lives.

NOTES

1. Janet Abbate, "Computer Networks," in *From 0 to 1: An Authoritative History of Modern Computing*, eds. Atsushi Akera and Frederik Nebeker (New York: Oxford University Press, 2002), 122–24.
   2. Ibid., 126.

3. Martin Campbell-Kelly and William Aspray, *Computer: A History of the Information Machine* (Cambridge, MA: Westview, 2004), 264–65.

4. Janet Abbate, *Inventing the Internet* (Cambridge, MA: MIT Press, 1999), 107.

5. Campbell-Kelly and Aspray, *Computer*, 265.

6. Abbate, *Inventing the Internet*, quote 201, 203.

7. Campbell-Kelly and Aspray, *Computer*, 266.

8. J. Klensin, "Request for Comments 5321: Simple Mail Transfer Protocol," Network Working Group, October 2008, https://tools.ietf.org/html/rfc5321.

9. P. Resnick, ed., "Request for Comments 5322: Internet Message Format," Network Working Group, October 2008, https://tools.ietf.org/html/rfc5322.

10. Ibid.

11. "MBOX—File Containing Mail Messages," Man Page, http://www.qmail.org/man/man5/mbox.html.

12. "Email (Electronic Mail Format)," Sustainability of Digital Formats: Planning for Library of Congress Collections, April 2017, https://www.loc.gov/preservation/digital/formats/fdd/fdd000388.shtml.

13. "Project Background: Introduction and Goals," Managing the Digital University Desktop, https://ils.unc.edu/digitaldesktop/Info/index.html.

14. "Chapter 132: Public Records," North Carolina General Assembly, General Statutes, http://www.ncga.state.nc.us/enactedlegislation/statutes/html/bychapter/chapter_132.html.

15. Nancy Adgent, *Collaborative Electronic Records Project: Introduction and Overview* (Sleepy Hollow, NY: Collaborative Electronic Records Project, 2008), 3, http://siarchives.si.edu/cerp/CERP_Overview_CC.pdf.

16. Ibid., 7.

17. ePADD Project Team, "Lexicon Working Group," Stanford Libraries, https://library.stanford.edu/projects/epadd/community/lexicon-working-group.

18. "A Guide to the Stephanie Strickland Papers, 1955–2015," David M. Rubenstein Rare Book and Manuscript Library, Duke University Finding Aids, http://library.duke.edu/rubenstein/findingaids/stricklandstephanie/.

19. Mark Greene and Dennis Meissner, "More Product, Less Process: Revamping Traditional Archival Processing," *American Archivist* 68 (2005): 208–63.

20. BitCurator, "BitCurator NLP," February 2018, https://bitcurator.net/bitcurator-nlp.

21. Andrew W. Mellon Foundation, "Mellon Foundation and Digital Preservation Coalition Sponsor Formation of Task Force for Email Archives," November 2016, https://mellon.org/resources/news/articles/mellon-foundation-and-digital-preservation-coalition-sponsor-formation-task-force-email-archives/.

22. Andrew W. Mellon Foundation Task Force on Technical Approaches to Email Archives, "Supplementary Documents," May 2018, http://www.emailarchivestaskforce.org/documents/.

Index

3D printing, 177, 180
3DsMax (software), 177

acquisitions and appraisal of digital
  materials, xii, xx, xxii, xxiii, 3, 5, 6, 7,
  8, 9, 10, 11, 12, 13, 14, 16, 19, 28, 32,
  33, 52, 54, 73, 83, 100, 111, 124, 125,
  129, 135, 170, 182, 186, 195, 197–198,
  201, 205, 206, 208, 211, 222, 225, 226,
  227; adapting paper-based practices,
  xviii, 3, 4, 185; and digital forensics,
  73, 74, 75, 76, 77, 80, 82, 85, 86, 87,
  88; and documenting white society, 4,
  7, 17; and donors, xxi, 7, 11, 12, 21, 53,
  55, 68, 84, 88, 89, 130, 133, 133–134,
  201–204, 205, 220; and empathy, 88,
  131; and metadata, 80; protocols before
  acquisition, 4, 11, 13, 215, 221,
  225–226
Actors Equity Association, 132
Adobe software, 137, 176, 182, 188, 208
Advanced Research Projects Agency,
  Department of Defense (ARPA), 216
Advisory Committee on the Records of
  Congress, 201
Affordable Care Act, 209
Aid4Mail, 218, 223
AIMS Project, 9, 83, 84, 87, 137
Amazon Glacier, 67
Amazon S3, 67
Amazon.com, xv, 67

American Archivist, xvii, 8, 125
American Institute of Architects (AIA),
  193n11
American Online, 217
American Society of Media Photographers,
  71n27
American Society for Theatre Research
  (ASTR), 135
Architect of the Capitol, 166, 193n10
Architecture and design records, xii, xxi;
  CAD/BIM Taskforce, Society of
  American Archivists, 165, 172, 185,
  191, 193n13; and digital preservation,
  165, 168, 176, 183, 184, 185, 186, 191;
  and donors, 165, 166, 167, 168,
  169–170, 182, 184, 185, 186, 189–191,
  files and formats, 165, 166, 172, 174,
  176, 186, 191; plans and models,
  172–176; project data, 172, 175,
  179–180, 193n15; rendering, 172, 175,
  176, 176–178, 179, 181, 185; and
  researchers, 169, 170, 172, 180, 185,
  186, 188, 189, 191, 192; and software,
  xxi, 165–167, 168, 169, 170, 171–172,
  173, 175, 176–178, 179–180, 182,
  183–184, 186, 188, 190, 191, 192,
  193n15, 193n22
archival information packages (AIP), 4, 56,
  221
Archive-It (software), 65, 133, 199
Archive Social, 199

231

Contributors

Douglas A. Boyd is director of the Louie B. Nunn Center for Oral History at the University of Kentucky Libraries Special Collections Research Center. He designed and created OHMS (Oral History Metadata Synchronizer), an open-source system for enhancing access to online oral history. He is the coeditor of *Oral History and Digital Humanities: Voice, Access, and Engagement* (New York: Palgrave MacMillan, 2014), author of *Crawfish Bottom: Recovering a Lost Kentucky Community* (Lexington: University Press of Kentucky, 2011), and he serves as editor and manager of the Oral History in the Digital Age initiative.

Heather Briston is head of curators and collections and university archivist at the UCLA Library Special Collections. She received an MS in information with a focus in archives and records management from the University of Michigan, and a JD from Syracuse University with a focus on intellectual property law. She is a current member and the past chair of the Intellectual Property Working Group of the Society of American Archivists and has taught three different SAA workshops on legal issues for archivists. She is the author of "Understanding Copyright Law" in *Rights in the Digital Era*, eds., Menzi L. Behrnd-Klodt and Christopher J. Prom (Chicago: Society of American Archivists, 2015). Her research explores legal issues and archives; accountability and archives; special collections and international studies; and teaching with primary sources.

Lisa Calahan is the head of archival processing at the University of Minnesota Libraries, Archives and Special Collections. She received an MLIS from Dominican University and an MA in public history from Loyola University, Chicago. She deals with the intersection of acquisitions management, collection appraisal, and arrangement as core functions of archival collection management for both analog and digital collections.

Danielle Emerling is assistant curator and congressional and political papers archivist at the West Virginia and Regional History Center at West Virginia University Libraries. She holds an MLS with an archives and records management specialization and an MA in history from Indiana University, Bloomington. She served as chair of the Congressional Papers Section of the Society of American Archivists in 2016–2017 and is the treasurer for the Association of Centers for the Study of Congress.

Matthew Farrell is digital records archivist with the Duke University Archives and David M. Rubenstein Rare Book and Manuscript Library. He holds an MLS with a concentration in archives and records management from the University of North Carolina School of Information and Library Science. His research interests include further applying digital forensics methods to descriptive practices and leveraging the capture of web-based communication to identify and capture additional web resources.

Martin Gengenbach is an archivist at the Gates Archive in Seattle, where he oversees processing and preservation activities for physical and digital materials. He holds an MLS with a concentration in archives and records management and a certificate in digital curation from the University of North Carolina School of Information and Library Science. Martin also teaches courses in digital forensics for the Digital Archives Specialist curriculum and certificate program of the Society of American Archivists.

Aliza Leventhal is the corporate librarian and archivist for Sasaki, an interdisciplinary design firm. In addition to supporting the firm's institutional memory and knowledge sharing with practitioners, she proactively engages designers and technical professionals to better understand the features, workflows, and challenges that digital design files pose for their long-term access. She is the author of *A Report on the Architecture, Design, and Engineering Summit*, published by the Library of Congress in 2018. Leventhal cofounded the CAD/BIM Taskforce of the Society of American Archivists in 2012 and continues to serve as its chair leading research and advocacy efforts for digital design files and software. Focused on expanding visual and technical literacy for design and architectural archivists, she works to lower the barriers for archivists to engage with digital design records and raise awareness within the design industry of the significance of the records produced.

Bertram Lyons, a certified archivist and senior consultant with AVP, specializes in the acquisition, management, and preservation of documentary, research, and cultural heritage collections. He holds an MA in museum studies with a focus in American studies and archival theory from the University of Kansas. He has worked at several archives programs, including the Alan Lomax Archive and most recently at the American Folklife Center at the Library of Congress. Lyons develops tools, policies, and partnerships around the preservation and management of analog and digital archival collections. He is active nationally and internationally with professional archival organizations, including the International Association of Sound and Audiovisual Archives, the Society of American Archivists, the Association of Recorded Sound Collections, and the Association of Moving Image Archivists.

Vincent J. Novara is curator of the Special Collections in Performing Arts, Michelle Smith Performing Arts Library, University of Maryland, where he earned an MM in music. A certified archivist, he has held archivist positions at UMD since 1994 and was appointed curator in 2005. His scholarly works include exhibitions, book chapters, and articles and reviews in the *American Archivist*, Music Library Association's *Notes,* ACRL's *CHOICE*, and *Educational Media Reviews Online*. In addition, Novara is a frequent panelist, presenter, and moderator at professional meetings. Novara also instructs the Project Management in the Archival Workplace workshop for the Mid-Atlantic Regional Archives Conference.

Aaron D. Purcell is professor and director of special collections at Virginia Tech. He earned a PhD in history from the University of Tennessee, an MLS with a focus in archives and records management from the University of Maryland, College Park, and an MA in history from the University of Louisville. Purcell has also worked at the National Archives and Records Administration, the National Library of Medicine, and the University of Tennessee. He has written seven other books in the fields of history and archives. Purcell's most recent book is *Digital Library Programs for Libraries and Archives: Developing, Managing, and Sustaining Unique Digital Collections* (Chicago: Neal Schuman, 2016). He is beginning work on an edited book about federal relocation projects in Appalachia during the mid-twentieth century.

Dorothy Waugh is a digital archivist at the Stuart A. Rose Manuscript, Archives, and Rare Book Library at Emory University where she is responsible for the acquisition and management of the Rose Library's born-digital collections. She received an MLS from Indiana University in 2012 and an MA in English Literature from the Ohio State University in 2010. Her current research interests include education and outreach opportunities related to born-digital archives and questions around how the born-digital format supports new types of archival research.